'Never has holism been more important than in this era of planetary crisis, polarized thinking, and the fragmenting of communities and the psyche. Never too has holism been so lauded and derided. So *Holism: Possibilities and Problems* is a necessary book for the twenty first century. With a wonderfully cogent introduction by Roderick Main, Christian McMillan, and David Henderson, the book focuses on the interrelated thought of Gilles Deleuze and C. G. Jung while also ranging richly between philosophy, the arts, clinical practice and the Anthropocene. For seekers of "the whole" in the context of emergence, complexity theory and transdisciplinarity, this is the place to start.'

– **Susan Rowland, PhD,** Pacifica Graduate Institute, California, USA

# HOLISM

*Holism: Possibilities and Problems* brings together leading contributors in a ground-breaking discussion of holism. The terms 'holism' and 'holistic' arouse strong emotional responses in contemporary culture, whether this be negative or positive, and the essays in this interdisciplinary collection probe, each in its own way, the possibilities and problems inherent in thinking holistically.

Christian McMillan, Roderick Main and David Henderson bring together established academics and emerging scholars across subject areas and disciplinary approaches to reveal the multiplicity and complexity of issues involved in holism. Divided into four parts, the chapters determine key strands of thinking explicitly or implicitly underpinning contemporary holistic thought, including what ethical conclusions might most reasonably be drawn from such thought. Accessible and diverse, this extensive volume contains chapters from the perspective of history, ecology, psychotherapy, poetry, mythology, and an especially strong representation of continental philosophy and Jungian depth psychology. Due to its multi-disciplinary nature, the book represents an unparalleled discussion of the meanings and implications of holism.

Written by an innovative and international calibre of contributors, this pioneering collection will be essential reading for practitioners in depth psychology and scholars of Jungian studies, as well as academics and students of philosophy, religious studies, spirituality, history, and the history of ideas. The book is a rich resource for the enhancement of critical reflection among all those with an interest in holism.

**Christian McMillan, PhD,** is Lecturer at West Suffolk College, University of Suffolk, and was formerly Senior Research Officer in the Department for Psychosocial and Psychoanalytic Studies, University of Essex, UK.

**Roderick Main, PhD,** is a professor in the Department of Psychosocial and Psychoanalytic Studies and Director of the Centre for Myth Studies at the University of Essex, UK.

**David Henderson, PhD,** is Lecturer in Jungian Studies in the Department for Psychosocial and Psychoanalytic Studies, University of Essex, UK. He is a member of the British Jungian Analytic Association (BJAA) and the International Association for Analytical Psychology (IAAP).

# PHILOSOPHY & PSYCHOANALYSIS BOOK SERIES
JON MILLS
Series Editor

*Philosophy & Psychoanalysis* is dedicated to current developments and cutting-edge research in the philosophical sciences, phenomenology, hermeneutics, existentialism, logic, semiotics, cultural studies, social criticism, and the humanities that engage and enrich psychoanalytic thought through philosophical rigor. With the philosophical turn in psychoanalysis comes a new era of theoretical research that revisits past paradigms while invigorating new approaches to theoretical, historical, contemporary, and applied psychoanalysis. No subject or discipline is immune from psychoanalytic reflection within a philosophical context including psychology, sociology, anthropology, politics, the arts, religion, science, culture, physics, and the nature of morality. Philosophical approaches to psychoanalysis may stimulate new areas of knowledge that have conceptual and applied value beyond the consulting room reflective of greater society at large. In the spirit of pluralism, *Philosophy & Psychoanalysis* is open to any theoretical school in philosophy and psychoanalysis that offers novel, scholarly, and important insights in the way we come to understand our world.

**Titles in this series:**

*Lacan on Psychosis: From Theory to Praxis*
Edited by Jon Mills and David L. Downing

*Ethics and Attachment: How We Make Moral Judgments*
Aner Govrin

*Jung and Philosophy*
Edited by Jon Mills

*Innovations in Psychoanalysis: Originality, Development, Progress*
Edited by Aner Govrin and Jon Mills

*Holism: Possibilities and Problems*
Edited by Christian McMillan, Roderick Main and David Henderson

# HOLISM

Possibilities and Problems

*Edited by Christian McMillan, Roderick Main and David Henderson*

LONDON AND NEW YORK

First published 2020
by Routledge
2 Park Square, Milton Park, Abingdon, Oxon OX14 4RN

and by Routledge
52 Vanderbilt Avenue, New York, NY 10017

*Routledge is an imprint of the Taylor & Francis Group, an informa business*

© 2020 selection and editorial matter, Christian McMillan, Roderick Main and David Hendersonm individual chapters, the contributors

The right of Christian McMillan, Roderick Main and David Henderson to be identified as the authors of the editorial material, and of the authors for their individual chapters, has been asserted in accordance with sections 77 and 78 of the Copyright, Designs and Patents Act 1988.

All rights reserved. No part of this book may be reprinted or reproduced or utilised in any form or by any electronic, mechanical, or other means, now known or hereafter invented, including photocopying and recording, or in any information storage or retrieval system, without permission in writing from the publishers.

*Trademark notice*: Product or corporate names may be trademarks or registered trademarks, and are used only for identification and explanation without intent to infringe.

*British Library Cataloguing-in-Publication Data*
A catalogue record for this book is available from the British Library

*Library of Congress Cataloging-in-Publication Data*
A catalog record has been requested for this book

ISBN: 978-0-367-42481-7 (hbk)
ISBN: 978-0-367-42482-4 (pbk)
ISBN: 978-0-367-82438-9 (ebk)

Typeset in Bembo
by Deanta Global Publishing Services, Chennai, India

 Printed in the United Kingdom
by Henry Ling Limited

# CONTENTS

*Acknowledgement* ix
*Contributors* x

Introduction 1
*Christian McMillan, Roderick Main and David Henderson*

**PART I**
**HISTORY AND CONTEXTS** 15

1 How do we think in terms of *wholes*? Holistic voices and
   visions after World War II 17
   *Linda Sargent Wood*

2 Irreducible responsibility: Applying holism to navigate the
   Anthropocene 31
   *Andrew Fellows*

3 Georg Ernst Stahl's holistic organism 42
   *Barbara Helen Miller*

**PART II**
**ANALYTICAL PSYCHOLOGY** 53

4 From the split to wholeness: The *'coniunctio'* in C. G. Jung's
   Red Book 55
   *Alessio De Fiori*

5  Science as a system: Connections between Carl Gustav Jung's holistic thoughts about science and his *Red Book* experience  67
   *Armelle Line Peltier*

6  The holistic wish: Migration of feeling, thought and experience  75
   *Phil Goss*

7  Holistic education: The Jungian dilemma  83
   *Robert Mitchell*

8  Simondon and Jung: Re-thinking individuation  91
   *Mark Saban*

**PART III**
**PHILOSOPHY**  99

9  A whole made of holes: Interrogating holism via Jung and Schelling  101
   *Gordon Barentsen*

10  Jung, Spinoza, Deleuze: A move towards realism  109
    *Robert Langan*

11  Kant's influence on Jung's vitalism in the *Zofingia Lectures*  118
    *Christian McMillan*

12  An emergent, critical realist understanding of holism  130
    *Ian Hornsby*

13  Synchronicity: Between wholes and alterity  141
    *Rico Sneller*

14  Why don't holisms describe the whole? The psyche as a case study  149
    *J. Linn Mackey*

**PART IV**
**PRACTICE AND THE ARTS**  157

15  A synchronistic experience in Serbia  159
    *Richard Berengarten*

16  The concept of *kami* in Shintō and holism: Psychotherapy and Japanese literature  170
    *Megumi Yama*

17  The CORE Trust: The holistic approach to addiction  180
    *Jason Wright*

*Index*  188

# ACKNOWLEDGEMENT

Work on this book was supported by the Arts and Humanities Research Council, UK [AH/N003853/1].

# CONTRIBUTORS

**Gordon Barentsen**, PhD, is a Doctor of English from Western University in London, Canada. His fields of interest are Romantic literature and philosophy, psychoanalysis (Freud/Jung/Lacan), and theory and criticism. He has given talks in the UK, Germany, the Czech Republic, and North America, he has lectured at the Melbourne School of Continental Philosophy and is a founding member of the North American Schelling Society (NASS). His particular interest is putting Jungian thought into dialogue with contemporary philosophy and theory. His book *Romantic Metasubjectivity: Rethinking the Romantic Subject Through Schelling and Jung*, is forthcoming on Routledge.

**Richard Berengarten** is a British poet who acknowledges elective affinities with Octavio Paz, George Seferis, and C. G. Jung. Berengarten has lived in Italy, Greece, Serbia, Croatia, and the USA. His *Selected Writings* number nine volumes. His writing has been translated into over one hundred languages; the *Critical Companion to his works* contains 34 essays from contributors in 11 countries; and his many awards include prizes in the UK, Serbia, and Macedonia. Formerly Visiting Professor at Notre Dame University (1982), British Council Lector in Belgrade (1987–1990), Royal Literary Fund Fellow, Newnham College, Cambridge (2003–2005), Berengarten is a Fellow of the English Association and Bye-Fellow at Downing College, Cambridge.

**Andrew Fellows** is a Zürich-trained Jungian Analyst with private practices in Bern and Zürich, a deep ecologist, and a writer. He is a Training Analyst at ISAPZURICH, holds a Doctorate in Applied Physics (Dunelm), and has two decades of international professional engagement with renewable energy, sustainable development and environmental policy. His special interests include the anima mundi, the mid-life transition, the new sciences, and the use of depth psychology to understand and address global collective problems, especially climate change. His book, *Gaia, Psyche and Deep Ecology: Navigating Climate Change in the Anthropocene* (Routledge, 2019), provides fuller and updated coverage of the themes he explores in his contribution to this volume. Further information is available at www.irreducible.world.

**Alessio De Fiori** is currently a PhD student in the department of German Studies (EA1341) at the University of Strasbourg and in the department of Educational Sciences ("R. Massa") at the University of Milan-Bicocca (Italy). He studied Philosophy and Human Sciences at the universities of Bologna (Italy), Lille (France), Strasbourg (France) and Freiburg (Germany). His PhD thesis examines C.G. Jung's relationship with German philosophy (from Meister Eckhart to Nietzsche). He is interested in the history of ideas (19th–20th centuries) and in the relations between depth psychology and philosophy.

**Phil Goss** is a Jungian Analyst (member AJA & IAAP) and Director of Counselling & Psychotherapy programmes at the University of Warwick. He was previously course leader for the Masters programmes in Counselling & Psychotherapy at the University of Central Lancashire. His publications include *A Complete Introduction to Jung* (Hodder and Stoughton 2015) and *Men, Women and Relationships, A Post-Jungian Approach* (Routledge, 2010) as well as analytically oriented chapters and papers on gender, education, spirituality, and landscape and loss. He has helped organise a number of conferences including 'Jung and Wordsworth' (Wordsworth Trust 2011) and 'The Notion of the Sublime: Jungian and Lacanian Perspectives' (University of Cambridge, 2014). He had a private practice in Cumbria and Lancashire, working with adults and children until 2016, but has since relocated to the Midlands with his family, where he is establishing an analytic practice.

**David Henderson**, PhD, is Lecturer in Jungian Studies in the Department for Psychosocial and Psychoanalytic Studies, University of Essex. He is a member of the British Jungian Analytic Association (BJAA) and the International Association for Analytical Psychology (IAAP). He is a convenor and regular contributor to the Jung-Lacan Research Network. He contributed chapters to *Re-Encountering Jung: Analytical Psychology and Contemporary Psychoanalysis*, R.S. Brown (ed.), Routledge and to *Depth Psychology and Mysticism*, T. Cattoi and D. Orodisio (eds.), Palgrave. Published papers include, 'Freud and Jung: The creation of the psychoanalytic universe,' and '"A life free from care": The hermit and the analyst,' in *Psychodynamic Practice*. His book *Apophatic Elements in the Theory and Practice of Psychoanalysis: Pseudo-Dionysius and C.G. Jung* is published by Routledge. He was the co-investigator on a two-year (2016–18) research project titled '"One world": logical and ethical implications of holism' funded by the Arts and Humanities Research Council, UK.

**Ian Hornsby** is a comic book writer and artist who specialises in creating comics that address complex ideas in new and accessible ways. He is Senior Lecturer in Critical and Cultural Theory within the Department of Theatre at the University of Chichester. Ian left school at age fifteen without qualifications or the ability to either read or write and worked for 10 years as an apprentice served boatbuilder. As a single parent, he was able to go back to learning when his son started school. His real education began after seeing Kenneth Branagh's production of *Look Back in Anger* at the Lyric Theatre in London in 1998 and after reading Robert M. Pirsig's *Zen and the Art of Motorcycle Maintenance*, a book which formed the basis of his MPhil Thesis *On Quality* (1998). His recent Publication …Comic Books, Möbius Strips, Philosophy and…. (2019) can be found on The Comics Grid: Journal of Comics Scholarship. His latest comic book *VOP* will be released 2020 and examples of his comic artwork can be seen at https://ihornsby.co.uk/ This site also includes the comic book *Emergence and 'Things in Themselves'* that should be read alongside his chapter in this collection: *An Emergent, Critical Realist, Understanding of Holism.*

**Robert Langan** is a PhD candidate with the Department of Psychosocial and Psychoanalytic Studies at the University of Essex. He received his MA in Jungian and Post-Jungian Studies from University of Essex, where he received the David Holt Prize for academic excellence. His research interests concern philosophical connections between Jung and Spinoza, as well as a metaphysical basis for psychological types. He is a speculative fiction writer and the author of *The Icons of Man* fantasy series.

**J. Linn Mackey**, PhD, is Professor Emeritus of Interdisciplinary Studies at Appalachian State. He now lives in Durham, NC, and is a member of The C. G. Jung Society of The Triangle. He has published a number of articles and book reviews in *Jung Journal*.

**Roderick Main**, PhD, is a professor in the Department of Psychosocial and Psychoanalytic Studies and Director of the Centre for Myth Studies at the University of Essex. His publications include *The Rupture of Time: Synchronicity and Jung's Critique of Modern Western Culture* (Brunner-Routledge, 2004), *Revelations of Chance: Synchronicity as Spiritual Experience* (SUNY, 2007), *Jung on Synchronicity and the Paranormal* (Routledge/Princeton, 1997), and *Myth, Literature, and the Unconscious* (Karnac, 2013). He was principal investigator on a two-year (2016–18) research project titled '"One world": logical and ethical implications of holism' funded by the Arts and Humanities Research Council, UK.

**Christian McMillan**, PhD, was a Senior Research Officer in the Department for Psychosocial and Psychoanalytic Studies at the University of Essex working on an AHRC funded project '"One world": logical and ethical implications of holism' (2016–2018). His doctoral thesis, 'The image of thought in Jung's whole-Self: A critical study' (2014) focussed on similarities and differences in the thought of depth psychologist C. G. Jung and French post-structuralist philosopher, Gilles Deleuze. Publications include: 'Jung, Literature, and Aesthetics' in *Jung and Philosophy* (ed. Jon Mills, Routledge, 2019); 'Jung and Deleuze: Enchanted Openings to the Other', *Internal Journal of Jungian Studies*, special issue (Dec, 2018); 'Archetypal Intuition: Beyond the Human' in *Psychoanalysis, Culture and Society* (ed. David Henderson, 2012). Forthcoming publications include: 'The 'image of thought' and the State-form in Jung's 'The Undiscovered Self' and Deleuze and Guattari's 'Treatise on Nomadology' in *Jung, Deleuze and the Problematic Whole* (eds. Roderick Main, Christian McMillan, and David Henderson).

**Barbara Helen Miller**, PhD, is a Jungian analyst in private practice in Hilversum (Netherlands). She was the second solo cellist with the Radio Philharmonic Orchestra of the Netherlands for thirteen years. On returning to academia, Barbara was awarded a Master of Arts in Psychology and Religion, and a PhD in Anthropology from Leiden University. Her research has focussed on the Sámi (Northern Norway) and their traditional healing practices, and continues to inform the Research Group Circumpolar Cultures, resulting in numerous publications. She is a member of the International Association for Analytical Psychology (IAAP), the Association of Graduate Analytical Psychologists (AGAP), and the Netherlands Association for Analytical Psychology (NAAP). Published works include: *Connecting and Correcting: A Case Study of Sami Healers in Porsanger* (2007). Leiden: CNWS Publications.

**Robert Mitchell** is an author, lecturer, teacher and independent scholar. He holds a BSc in mathematics, with post-graduate work in education and doctoral studies in the history of consciousness. He taught maths, English, and history at the secondary level for 27 years. Additionally, he has published a two-volume memoir of his 12-year transformative odyssey following combat service in the Vietnam War: *Journey to Mytros* (2011) and *The Trials of the Initiate* (2012). Based on his doctoral work, he is currently writing a two-volume series for a general audience: *Seeking the Archetype of the Teacher* and *Education, Culture and Democracy: the American Experiment*. His main interests are in developmental individuation, education and the culture of democracy.

**Armelle Line Peltier** is a Doctor of Epistemology and History of Sciences at the Archives Henri Poincaré—Philosophie et Recherches sur les Sciences et les Technologies—Université de Strasbourg. Published papers include: '*Le Livre Rouge de Carl Gustav Jung: processus créateur et connaissances*', Delforge, Nicolas et Dörries, Matthias (dir.), *Limites de la créativité*, Paris, Kimé (2016). The title of her thesis is: Une pensée créatrice en science. L'élaboration de la connaissance chez Carl Gustav Jung (1875–1961) à travers l'étude du *Livre Rouge* (1913–1961).

**Mark Saban** is a lecturer in the Department of Psychosocial and Psychoanalytic Studies, University of Essex. He is also a Senior Analyst with the Independent Group of Analytical Psychologists (UK). He has published numerous papers and chapters.

**Rico Sneller** is a senior lecturer of Ethics/Philosophy at the Technical University of Eindhoven (Netherlands). His research interests lie in the field of Continental Philosophy, especially 19th- and 20th-century approaches to human consciousness, and altered states of mind (inspiration, genius, mysticism, ecstasy, telepathy, etc.). He is Vice President of the International Society of Alternative Perspectives and Global Concerns (APGC): see https://ap-gc.net.

**Linda Sargent Wood** is an Associate Professor of History at Northern Arizona University and the author of *A More Perfect Union: Holistic Worldviews and the Transformation of American Culture After World War II* (Oxford, 2010) and 'Contact, encounter, and exchange at Esalen: a window onto late twentieth-century American spirituality.' Her current project on the disability rights movement invests her in questions about who merits membership in the community and how difference is factored into the whole. Recently, she published 'We had to start treating them as human beings: Dr. Philip Pallister, clinical genetics and the Montana State Training School.'

**Jason Wright** is currently the Clinical and Founding Director for number 42 psychotherapy and well-being. Previously he worked as Clinical Director and CEO for the CORE Trust addictions charity. He has also chaired and or served on the board of the Psychoanalytic Consortium, the College of Psychoanalysts, London drug and Alcohol Network, Drugscope, Centre for Transpersonal Psychology and the UKCP psychoanalytic section (now CPJA). He has taken various consulting roles in the corporate and voluntary sectors and practices as a psychotherapist.

**Megumi Yama** is professor of clinical psychology and depth psychology at Kyoto University of Advanced Science. She was a visiting researcher at Harvard University in 2015 and Essex University 2008–2009. She is also engaged in clinical work as a psychotherapist based on Jungian principles. She was educated in clinical psychology at Kyoto University under Prof. Hayao Kawai, where she received her PhD. Her interest is in images and words; what is taking place in the invisible silence. She deals with the theme by exploring clinical materials, formative art, myth, literature and Japanese culture. She has written many articles and books including translations. Her publications include *To the Depth of Words* (Seishinshobo, 2003) and *Yasuo Kazuki: his work and creative activity* (Tomishobo, 2016). Her articles (in English) include: 'The artist's experience of formative work: Japanese painter Yasuo Kazuki and his *Siberian Series*': 'Ego consciousness in the Japanese psyche: culture, myth and disaster': 'Haruki Murakami: modern myth-maker beyond culture': The Meaning of Mystical Experiences on the Boundary between Life and Death. Her chapter 'Listening to the narratives of a pre-modern world: beyond the world of dichotomy' is included in *Jungian and Dialogical Self Perspective* (Palgrave Macmillan, 2011) : 'Non-fixed multiple perspectives in the Japanese Psyche: traditional Japanese art, dream and myth' is included in *Contemporary Influences of C. G. Jung's Thought* (Brill, 2018): 'Listening to a dream narrative: a language for narrating boundaries' is included in *Narratives of Individuation* (Routledge, 2019): '*The Red Book*: A Journey from West to East via the Realm of the Dead' is included in *Jung's Red book for our time: Searching for Soul under Postmodern Conditions* Vol.3 (Chiron Pub., 2019).

# INTRODUCTION

*Christian McMillan, Roderick Main and David Henderson*

On reading the book *Holism and Evolution* by the South African soldier, statesman, and philosopher Jan Christiaan Smuts (1926), in which the term 'holism' was coined, Albert Einstein remarked that holism, along with his own notion of relativity, would become one of the defining concepts of the third millennium (Einstein 1936). While it would be unwise to attach too much importance to this perhaps lightly made prediction, it is certainly the case, almost a century after the publication of Smuts's book, that the terms 'holism' and 'holistic' are used regularly in numerous areas of contemporary life, including medicine (House 2016), therapy (Beckman and Le Quesne 2005), spirituality (Hanegraaff 1998, pp. 119–58), education (Forbes 2003), and ecology (Marietta 1994). Though predominantly countercultural, many of these accumulating uses have by now been partially integrated into mainstream cultural discourses and practices (Heelas and Woodhead 2005). Meanwhile, in academic contexts, there continues to be lively discussion of holistic methodologies in the social sciences (Hanson 2014; Zahle and Collin 2014), and strong cases have been advanced in favour of holism in areas such as the philosophy of physics and the philosophy of mind (Esfeld 2001). Some influential general approaches to working holistically have also appeared, such as General System Theory (Bertalanffy 1968), Batesonian cybernetics (Bateson 1973), and complexity theory (Bertuglia and Vaio 2005).

Whether in popular or intellectual contexts, the use of the language of holism often provokes strong positive or negative responses. To some, holistic approaches are associated with desirable qualities such as inclusion, integration, balance, and wider vision, and are championed as remedies for the fragmentation and alienation that are considered to beset the modern world (Bohm 1980, pp. 1–26; Berman 1981). To others, however, holistic approaches bespeak vagueness, the erasure of differences, and, where individual elements are subordinated to a deemed superior whole, a tendency towards totalitarianism (Popper 1957, p. 73; Phillips 1976; Harrington 1996).

The wide incidence, diverse use, and ambivalent emotional charge of the term 'holism' and its adjectival form 'holistic' make it pressing to understand these terms better. However, this is no easy task. While it is clear that holism (from the Greek ὅλος/*holos* = whole) is a perspective that in some sense attaches importance to a thing or system 'as a whole', over and above its nature as a composite of parts—as in the common adage 'the whole is more than the sum of its parts'—holistic thinkers themselves are often not clear, let alone unanimous, about the ontological status of any particular whole, the relation of the composite parts of that whole among themselves and in relation to the whole, and the importance of taking a holistic perspective.

Scholars of holism have approached these issues in a variety of ways. Some have tried to extrapolate analytic definitions of holism that could then be applied to any case (Phillips 1976; Esfeld 1998, 2001). Others have attempted to reconstruct through careful historical work the actual understandings and uses of holism (or its equivalents) by particular thinkers or groups of thinkers; for example, in relation to *Gestalt* psychology (Ash 1995; Harrington 1996), biology, neurology, and neuropsychiatry (Harrington 1996), or biomedicine (Lawrence and Weisz 1998). Another approach has been to sample classic and/or contemporary usages by focusing on a single discipline, such as education (Forbes 2003), psychology (Diriwächter and Valsiner 2008), or anthropology (Otto & Bubandt 2010). There are also studies that take a deliberately broad view of 'holistic worldviews' in order to capture the overall holistic character of a particular period of a culture, such as post–Second World War America, regardless of whether the actors involved all used the language of holism themselves (Wood 2010).

Indeed, almost any study of holism has to contend with the fact that the set of ideas signalled by the term 'holism' has often been expressed, more or less nearly, in a variety of other terms. As Christopher Lawrence and George Weisz remark with reference to their study of medical holism between 1920 and 1950:

> It is almost impossible to articulate fully the relationship among the many diverse terms with holistic implications that gained popularity—organicism, vitalism, totality, synthesis, community, *Ganzheit*, *Gestalt*, *médecine humaine*, to name but a few. One can at best point to Wittgensteinian family resemblances, the full exploration of which would require something like an intellectual history of the Western World during the nineteenth and twentieth centuries.
>
> (*Lawrence and Weisz 1998, p. 6*)

The actual term 'holism', as already noted, was coined by Smuts in his 1926 book *Holism and Evolution*. However, the major themes with which Smuts engaged had already been under discussion for several decades in disciplines such as physics, biology, psychology, and sociology, using some of the terms mentioned by Lawrence and Weisz (Phillips 1976; Weber and Esfeld 2003; Esfeld 2003)—Smuts himself drew particularly on recent physics, biology, and psychology (1926). Some of these discussions addressed scientific problems that had arisen internally to the disciplines, principally concerning the adequacy of reductive materialistic, atomistic, and mechanistic principles for explaining complex phenomena of life, mind, and society (Ash 1995; Lawrence and Weisz 1998). But other discussions, as well as some of the same discussions registered differently, were driven by more cultural concerns, such as with the perceived social and political consequences of materialism and mechanism—the problem of 'disenchantment', as Max Weber named it (Harrington 1996). There were thus both cognitive and cultural dimensions to work on holistic themes (Lawrence and Weisz 1998, pp. 6–7). Both dimensions can in fact be traced much further back in the cultural history of the West, through German Romanticism and Renaissance esotericism to the philosophy of the ancient Greeks (Dusek 1999). But the success of materialistic and mechanistic principles in the physical and chemical sciences at the end of the 19th century prompted a particularly intense period of reflection and work on these issues in the subsequent decades.

There does not appear to have been any uniformity in the kind of social and political agendas holistic thought was made to serve during this period. Undoubtedly, the most nefarious political appropriation of holistic thought was by the Nazis (Harrington 1996). This association has contributed to the perception that there may be an intrinsic relationship between holistic thought and totalitarianism (Popper 1957, p. 73; Keulartz 1998, p. 141), a perception only reinforced at the other end of the political spectrum by the shared influence of Hegelian thought on both Marxist ideology and holism (Phillips 1976, pp. 5–20), as well as by such holistic utterances as Vladimir Lenin's that 'Everything is connected to everything else' (cited in Woods 2010, p. 14). But several historians of the period have argued that these linkages with totalitarianism were contingent: 'the history of German holism', writes Harrington, 'is a history of many stories, and the prominent cases of Goldstein, Wertheimer, and Driesch show that other political voices [than conservative and totalitarian] were possible and, in various ways, persuasive' (1996, p. 208). Similarly, Mitchell Ash cites Martin Leichtman's view that 'the Gestalt theorists […] advanced a "liberal humanistic" or "liberal democratic world view" rooted in Enlightenment values that was opposed to the prevailing conservatism of the German academic elite' (Ash 1998, pp. 2–3). Beyond this specific period, Harrington further notes the influence on American post–Second World War culture of 'left-leaning, holistically oriented immigrants to the United States, like Kurt Goldstein, Herbert Marcuse, and Fritz Perls' (1996, p. 211). More generally still, Val Dusek (1999) argues for the role of women, peasants, and déclassé intellectuals in stimulating currents of holistic thought at various periods in the development of Western culture (1999, pp. 5–11).

A helpful perspective on some of these ambivalent ethical attitudes toward holism is provided by Lawrence and Weisz, who observe that 'there have been two rather different holistic responses to modernity':

> On the one hand, there has been an emphasis on the need for *individual* wholeness, plenitude, or authenticity, despite the fragmenting and distorting quality of modern social life. A contrasting response has emphasised the submergence of the individual within a larger entity—nation, race, religious community, nature.
>
> *(Lawrence & Weisz 1998, p. 7)*

It is often possible to see ethical and political claims in relation to holism as stemming from the extent to which they stress one or the other of these two possible responses.

Anne Harrington has examined how various holists in the interwar years in Germany made connections between clinical and cultural phenomena by exploiting 'the rich metaphorical language of Wholeness' (1996, p. xxiv); and Linda Sargent Wood, focusing on the later period and different geographical area of post–World War II America, has remarked on the 'episodic' nature of the notion of holism, the way it 'rises and falls at varying historical intervals', as well as on its 'slippery' literal meaning and 'amazing plasticity' (2010, pp. 15–16). Together with the plurality of contextually dependent understandings and uses of the term and the existence of closely related alternative terms, this all makes it difficult to define holism with any precision.

Several commentators have noted that rather than define holism positively, it is easier to characterise it by what it opposes. Marcel Weber and Michael Esfeld, for instance, in their overview of holism in the natural and social sciences, highlight the opposition of holism to the epistemological assumptions of reductionism, mechanism, and individualism (2003, p. 2). For Val Dusak, discussing the holistic inspirations of electromagnetic theory in physics, the main opposed viewpoint is atomism (1999, pp. 17–19). And Wouter Hanegraaff, writing about the New Age movement from the later 1970s, identifies various manifestations of dualism and reductionism as the non-holistic orientations that holism opposes: specifically, the assumption of a fundamental distinction between Creator and creation, between humans and nature, or between spirit and matter; and the tendency to reduce organic wholes to mechanisms and spirit to matter (1998, p. 119).

Nevertheless, there have been sophisticated attempts to provide analytic definitions of holism (Phillips 1976; Esfeld 1998, 2001). Perhaps the most lucid treatment remains that of Denis Phillips in his book *Holistic Thought in Social Science* (1976). Phillips identifies three kinds of holism, which he calls Holism 1, Holism 2, and Holism 3. Holism 1, which Phillips equates with 'organicism', involves five propositions:

1. The analytic approach as typified by the physicochemical sciences proves inadequate when applied to certain cases—for example, to a biological organism, to society, or even to reality as a whole.
2. The whole is more than the sum of its parts.
3. The whole determines the nature of its parts.
4. The parts cannot be understood if considered in isolation from the whole.
5. The parts are dynamically interrelated or interdependent.

(Phillips 1976, p. 6)

The first proposition states the need for a holistic approach, while the remaining four propositions articulate how the parts of a whole or 'organic system' are related both to the whole and to one another within the whole (Phillips 1976, p. 7).

Within Holism 1, while it is not possible to predict the properties of a whole based solely on knowledge of its parts, it is still in principle possible, once the whole has been sufficiently studied, thereafter to explain the whole in terms of the parts. Some holists, however, make the stronger claim that there are cases where it is not possible to explain the whole in terms of the parts no matter how thoroughly the whole has been studied. To cover claims such as these Phillips formulated Holism 2, which states that 'a whole, even after it is studied, cannot be explained in terms of its parts' (1976, p. 36).

Finally, there are holists who claim that special concepts are needed to discuss systems as wholes. As examples, Phillips refers to Paul Weiss's use of the concept of 'hierarchies' (1976, p. 35), to the widespread use of 'concepts pertaining to field theory' (1976, p. 36), and to Arthur Koestler's coinage of the term 'holon' to express the idea that things can be simultaneously both wholes and parts depending on whether they are being considered from above or from below in the hierarchy of a system (1976, p. 70). These kinds of claims are covered by Phillips's Holism 3, which states that 'it is necessary to have terms referring to wholes and their properties' (1976, p. 37).

It reveals a lot about the complexity of holism that this attempt to provide a clear and comprehensive definition needs to be broken into three variants, one of which itself involves five subsidiary propositions. Nor are Phillips's formulations the only possible ones (Esfeld 1998, 2001) or beyond dispute (Bailis 1984). There may even be an inherent impossibility in trying to articulate analytically a methodological and epistemological principle—holism—that expressly challenges the adequacy of analytical thinking. This would not be a view shared by Phillips, though, for whom Holism 1 and Holism 3 are not essentially incompatible with the analytic or reductive method (1976, pp. 122–3).

In presenting Holism 1 Phillips explains at length the philosophical reasoning underpinning the way holists understand the relationships of the parts of a whole both to the whole that they constitute and to one another (1976, pp. 6–20). He concludes that the form of holism based on these relationships, 'modern organicism', is 'in a sense, no more than the Hegelian theory of internal relations writ large' (1976, p. 20). This reference to Hegelian theory signals the metaphysical or ontological dimension of holism, beyond the methodological and epistemological dimensions on which Phillips primarily focuses. It is a particularly interesting observation in light of subsequent scholarship which has shown that the Hegelian doctrine of internal relations itself parallels and may well have been influenced by Hermetic thought (Magee 2001, pp. 13–14).

Thus, even Phillips's sober, analytical study points to a set of fundamental metaphysical questions about ultimate reality and the relationship between the One and the Many, and these questions are indeed frequent preoccupations of holists and of scholars discussing holism. For example, the principal targets of much holistic thought—reductionism, mechanism, individualism, atomism, and dualism—are often perceived to stem from a particular metaphysical assumption associated with theism: the ontological separation of the divine from the world (Berman 1981; Hanegraaff 1998, p. 119). Many holists, explicitly or implicitly, tend to support the different metaphysical perspectives of pantheism or panentheism, in which the divine is considered not to be separate from the world (even though, in panentheism, it may still exceed the world) (Main 2017). The Hermetic philosophy informing holism via the Hegelian doctrine of internal relations is a classic expression of panentheistic thought (Magee 2001, pp. 8–9; Hanegraaff 2012, p. 371).

Metaphysical preoccupations such as these are often considered important to holists in that the assumed relation between the divine and the world (or whatever other terms are used to frame the relation of ultimate reality to the multiplicities of experience) sets the pattern for relations within the world: a metaphysics enshrining inherent ontological division is considered to result in a divided and disconnected world picture, marked by relations of dominance and conflict; while a metaphysics enshrining inherent ontological unity is considered to result in a unified and interconnected world picture, more marked by equality and co-operation. The theoretical importance of such considerations is indicated, for example, by Hanegraaff's identification of four main 'structural types' of holism within New Age thought, the titles of which signal some of the metaphysical assumptions on which they are based: ultimate source holism, universal interrelatedness, dialectical or polarity holism, and organicistic holism (1998, pp. 120–58).

Holism, then, is a complex and highly charged term. The present volume does not legislate any particular definition or valuation, but rather allows the author of each of the contributed essays to take her or his own approach to address the specific possibilities and problems that the concept of holism is perceived to hold. The essays originated in an international conference held at the University of Essex in 2017, which was supported by the Arts and Humanities Research Council, UK, as part of a research project titled '"One world": logical and ethical implications of holism' (AHRC reference: AH/N003853/1). A central task of that project was a comparison of the concept of the whole in the work of the Swiss psychiatrist Carl Gustav Jung (1875–1961) and the French post-structuralist philosopher Gilles Deleuze (1925–1995). This origin explains why a large number of the papers in the present volume focus on the work of Jung and, to a lesser extent, Deleuze. However the remit of the conference was open as regards what presenters understood by holism and with what historical contexts, theoretical frameworks, and specific thinkers they wished to engage. As a result, the essays collected here cover a wide range of issues associated with the concept of holism, and take a correspondingly wide range of approaches. Together they provide a rich, albeit inevitably still partial, picture of this complex topic of inquiry and offer a plethora of stimulating insights and provocations. (A more focused study of the thought of Jung and Deleuze in relation to the concept of the whole, emerging from the same research project, can be found in the companion volume *Jung, Deleuze, and the Problematic Whole* [Main et al. 2020].)

## Outline of the volume

The contributions of this volume are divided into four parts. Part I, 'History and contexts', focuses on the history of the concept of holism in relation to multiple contexts as well as its continuing relevance today as a way of thinking capable of negotiating the damaging effects of the Anthropocene. Part II, 'Analytical psychology', concentrates on the engagement between C. G. Jung's thought and holism, especially with respect to Jung's notion of the conjunction of opposites and the process of individuation. Part III, 'Philosophy', examines 'holistic' aspects of the philosophy of Gilles Deleuze and the thought of Jung in relation to concepts of key thinkers in Western philosophy including, but not limited to, Spinoza, Kant, Schelling, Klages, and Bhaskar. The final part of this collection, 'Practice and the arts', offers personal and professional perspectives on holism in practice in relation to artistic production, mythological thinking, and psychotherapy. Each part of this volume addresses itself to a common theme that is evident throughout the whole volume: how to *think* holistically.

### *Part I: History and contexts*

For the volume's opening chapter (Chapter 1) 'How do we think in terms of *wholes*? Holistic voices and visions after World War II', Linda Sargent Wood poses some crucial questions: how will holistic ideas be used—for good or ill, for solving or creating problems? Will we aim to protect and bolster our own little corner of the world, championing a particular race or nation at the expense of others? Will we work together—across cultures and geographies—on mutual projects that protect the planet and lead to greater quality and justice? Wood's survey of holistic thought in the 20th century demonstrates how these questions have galvanised and motivated thinkers from across several fields: the psychologist

Abraham Maslow, French Jesuit priest and palaeontologist Teilhard de Chardin, environmentalist Rachel Carson, civil rights leader Martin Luther King, and architect Buckminster Fuller. Whilst these figures offered complementary perspectives on how to think holistically, Wood's survey of the history of holism does not limit itself to recent times. The concept has deep historical roots and Wood charts its emergence from Plato, Hippocrates and Aristotle into Medieval Europe and the modern period. The questions that close her chapter have not yet been answered and definitive conclusions are unlikely to be found. Nonetheless, the contributors to this volume all, in one form or another, follow in the spirit of those who have sought an answer to one or several of these questions, serving as a timely reminder that although holism may be an 'episodic notion', as Wood relates, it is certainly not an irrelevant one.

In Chapter 2, 'Irreducible responsibility: Applying holism to navigate the Anthropocene', Andrew Fellows investigates how analytical psychology and Gaia theory view the mental and physical domains in broadly similar ways. Dynamically, both psyche and Gaia appear to be teleological, capable of reconciling the conflicting requirements of stability and change. Structurally, their potential pathologies, together with independent but similar conclusions by Jung and Lovelock about the global role of human consciousness, suggest equivalent relationships of ego to self and of *homo sapiens* to the natural world. The mind-matter properties evince a new ethos equivalent to Jung's concept of individuation. Specifically, the psychological shift of the centre of the personality from the ego towards the self translates into a cultural shift of our worldview from anthropocentrism to biocentrism. Fellows argues that this shift was independently proposed by the Norwegian philosopher Arne Næss in the 1970s as the basis of the long-range deep ecology movement.

In her chapter 'Georg Ernst Stahl's holistic organism' (Chapter 3), Barbara Miller asks, 'how is life organised?' Her chapter responds by focussing on the work of 17th-century pietist, philosopher and physician Georg Ernst Stahl and his anti-mechanistic theory of the organism, which emphasised that the soul and the body are a unity, that life is organic, and that life is the active soul working within the structures and substances of the body. According to Miller, this view was at odds with the proponents of the 'new' philosophy of Descartes and of Newtonian physics. Stahl proposed a theory of a holistic, self-determined organism and in his definition of organism, he equated 'life' with the ability of the whole organism to organise change. The 'organ' of perception is the sum of all perceptual processes (including sensory impressions, mental images and emotions), which Stahl referred to as the 'soul'. Within radical Protestant movements (leading influences on which were Gottfried Arnold and Jacob Böhme) Stahl's theory was 'enthusiastically' embraced, answering their need to legitimise the inspirational freedom of the spirit, whilst challenging the notion that 'pure' reason could lead to spiritual growth. Legitimate inspiration facilitated the experience of conversion and 'rebirth.'

## Part II: Analytical psychology

Between 1913 and 1916 C. G. Jung underwent a period of intense psychic transformation or 'rebirth' during which he investigated the contents of his own unconscious in the form of a 'night sea journey' or Neykia. Jung vividly documented many aspects of this journey in pictorial form and his experiences have only recently been published in *The Red Book: Liber Novus* (2009). The book illustrates Jung's own engagement with the process he would eventually come to refer to as individuation: a holistic transformation in which the ego engages with wider aspects of the psyche to become 'whole'. In Chapter 4, 'From the split to wholeness: The "*coniunctio*" in C. G. Jung's *Red Book*', Alessio De Fiori investigates a central theme from Jung's *Red Book*, the conjunction of opposites (*coniunctio oppositorum*) as it appears at different levels within the text: ontological, eschatological and cosmological. De Fiori refers to this as a 'holistic vision of psychic development, [establishing unities] between the different parts of the personality and Self, between the One and the All, between human and God.' For a vision of what holistic thinking might entail, Jung's *Red Book* may serve as a preparatory text.

In Chapter 5, 'Science as a system: Connections between Carl Gustav Jung's holistic thoughts about science and his *Red Book* experience', Armelle Line Peltier argues that throughout all of Jung's work one can identify the idea of a whole: science, psychology, psyche are all systems that cannot be reduced to their parts. The relation between Jung's holistic discourse about science and his practice of it are examined, eliciting the following questions: Are Jung's holistic thoughts about the elaboration of knowledge consistent within his *Red Book* experience? Does the *Red Book* experience enable Jung to create a holistic methodology? The similarities and differences between Jung's holistic discourse and his way of elaborating knowledge are addressed in three ways: through an analysis of his discourse about science, psychology, and psychological methods; through an analysis of his practice of science (psychology) in the *Red Book* experience; and through a comparison from an (anarchic) epistemological and systemic perspective.

The following three chapters of Part II crystallise around the theme of individuation, a central concept in analytical psychology. In Chapter 6, 'The holistic wish: Migration of feeling, thought and experience', Phil Goss elaborates on the holistic nature of wishing, irrespective of whether that desired in the wish is fulfilled or not. Applying a predominantly Jungian lens to this exploration, with Fordham's de/re-integration dynamic as a guide, but also drawing on other frames of reference including neuroscience to approach questions about holism, the chapter posits that the human instinct to wish reflects the presence of a searching function ('the holistic wish') which seeks a sustained sense of organismic integrity.

Robert Mitchell's contribution 'Holistic education: The Jungian dilemma' (Chapter 7) argues that the journey of individuation does not have to be considered a process common only to the 'second half of life', as Jung frequently advocated. The Jungian formula for the first half of life is ego development. By default, childhood development is conceded to the Freudian model. This seeming contradiction has not escaped holistic educators, for many of whom Jung is considered the primary psychological author of the holistic paradigm. The 'dilemma' lies in the suggestion that child development cannot be both egocentric and holistic. Mitchell asks, can it? Modifications to Jung's theory of individuation suggest that personality development and individuation begin in the earliest stages of life and continue through the educative years as what might be called *Developmental Individuation*. In line with many other contributions in this volume, the notion of a kind of holistic thinking, instilled early, is implicitly negotiated in this chapter.

Mark Saban closes Part II with 'Simondon and Jung: Rethinking individuation' (Chapter 8), which introduces the work of a French philosopher and biologist on whom Jung's thought had a profound influence. It is also noteworthy that Gilles Deleuze began the process of making aspects of Simondon's work more visible, being partly responsible for the resurgence in philosophical scholarship on Simondon more recently. Simondon's and Deleuze's sympathies with aspects of Jung's work make their appearance in Saban's analysis. Although Simondon's ideas about individuation were influenced by Jung's, the range, complexity, and rigour of his thought offer the possibility of a deepening critical understanding of the limitations and contradictions found in Jung's ideas. The chapter focuses on the crucial importance for Simondon of the relational, the affective/emotional and Simondon's emphasis upon participation in the collective, and the problem-solving aspect of individuation. It is claimed that a creative re-visioning in the light of these ideas has the capacity to provide a philosophical grounding for a concept that is central to Jung's psychology – and central to the clinical engagements of analytical psychology.

## *Part III: Philosophy*

This part of the volume, which embarks on a number of Jungian and Deleuzian adventures under the guidance of scholars who work across these domains, begins with Gordon Barentsen's 'A whole made of holes: Interrogating holism via Jung and Schelling' (Chapter 9). He examines the idea of an ethical holism by articulating the theoretical countertransferences between Jungian thought and the *Naturphilosophie* of German philosopher Friedrich Schelling, which offers crucial insight into Jung's embattled attempts to articulate the psyche–nature relationship. The chapter begins with Schelling, who conceives nature's products as composed from an infinite matrix of 'dynamic atoms', mutually entangled points of intensity called *actants*. Barentsen then articulates the isomorphism between the actants' dynamism and Jung's mature formulation of the *archetype*. What he refers to as Jung's 'therapeutics of presence' (archetypes concretized for the sake of a linearized therapy) is troubled by the open energic economy of Jung's metapsychology, which entangles archetypes with each other like Schelling's actants. The chapter closes by addressing two questions: *can* we ethicize this 'whole made of holes', a totality ostensibly more than the sum of its parts but nevertheless destabilized by its constituent seethe of nonmolar intensities? And if we cannot escape ethics in the symbolic order, must we not look to its (Derridean) dangerous supplement?

From Schelling to Spinoza, Chapter 10, 'Jung, Spinoza, Deleuze: A move towards realism', by Robert Langan outlines key differences between the dual-aspect monism established by C. G. Jung in his work with Nobel Prize–winning physicist Wolfgang Pauli on the one hand, and the metaphysics of the 17th-century rationalist Baruch Spinoza on the other. Spinoza is often credited as a key predecessor to the Jung–Pauli model; yet Jung himself is curiously dismissive of Spinoza throughout his *Collected Works*. Using the distinction between *realist* and *anti-realist* philosophy as established by the speculative realist philosophers Manuel DeLanda and Graham Harman, Langan argues that the Jung–Pauli model requires the intervention of the human mind for reality to exist and that this amounts to an *anti-realist* philosophy; while the ontology of Spinoza treats the human as no more important than the nonhuman, and thus is a *realist* philosophy. Criticisms of anti-realist philosophy, as raised by Deleuze, illustrate the problems of making the human mind into a mediator and microcosm of the whole—it robs the nonhuman of its creative power and fails to account for the genesis of all that exists. The chapter concludes by asking if there are resources in Jung's thought that run counter to this anti-realist tendency and that allow Jung's monism to be reworked in a way closer to the realism of Spinoza and Deleuze.

Chapter 11, 'Kant's influence on Jung's vitalism in the *Zofingia Lectures*', continues to draw from important philosophical writers in the Continental tradition. Christian McMillan focuses on Kant's *Third Critique* to interrogate its influence, from a post-Deleuzian perspective, on Jung's earliest work, *The Zofingia Lectures*. Jung's vitalism owes a debt to the influence that Kant's holistic organicism had over many 19th-century philosophers and natural scientists. It has been argued by some Jungian scholars that Jung's vitalism remains largely consistent between the views he expressed in the *Zofingia Lectures* and views concerning the nature of the psychoid expressed over 50 years later in 'On the nature of the psyche'. If this is so, then the historical basis of this consistency bears further elaboration.

Robert Langan's focus on Spinoza and realism is complemented by Ian Hornsby's innovative contribution 'An emergent, critical realist understanding of holism' (Chapter 12). Incorporating small sections of sequential art to elucidate his broader narrative, Hornsby sets out to construct a critical realist framework, taken from the early writings of Roy Bhaskar (an alternative to poststructuralism's solipsistic 'linguistic turn' and positivism's 'epistemic fallacy'), as a philosophical strategy for investigating holism in the writings of both Deleuze and Jung. The construction of bronze, from the melding of tin and copper, has been used as a metaphor through which to observe holism as a form of emergence. This can be seen in Deleuze's collaboration with Guattari and how their writing points to the emergent properties within art as containing the ability to reterritorialize our relations with the world. A form of emergence can also be seen in Jung's writings on the formation of the transcendent function.

In Chapter 13, 'Synchronicity: Between wholes and alterity', Rico Sneller suggests that synchronistic experiences, of the kind elaborated in Jung's 1952 essay 'Synchronicity: An acausal connecting principle', gesture towards a re-conception of nature, language, and consciousness. This allows him to explore the possibility of thinking 'wholes' without the exclusion of alterity, a theme common to French poststructuralists such as Deleuze, Derrida, and Levinas. Employing Jung's mature notion of the psychoid, Sneller challenges the possibility of being able strictly to demarcate the boundaries of consciousness and the psyche, reimagining the relationship between nature, consciousness, and psyche as fluid. Drawing from several Eastern and Western writers (Yasuo Yuasa, Carl du Prel, Ludwig Klages, and Gustav Fechner) he proposes that synchronistic experiences require that we resort to images rather than concepts for their articulation, in order to facilitate a re-conception of nature, language, and consciousness. These experiences are the very catalyst for such a re-conception.

John Mackey's chapter, 'Why don't holisms describe the whole? The psyche as a case study' (Chapter 14), concludes this section of the volume. He reviews the perspectives of John Macmurray, Georg Henrik von Wright and the Pauli-Jung conjecture of dual-aspect monism, arguing critically that 'holisms never describe the whole'. Mechanistic and teleological approaches to the formation of 'unity patterns'—biological, organismic, psychological, and 'personhood' patterns—are summarised in the accounts presented by Mackey and complemented by findings in the 'new' mathematics of fractals and non-linear dynamics, which reveal a 'new kind of holism' otherwise known as 'emergence'. Mackey, in common with other contributors to this volume (Fellows and Langan), refers to Jung's collaborative work with physicist Pauli to elaborate on an alternative perspective—dual-aspect monism— which complements but does not fully address the biological and organic perspectives of Macmurray.

## *Part IV: Practice and the arts*

The final part of this volume seeks to offer artistic, spiritual and psychotherapeutic perspectives on the nature of holism in practice. The opening chapter of Part IV is written by acclaimed poet Richard Berengarten and consists of an autobiographical account of a synchronistic event that gave rise to a poetic work that changed his life. In 'A synchronistic experience in Serbia' (Chapter 15) what happened before, during, and after the event unfolds in an evocative narrative that Berengarten shares with the reader. The external catalyst event, in May 1985, occurred in central Serbia, at the same location as the external primary event, a wartime massacre perpetrated 44 years previously by Nazi occupiers, in October 1941.

Megumi Yama's chapter, 'The concept of *kami* in Shintō and holism: Psychotherapy and Japanese literature' (Chapter 16), reviews how the ambiguous nature of *kami* itself is unique in religious and cultural meaning and with respect to its deep roots in the Japanese psyche. The Japanese word *kami* is usually translated into English as deity, god, or spirit; yet none of these words precisely capture its full meaning. According to Yama, many Japanese accept the concept of *kami* without even being conscious of its historical religious basis. She argues that we can find these *kami* in the *Kojiki*, the oldest Japanese creation myth, and that such a concept may finally lead to the Buddhist idea of *jinen*—a state in which everything flows spontaneously, or just as it is. She concludes that given we cannot have direct contact with this *kami*, all that we can do is to try to have a relationship with Ame-no-minaka-nushi, as one *kami* as a whole, through the channels of multiple *kami*.

Finally, Jason Wright's chapter 'The CORE Trust: The holistic approach to addiction' (Chapter 17) explores the work of a Central London voluntary sector organisation which treated addicts 'holistically' between 1985 and 2014, using depth psychological and psychoanalytic insights from Jung's analytical psychology, James Hillman's archetypal psychology, and the work of Donald Winnicott. The process philosophy of Whitehead and Bohm and group analytic and complementary healthcare models were also central to this holistic approach. Wright describes how internal and external processes of containment were necessary when working with the experiences of a diverse therapeutic community. The underpinning model or frame for the practice was one of community articulated through Hillman's archetypal framework. This psychotherapeutic frame was in negotiation with other traditions, particularly acupuncture, qi gong, and Chinese herbalism form 'the east' and herbal medicine, homeopathy, and physical treatments such as Alexander technique and cranio-sacral therapy from 'the west'. These treatments, taken together, formed a physical, mental, and spiritual frame, with aspects of Whitehead's and Bohm's ideas of process offering a useful description of the relational dynamics of people, philosophies, and practices.

## References

Ash, M. (1995) *Gestalt Psychology in German Culture, 18901967: Holism and the Quest for Objectivity*, Cambridge: Cambridge University Press.
Bailis, S. (1984) 'Against and for holism: a reply and a rejoinder to D. C. Phillips', *Issues in Integrative Studies* 3: 17–41.
Bateson, G. (1973) *Steps to an Ecology of Mind*, London: Paladin.
Beckman, H. and Le Quesne, S. (2005) *The Essential Guide to Holistic and Complementary Therapy*, London: Thompson Learning.
Bertuglia, C. S. and Vaio, F. (2005) *Nonlinearity, Chaos, and Complexity: The Dynamics of Natural and Social Systems*, Oxford: Oxford University Press.
Bohm, D. (1980) *Wholeness and the Implicate Order*, London and New York: Routledge and Kegan Paul.
Berman, M. (1981) *The Reenchantment of the World*, Ithaca, NY: Cornell University Press.

Bertalanffy, L. von (1968) *General System Theory: Foundations, Development, Applications*, New York: Braziller.
Diriwächter, R. and Valsiner, J. (eds.) (2008) *Striving for the Whole: Creating Theoretical Syntheses*, New Brunswick, NJ: Transaction Publishers.
Dusek, V. (1999) *The Holistic Inspirations of Physics: The Underground History of Electromagnetic Theory*, New Brunswick, NJ: Rutgers University Press.
Einstein, A. (1936) Letter to Jan Smuts, 24 June 1936, Vol. 54, Folio 33, Cambridge University Library.
Esfeld, M. (1998) 'Holism and analytic philosophy', *Mind* 107: 365–80.
Esfeld, M. (2001) *Holism in Philosophy of Mind and Philosophy of Physics*, Berlin: Springer.
Esfeld, M. (2003) 'Philosophical holism', *Encyclopedia of Life Support Systems*, Paris: UNESCO/Eolss Publishers. [http://www.eolss.net].
Forbes, S. (2003) *Holistic Education: An Analysis of Its Ideas and Nature*, Brandon, VT: Foundation for Educational Renewal.
Hanegraaff, W. (1998) *New Age Religion and Western Culture: Esotericism in the Mirror of Secular Thought*, Albany, NY: State University of New York Press.
Hanson, B. (2014) *What Holism Can Do for Social Theory*, New York and London: Routledge.
Harrington, A. (1996) *Reenchanted Science: Holism in German Culture from Wilhelm II to Hitler*, Princeton, NJ: Princeton University Press.
Heelas, P. and Woodhead, L, with Seel, B., Szeszynski, B. and Tusting, K. (2005) *The Spiritual Revolution: Why Religion in Giving Way to Spirituality*, Oxford: Blackwell.
House, W. (2016) 'Being holistic: the new focus of the BHMA', *Journal of Holistic Healthcare* 13(1): 4–6 .
Keulartz, J. (1998) *The Struggle for Nature: A Critique of Radical Ecology*, trans. R. Kuitenbrouwer, London: Routledge.
Lawrence, C. and Weisz, G. (eds.) (1998) *Greater than the Parts: Holism in Biomedicine 1920–1950*, New York and Oxford: Oxford University Press.
Magee, G. A. (2001) *Hegel and the Hermetic Tradition*, Ithaca, NY: Cornell University Press.
Main, R. (2017) 'Panentheism and the undoing of disenchantment', *Zygon: Journal of Religion and Science* 52(4): 1098–1122.
Main, R., McMillan, C. and Henderson, D. (2020) *Jung, Deleuze, and the Problematic Whole*, London and New York: Routledge.
Marietta, D. (1994) *For People and the Planet: Holism and Humanism in Environmental Ethics*, Philadelphia, PA: Temple University Press.
Otto, T. and Bubandt, N. (eds.) (2010) *Experiments in Holism: Theory and Practice in Contemporary Anthropology*, Oxford: Wiley-Blackwell.
Phillips, D. C. (1976) *Holistic Thought in Social Science*, Stanford, CA: Stanford University Press.
Popper, K. (1957) *The Poverty of Historicism*, London: Routledge, 2002.
Smuts, J. (1926) *Holism and Evolution*, London: McMillan.
Weber, M. and Esfeld, M. (2003) 'Holism in the sciences', *Encyclopedia of Life Support Systems*, Paris: UNESCO/Eolss Publishers. [http://www.eolss.net].
Wood, L. S. (2010) *A More Perfect Union: Holistic Worldviews and the Transformation of American Culture after World War II*, Oxford: Oxford University Press.
Zahle, J. and Collin, F (eds.) (2014) *Rethinking the Individualism-Holism Debate: Essays in the Philosophy of Social Science*, Dordrecht: Synthese Library Springer.

# PART I
# History and contexts

# 1

# HOW DO WE THINK IN TERMS OF *WHOLES?* HOLISTIC VOICES AND VISIONS AFTER WORLD WAR II

*Linda Sargent Wood*

NASA's first photos of earth shifted our vantage point. "Earthrise" especially captured the imagination in its shot of earth as a bright blue and white sphere against the pitch-black setting of space. Taken in 1968, a year of tremendous tumult around the world, the image gave humanity a startling view. Physicist Stephen Hawking called this new perspective one of the "great revelations of the Space Age" and an invitation to "see ourselves as a whole." For him, the image of earth from space reinforced unity and beckoned us to act accordingly: "One planet. One human race. We are here together and we need to live together with tolerance and respect. We must become global citizens." Our only boundaries, Hawking mused, are the borders we create.[1] Such messages resonated in 1970 when historic numbers gathered on the mall in Washington, DC, to celebrate the first Earth Day. Environmentalists spoke of ecological wholeness and harmony and encouraged all to think globally and act locally. This world—sea, soil, and sky—was one ecosystem, one society. An entire generation, one college student exclaimed, was "seeing, thinking, feeling wholes."[2] NASA photographs only seemed to confirm this; the planet was one, interconnected whole.[3]

Earth Day offered a celebration of holistic ideas in a time when holistic sensibilities reverberated throughout significant subsections of post–World War II America with particular power. This manifestation of holism—a view that held that reality can only be understood as a whole, can only be comprehended by focusing on relationships between the parts and the whole—emphasized unity, interdependencies, integration, and community.[4]

One popular holistic articulation came from zoologist and nature writer Rachel Carson. In her successful trilogy of books on the sea she wrote about a "web of life" that connected humans to the world around them and argued that actions taken in one segment of the ecosystem had dramatic consequences elsewhere. She used this holistic reasoning in her 1962 book, *Silent Spring*, to chastise the chemical industry. Pesticides sprayed over croplands seep into groundwater and move throughout the ecosystem, harming the entire environment in the process. "In the ecological web of life," the zoologist explained, "nothing existed alone."[5] *Silent Spring* set off a storm of controversy, shot to the top of the *New York Times* bestseller list, and ignited the modern environmental movement. Thousands accepted her message, joined environmental groups, and lobbied for clean air and water.[6]

Carson thought in terms of "wholes." She focused on entire systems. Her training in biology taught her to examine individual species with great care but she focused on how one species was affected by another and how actions in one place could have long lasting consequences elsewhere. Her interest was in the big picture and she was not alone in environmental circles and elsewhere.

In the 1960s and 1970s, holistic conceptions resounded throughout significant subsections of American culture with particular power, changing the ways people understood themselves and their relationship with other people and the environment, drove social reform, and altered conceptions of science and religion. Making connections between spraying apple trees with chemicals and no birds singing was only one of the arenas where Americans embraced this train of thought.

Turning to structural engineer and futurist R. Buckminster Fuller reveals another holistic expression. A year after Carson broadcast her holistic world view in *Silent Spring*, Fuller published *Operating Manual for Spaceship Earth* and joined others in asking, "How do we think in terms of wholes?" To posit solutions to the problems we face, we can't be specialists that only think in terms of parts, Fuller contended. We must eschew specialization and reductionistic approaches. We have to think of the whole system—the whole earth—and "make the world work for 100% of humanity…without ecological offense or damage to anyone."[7] In an age of plenty that was also fraught with division and disparity, he aimed to distribute resources fairly and to provide food and shelter for all. Through his speeches, books, maps, and businesses, he called for a just allocation of assets, an end to the Cold War, and more harmony between East and West. We must "explore ways to make it possible for anybody and everybody in the human family to enjoy the total Earth without … gaining advantage at the expense of another."[8]

His innovative geodesic dome became part of his solution, as he fashioned the economical units to serve as everything from homes to stadiums, storage sheds to churches, greenhouses to planetariums. Geodesics offered an answer to worldwide housing shortages and more. Held together in synergetic wholeness, each part relying on neighboring parts for stability, geodesics became his holistic representation, a metaphor for the interdependency he found at the heart of his holistic philosophy. They were the embodiment of his belief that the machine belonged in the garden, his affirmation that the relationship between technology and nature was complementary. Both, he felt, had a place on this planet he dubbed "spaceship earth." His proposed dome over New York

City, though fantastic and impractical, offered a palpable way to control the climate.[9]

Fuller's maps, sometimes flat representations, sometimes globes, also communicated his holistic vision. They, too, emphasized connections, interdependencies and oneness. Just as each part of his dome relied on adjacent parts to form the whole structure, so, too, he felt that each sea and land mass was crucial to the whole planet. *Life* magazine published a cut-out of one map with 20 different, separable triangles and instructions for assembling. *Life* called the map "pure invention" but readers responded enthusiastically. The issue sold a record-breaking 3 million copies. As a manipulable, it could be laid out flat or folded into a globe.[10] There was no up, down, north, south, east, or west. The parts could be rearranged to give any region—or no region—center stage. Differing perspectives and interests could thus be highlighted. To encourage thinking of the globe as one comprehensive whole, Fuller's maps could be arranged to line up the continents and showcase one stream of land. Conversely, his "One-Ocean World" map highlighted the interconnectedness of the earth's water by showing it as one united body, dispelling assumptions of oceans as separate and isolated. He called his domes "world-around structures" to fit his global vision of "one world town." By merging the dome and globe together in a "geoscope," he depicted his idea of one global village.

Maps are abstracts that may be used as both *models of* and *models for* something, a tangible, objective reality or a vision.[11] Fuller's maps did both, though they were largely visionary. He designed his maps to help others see as he did, that we are aboard one spaceship earth. We are one planet, one human race in a global village not divided by east and west or other human boundaries. Hawking's words in 2015 echo such declarations.

Fuller attracted a sizeable following, even ones willing to listen to his six-hour lectures peppered with words he invented. His geodesics became colorful domiciles for counterculture enthusiasts as well as practical spaces for fairs, military operations, scientific experiments, and sporting events. His maps became a forum for playing his World Game—his antidote to Cold War military games—where people puzzled through ways to justly allocate resources and make peace.[12]

Other individuals from multiple socioeconomic and racial backgrounds joined Carson and Fuller in challenging their era's most pressing problems and calling on holistic understandings to bring an end to mushroom clouds, military-industrial complexes, racial and gender discrimination, and inequities of wealth and power. To follow the story of this particular cultural response even further, several serve as illustrations of holism's power in their own spheres of influence: civil rights leader Martin Luther King, Jr.; French Jesuit priest and paleontologist Pierre Teilhard de Chardin; and psychologist Abraham Maslow.

While these five do not provide definitive renderings of holism in any kind of absolute sense, they do offer examples of holistic ideas in different fields of knowledge and highlight some of the ways that holism can be used and bent for various agendas. Together they comprise a small, yet suggestive, sampling of a broader cross-section of American society. Each spoke to similar concerns and offered complementary answers. Troubled by what seemed to them a fragmented world, they reprimanded a science that had led to atomic war. They balked at medical approaches that treated humans as parts, systems that compartmentalized life, and huge corporations that, in quest of profit, ignored their products' harm. Some defied accepted social codes, rebelling against hierarchical distinctions of race and sex. With zeal, each strove to create a better world, infusing their spiritual values and holistic outlook into some of the century's most powerful social movements: the counterculture, environmentalism, the struggle for racial and gender equality, and the push for alternative medicine. Holistic concepts provided an ethical framework and practical solutions for handling a variety of crises.

Though contested and controversial, their influence can be measured through their bestselling books; large turnouts at speeches, rallies, and marches; popular architectural designs; prominent academic work in journals and institutes; legal reforms; an increase in the number of businesses offering holistic health; and changing spiritual practices and beliefs. Their success impacted some of the ways that ordinary individuals, rich and poor, male and female, perceived race, gender, nature and technology; and it contributed to the persistence of religion in a scientific age.

Before exploring the other holistic expressions within this select group, it is worth pausing to survey holism historically. Holism has a history. As an intellectual and social construct, it has waxed and waned in influence and power. Episodically, the worldview enjoys time in the sun, then fades only to resurface at another time and place.

South African General Jan Christiaan Smuts coined the word "holism" in 1926 to reflect his interests in evolution, philosophy, and Gestalt psychology, which expressed holistic, anti-reductionistic thought. Gestalt psychologists claimed that the mind perceives reality in terms of organized wholes. People, they contended, do not understand experience in a piecemeal fashion. When we perceive a pattern, solve a problem, answer a riddle, we exclaim "aha." We see the whole. Austrian philosopher Christian von Ehrenfels laid the groundwork for Gestalt psychology by explaining that a melody is comprised of musical notes; yet, it is more than a collection of notes. It follows a distinct form. If the notes are rearranged, the melody is lost. Hence, the melody is a whole that is more than the sum of its parts.[13] Max Wertheimer and other Gestalt psychologists working in the twentieth century voiced adherence to organic wholes and the interdependencies of the parts, then they influenced other holists, such as Ruth Benedict, Frederick Perls, Abraham Maslow, and Smuts. But holism was not unique to this era either.

Smuts derived the word from the ancient Greek word, "holos," meaning whole. Holos abounded in the writings of Plato, Aristotle, Hippocrates, and Paul, often conveying a holistic meaning. Plato, in *Dialogues*, critiqued medicinal practices that did not treat the "whole" patient, and he quoted favorably from

Hippocrates who wrote that "the nature of the body can only be understood as a whole."[14] Aristotle wrote what has become today's common understanding of holism in *Metaphysics*: "The whole is more than the sum of its parts." The Apostle Paul used the term in his biblical letters to express that the person should be viewed as wholly integrated in spirit, body, and mind, linking his ontology with other New Testament passages that referred to wholeness of life in terms of salvation and sanctification. In this way, he united holiness with wholeness.

Holistic ideas have surfaced in a variety of cultures and diverse places and times. Medieval European philosophers employed holistic conceptions to explain life as a "great chain of being." Hildegard of Bingen, a twelfth-century mystic and patron saint of the 20th-century New Age movement, developed a holistic theology of immanence, exclaiming, "O Holy Spirit, you are the mighty way in which everything that is in the heavens, on the earth, and under the earth, is penetrated with connectedness, penetrated with relatedness." Human beings, in synergetic relation with God and a fundamental part of this organic whole, were, she professed, "co-creators with God in everything we do."[15] In India, holistic thought found expression in Vedanta philosophy and Hindu culture. The Yin and Yang as complementary visions of the whole in Chinese adhere to a holistic framework.

As the many appropriations of holism in various disciplines and times suggest, the concept of holism, like other intellectual constructs and sensibilities, is malleable.[16] Across time and space, individuals and groups invented, borrowed, and reclaimed holistic understandings as their own, manipulating the sensibility to fit multiple agendas. The 20th century alone contains many manifestations. Alternative or complementary medicine, for example, has viewed the person (emotional, mental, physical, and spiritual) and the person's environment as a whole in the diagnosis and treatment of disease.[17] In philosophy, semantic holists have argued that meaning can only be derived from the context of the language as a whole. The parts—syllables, words, sentences—are derivative.[18] In biology, theoretical biologist Ludwig Bertalanffy (1901–1972), father of General Systems Theory, applied a holistic approach by focusing on the integration of the parts to the whole organism. The systems model became a guiding paradigm for a variety of disciplines, from the sciences and social sciences to corporate management and public administration. The ecosystem, which posits that the organism continuously interacts with its environment, reflects this approach.[19] Cybernetics studies, especially under the hand of Norbert Wiener, employed another systems methodology using mathematical feedback theories and self-organizing assumptions that was foundational for computer designers and some psychologists.[20]

Social and political theories have, at times, also reflected organic, holistic thinking. Sociologist Emile Durkheim's view of society as an organic whole is one example. Socialism is another. Even as it focuses on the uneven distribution of power among the classes, socialist theory prioritizes the communal whole. In 1914 Vladimir Lenin wrote, "Everything is connected to everything else."[21] Totalitarianism in its demand for subservience by all members to the centralized state reveals how holism may be appropriated for ill. Adolf Hitler's vision of a superior Aryan race and his ideal of a unified world legitimized in his eyes the subordination of the one for the many, the sacrifice of some for the good of the whole. His manipulation of holism, in stark contrast with other versions, demonstrates the idea's pliability.

In American history, holistic thought permeated sundry utopian experiments and reform impulses from the Romantic movement in the 19th century to the conservationists of the 20th century. While responding to unique concerns of their particular generation, comparisons between Transcendentalist journal *Dial* editor, Margaret Fuller, and her grandnephew Buckminster Fuller hint at more than generational differences. Other 20th-century holists also found their 19th-century ancestors inspirational to the extent that many parallels can be drawn between the eras. Both borrowed from organic models of nature; presumed connectedness, unity, and harmony with nature; and catered to pantheistic religious conceptions or, at least, a belief in divine immanence rather than transcendence. Twentieth-century figures concerned about human relationships with nature also articulated holistic ideas. Conservationist John Muir summed up his view in a statement frequently quoted by later environmentalists and sustainability experts: "When we try to pick out anything by itself, we find it hitched to everything else in the Universe."[22]

In these and other instances, individuals and groups over time and place bent and employed holistic understandings for their own purposes. In this way, holism is, to borrow from historian James Gilbert's lexicon, an "episodic notion," a cyclical idea that rises and falls at varying historical intervals.[23]

Holism's rise in American culture in the post–World War II era was one of these episodic moments. It resonated in powerful ways across society. Seeing how it manifest itself within the civil rights movement illustrates, too, that it was not a fringe movement or one isolated to the environmental movement or to Buckminster Fuller's geodesic renderings.

Martin Luther King, Jr.'s vision of a beloved society made a holistic declaration. "In a real sense all of life is interrelated," he contended, as he sought to unite race-divided America. "We are," he affirmed, "tied together in the single garment of destiny, caught in an inescapable network of mutuality."[24] He recognized healing required change not just in one part but in all. Prompted to action by discrimination and poverty at home and decolonization and war abroad, King promised racial healing and a brotherhood that was more than a sum of its parts, more than a negation of the customs of segregation. His work helped trigger a revolution in racial relations, the Civil Rights Act of 1964, and the Voting Rights Act of 1965.[25]

Dreams of community did not stop with the physical universe. The web of life, according to Teilhard de Chardin, joined spirit and matter. The French priest, who gained a significant American following in the 1960s, advocated a panentheistic belief system that *all is in God,* and postulated that everything had a part in the evolutionary process. Speaking to concerns about the role of faith in an increasingly modern, scientific, and technological society, Teilhard merged Catholicism with evolutionary theory and called his ideas "A Religion of Evolution." He envisioned the universe progressing toward a place of unity, a mystical state that he named the "omega point."[26]

Though the Vatican banished him to China because of his evolutionary ideas for most of his adult life, Teilhard wrote prolifically. He attracted progressive Catholics and proved to be one of the most inspirational voices for the human potential movement. The American and British Teilhard Associations and the journal *Zygon* disseminated Teilhard's synthesis, and the priest's ideas influenced Gaia science, cosmological viewpoints in physics, Deep Ecology, and New Age religion.

Outlining the contours of Teilhard's holistic synthesis in this era of high scientific achievement helps explain how some continued to maintain their strong religious allegiance. Instead of opting for science over religion, Teilhard and his followers merged scientific and religious tenets.

Holism during this era was about imagined communities. Carson connected humans to an ecosystem of elm leaves, earthworms, and robins to create an idyllic web of life. Fuller envisioned a highly efficient built environment that yielded greater individual happiness, social harmony, and global sustainability. King dedicated himself to the formation of a "beloved community," marked by interracial equality. Teilhard, in his creative amalgamation of Catholicism and evolution, wrote of a final day of love and brotherhood at the "Omega Point."

Psychologist and self-proclaimed holist Abraham Maslow was no different. Though best known as one of the founders of humanistic psychology and a proponent of "individual growth," his holism had a strong, communitarian thrust. Hand-in-hand with his hope to foster "self-actualized" people—his expression for emotionally healthy, fully integrated, and self-fulfilled individuals—he dreamed of the establishment of democratic, just, and peaceful societies and "construction of the One Good World."[27] He called his utopia "eupsychia" (pronounced, he said, "yew-sigh-key-a").[28] Hence, in understanding his psychology, community was fundamental.

Maslow claimed that his vision of Eupsychia began to jell in the days following Japan's attack on Pearl Harbor. Driving home one day, a "poor, pathetic parade" crossed before him at an intersection. "Boy scouts and fat people and old uniforms and a flag and someone playing a flute off-key" formed a ragged patriotic procession and symbolized to him a world in disarray. The tears began to flow: "I felt we didn't understand—not Hitler, nor the Germans, nor Stalin, nor the Communists. We didn't understand any." In response, Maslow called for psychological enlightenment. He "had a vision of a peace table, with people sitting around it, talking about human nature and hatred and war and peace and brotherhood" and determined "that the rest of my life must be devoted to discovering a psychology for the peace table ... I wanted to prove that human beings are capable of something grander than war and prejudice and hatred."[29]

In his advocacy for peace and his embrace of humanism, Maslow took a holistic perspective of the person as sacred and whole. He denounced reductionism. A brief stint in medical school fortified this view. One physician showed students how to remove a cancerous breast but did so without respect, "He cut off the breast, tossing this object off through the air onto a marble counter where it landed with a plop," Maslow recalled, "I have remembered that plop for thirty years. It had changed from a sacred object into a lump of fat, garbage, to be tossed into a pail."[30] In his book, *Motivation and Personality*, the psychologist wrote, "Holism is obviously true—after all, the cosmos is one and interrelated; any society is one and interrelated; any person is one and interrelated. … Recently I have become more and more inclined to think that the atomistic way of thinking is a form of mild psychopathology."[31]

Such holistic expressions helped reshape American notions of spirituality and stimulated organizations, institutions, and movements that embodied and popularized holistic understandings. Clinics opened to treat the whole person—mind, body, and spirit—and Maslow's convictions were at the forefront of this approach. He became beloved by holistic health practitioners for his rebellion against the treatment of the body as just a bunch of parts.[32]

The psychologist served as one of the inspirations for the human potential movement, particularly strong in such places as the Esalen Institute. Situated on California's rugged coast, Esalen reflected some of the ways holism permeated the culture, and it served as one of the most prominent venues for spreading and shaping holistic thought.

Famous in the 1960s for its individualistic excesses and Dionysian explorations of self through encounter groups, psychodramas, spontaneity theatre, transactional analysis, sexual adventures, and psychedelic drugs, rumors spread quickly through the media and counterculture that Esalen was a "happening place." Indeed, leaders trumpeted personal freedom and gave participants a chance to experiment with psychological techniques designed to help one "get in touch" with body, mind and spirit.[33]

Yet, while Esalen attracted those in search of what one attendee called the "very honey pot of eroticism," it was always more than mineral springs and narcissistic exploits.[34] From its beginning in 1962, co-founders Michael Murphy and Richard Price plotted human transformation in conjunction with social solidarity and spiritual oneness. Workshops promoted communalism, spiritual harmony, environmentalism, and the creation of a better society. Even the pursuit of "peak experiences" and "self-actualization," according to one of Esalen's early proponents and influences, Abraham Maslow, was perceived as a path to creating a synergistic world. Maslow and Fuller spoke there; the ideas of Teilhard, Carson, MLK, and other holists found a welcome audience there. The result was a center that cultivated holistic connections and married eastern mysticism with Western religious and scientific notions. As such, it became a sort of Western ashram where participants blended Buddhism, Christianity, Judaism, evolution, and humanistic psychology. Workshops offered a mix of practices that anticipated the New Age movement.

Studying any one of these holists or phenomena in isolation misses the larger significance. Congregating them highlights the fundamental role that holism played in the culture at mid-century. As these individuals declared their holistic worldviews, they articulated cultural tensions Americans experienced during the Cold War. Their understandings of the world challenged Cold War animosities, an ethos of containment, nuclear fear, and Levittown sameness. They expressed hope for creating meaningful communities, maintained faith in an increasingly scientific world, and made space for technology while preserving a harmonious relationship with nature. In doing so, they both reflected and shaped American culture.

While these holistic ideas hit with particular power, produced tangible results and sparked "seeing, thinking, feeling wholes," the communitarian impulse within this holistic moment did not last. Holism took an individualistic turn in the 1970s. Showing the very manipulability of this constellation of ideas, other holistic thinkers again remade the concept and crafted holistic projects to meet new times and circumstances. Consequently, this anthology of ideas lost much of its communitarian drive, optimistic impulse, and utopian thrust in exchange for more personal articulations. These holists turned their attention inward to the integration of the individual mind and body and marketed it for a new day.

Hence, holism did not fade completely. Today, at two decades into the 21st century, the word "holism" seems to be everywhere from agriculture to architecture, from psychology to education, from religion to science, from financial wellness to marketing to tourism. Health care adopts Eastern and Western medicine and some practitioners advocate a holistic mindset. Like past iterations, many use this kaleidoscope of ideas today to understand reality and to confront current troubles. Scientists, for example, stress holistic connections between disappearing glaciers, the devastating collapse of Australia's Great Barrier Reef, and humanity's footprint.

The question persists. How will holistic ideas be used: For good, for ill, for solving or creating problems. Will we aim to protect and bolster our own little corner of the world, championing a particular race or nation at the expense of others? Will we work together—across cultures and geographies—on mutual projects that protect the planet and lead to greater equality and justice? In our answers and work, we might do well to take the vantage point of Hawking in seeing earth from space, in seeing ourselves as a whole, as one human race on one planet aiming for harmony, tolerance and respect.

## Notes

1 Stephen Hawking, "It Can Be Done," speech given at the 2015 World Economic Forum's Annual Meeting, as quoted by Lillian Gregory, "A Message from Stephen Hawking: 'It Can Be Done," September 24, 2015, https://www.linkedin.com/pulse/message-from-stephen-hawking-can-done-lillian-gregory.
2 Phil Nelson, "Environment and Establishment: A Student Letter," *National Parks and Conservation Magazine* 44 (1970): 11–12, quote on page 11. Also quoted in Roderick

Nash, *Wilderness and the American Mind*, rev. ed. (New Haven, CT: Yale University Press, 1973), 252.

3 Andrew Kirk, *Counterculture Green: The Whole Earth Catalog and American Environmentalism* (Lawrence: University Press of Kansas, 2007), 41–42; Neil Maher, "Gallery: Neil Maher on Shooting the Moon," *Environmental History* 9 (July 2004): 526–31.

4 To miss this holistic mentalité would discount vital aspects of American life and lead to only partial explanations of the time. Yet, while declaring holism's importance, I do not mean to suggest that holism explains everything about any one person nor do I presume that holism singularly defined the era. People and history defy such simplicity. Rather, in calling this a key period for holistic thinking and action, I seek to capture—as students of the Enlightenment, Romanticism, or Modernism have done for their study eras—a broad framework, sensibility, sentiment, mood, and intellectual configuration. I have written about this holistic moment, developing the ideas in more depth and detail, in *A More Perfect Union: Holistic Worldviews and the Transformation of American Culture After World War II* (New York: Oxford University Press, 2010). Some of this chapter was originally published in the introduction of my book and has been reproduced by permission of Oxford University Press [https://global.oup.com/academic/product/a-more-perfect-union-9780195377743?cc=us&lang=en&]. Please see it also for ways in which each of these individuals constructed their holistic views, used them for different projects, and their impact on the culture.

5 Rachel Carson, *Silent Spring* (Boston: Houghton Mifflin, 1962), 51.

6 Many have written about Carson, see especially Linda Lear's biography, *Rachel Carson: Witness for Nature* (New York: Holt, 1997); Paul Brooks, *The House of Life: Rachel Carson at Work* (Boston: Houghton Mifflin, 1972); Carol B. Gartner, *Rachel Carson* (New York: Ungar, 1983); Maril Hazlett, "'Woman vs. Man vs. Bugs': Gender and Popular Ecology in Early Reactions to *Silent Spring*," *Environmental History* 9 (Oct. 2004), 701–29; H. Patricia Hynes, *The Recurring Silent Spring* (New York: Pergamon Press, 1989); and Hynes, "Ellen Swallow, Lois Gibbs and Rachel Carson: Catalysts of the American Environmental Movement," *Women's Studies International Forum* 8 (1985): 291–98; Ralph H. Lutts, "Chemical Fallout: Rachel Carson's *Silent Spring*, Radioactive Fallout, and the Environmental Movement," *Environmental History Review* 9 (Fall 1985): 210–25; reprinted in *And No Birds Sing: Rhetorical Analyses of Rachel Carson's Silent Spring*, ed. Craig Waddell (Carbondale, Ill.: Southern Illinois University Press, 2000), 17–41; Mark Hamilton Lytle, *Gentle Subversive: Rachel Carson, Silent Spring, and the Rise of the American Environmental Movement* (New York: Oxford University Press, 2007); Mary A. McCay, *Rachel Carson* (New York: Twayne, 1993); Vera Norwood, "Heroines of Nature: Four Women Respond to the American Landscape," *Environmental Review* 8 (1984): 34–56; and Philip Sterling, *Sea and Earth: The Life of Rachel Carson* (New York: Crowell, 1970).

7 R. Buckminster Fuller, *Operating Manual for Spaceship Earth* (New York: E. P. Dutton, 1963), 59.

8 R. Buckminster Fuller, *Critical Path* (New York: St. Martin's Press, 1981), 169. Fuller was prolific, publishing multiple books and articles. For biographies, see Lloyd Steven Sieden, *Buckminster Fuller's Universe: An Appreciation* (New York: Plenum Press, 1989); E. J. Applewhite, *Cosmic Fishing* (New York: Macmillan, 1985); Baldwin, *Bucky Works*; Alden Hatch, *Buckminster Fuller: At Home in the Universe* (New York: Dell, 1974); Hugh Kenner, *Bucky: A Guided Tour of Buckminster Fuller* (New York: Morrow, 1973); Robert W. Marks, *The Dymaxion World of Buckminster Fuller* (New York: Reinhold, 1960); John McHale, *R. Buckminster Fuller* (New York: Braziller, 1962); Robert Snyder, ed., *R. Buckminster Fuller: An Autobiographical Monologue/Scenario* (New York: St. Martin's Press, 1980); Calvin Tomkins, "Profiles: In the Outlaw Area," *New Yorker*, January 8, 1966, 35; and Calvin Tomkins, "Architecture: Umbrella Man," *Newsweek*, July 13, 1959, 84–87.

9 For Fuller's domes and its many uses, start with J. Baldwin, *Bucky Works: Buckminster Fuller's Ideas for Today* (New York: Wiley, 1996).
10 "Life Presents R. Buckminster Fuller's Dymaxion World," *Life*, March 1, 1943, 41–55; Buckminster Fuller, *Ideas and Integrities: A Spontaneous Autobiographical Disclosure*, ed. Robert W. Marks (Englewood Cliffs, N.J.: Prentice-Hall, 1963), chapter 6. Hatch reports the popularity of the maps in *Buckminster Fuller*, 167. Fuller's patent lawyer Donald Robertson traces the story of the map's creation in *Mind's Eye of Richard Buckminster Fuller* (New York: Vantage Press, 1974), chapter 2.
11 Political scholar Benedict Anderson, relying on the works scholar Thongchai, developed this categorization of mapmaking in his book *Imagined Communities: Reflections on the Origin and Spread of Nationalism*, rev. ed. (London: Verso Books, 1991), 173–74.
12 R. Buckminster Fuller, *The World Game: Integrative Resource Utilization Planning Tool* (Carbondale: Southern Illinois University Press, 1971). Fuller discusses his World Game in multiple places. See, for example, Buckminster Fuller, *Education Automation: Freeing the Scholar to Return to His Studies* (Carbondale: Southern Illinois University Press, 1962); Fuller, *Critical Path*, chapter 6;
13 Jan C. Smuts, *Holism and Evolution* (New York: Macmillan, 1926). D. Brett King and Michael Wertheimer, *Max Wertheimer and Gestalt Theory* (New Brunswick, New Jersey: Transaction Publishers, 2005), 41. Ehrenfels published his remarks in "On Gestalt Qualities," in Richard Avenarius's *Quarterly for Scientific Philosophy*; for the English translation, see *Foundations of Gestalt Theory*, trans. and ed. Barry Smith (Munich: Philosophia Verlag, 1988): 82–117. Ehrenfels also drew from the Scottish Common Sense school, particularly Thomas Reid, who suggested that complex ideas are apprehended as meaningful wholes; see Thomas H. Leahey, *A History of Psychology: Main Currents in Psychological Thought* (Upper Saddle River, N.J.: Prentice Hall, 1997), 136–38, 209. The German poet Goethe came to similar conclusions as expressed in his organic view of nature; see Mitchell G. Ash, *Gestalt Psychology in German Culture, 1890–1967: Holism and the Quest for Objectivity* (New York: Cambridge University Press, 1995), 85–86. For a historical and Catholic treatment of Smuts's work, see Frederick C. Kolbe, *A Catholic View of Holism: A Criticism of the Theory Put Forward by General Smuts in His Book, Holism and Evolution* (New York: Macmillan, 1928). For historical and philosophical accounts of the holistic worldview, see Stephen G. Brush, "The Chimerical Cat: Philosophy of Quantum Mechanics in Historical Perspective," *Social Studies of Science* 10 (1980): 393–447; Stephen C. Pepper, *World Hypotheses: A Study in Evidence* (Berkeley: University of California Press, 1942); and Harry Settanni, *Holism—A Philosophy for Today: Anticipating the Twenty-first Century* (New York: Peter Lang, 1990).
14 Plato, "Phaedrus," *The Dialogues of Plato*, trans. Benjamin Jowett, The Classical Library online http://www.classicallibrary.org/plato/dialogues/7_phaedrus.htm (accessed September 29, 2018). See Richard H. Svihus, "On Healing the Whole Person: A Perspective," *The Western Journal of Medicine* 131 (1979): 479, for a discussion of Plato and Hippocrates. For another helpful discussion on Plato's thoughts and how his thought has influenced the modern environmental movement and conceptions of the earth as a living organism, most notable in the "Gaia Hypothesis," see J. Donald Hughes, *Pan's Travail: Environmental Problems of the Ancient Greeks and Romans* (Baltimore: Johns Hopkins University Press, 1994). In these and other instances, Plato voiced a holistic view, but in his division of the world into ideas and matter, he expressed a mind-body dualism.
15 Hildegard of Bingen, as quoted in Carol MacCormack, "Hildegard of Bingen: A 12th Century Holistic World View," in Carol MacCormack and Jack Monger, *The Blossoming of a Holistic World View* (Landenberg, Pennsylvania: Quaker Universalist Fellowship, 1992), 9.
16 Exposing the plasticity of an idea is, to some extent, shaped by postmodernism which illuminates the frail nature of metanarratives. See Jean-François Lyotard, *The Postmodern Condition: A Report on Modernity* (Paris, 1979; Manchester, 1984).

17 For histories of alternative, complementary, and holistic health in American history, see Robert H. Abzug, *Cosmos Crumbling: American Reform and the Religious Imagination* (New York: Oxford University Press, 1994); especially 163–182; Kristine Alster, *The Holistic Health Movement* (Tuscaloosa: University of Alabama Press, 1989); Norman Cousins, *Anatomy of an Illness as Perceived by the Patient* (New York: Norton, 1979); and Norman Cousins, "The Holistic Health Explosion," *Saturday Review* 6 (March 31, 1979): 17–20; Christopher Lawrence and George Weisz, *Greater than the Parts: Holism in Biomedicine, 1920-1950* (New York: Oxford University Press, 1998); June Lowenberg, *Caring and Responsibility: The Crossroads between Holistic Practice and Traditional Medicine* (Philadelphia: University of Pennsylvania Press, 1989); Phyllis Mattson, *Holistic Health in Perspective* (Palo Alto, California: Mayfield, 1982); J. Warren Salmon, "The Holistic Alternative to Scientific Medicine: History and Analysis," *International Journal of Health Services* 10 (1980): 133-47; James C. Whorton, *Crusaders for Fitness: The History of American Health Reformers* (Princeton, NJ: Princeton University Press, 1982); and James C. Whorton, *Nature Cures: The History of Alternative Medicine in America* (New York: Oxford University Press, 2002), especially chapters 11–12.

18 For semantic holism, see Jerry Fodor and Ernest Lepore, *Holism: A Shopper's Guide* (Cambridge, Massachusetts: Basil Blackwell, 1992); and Jerry Fodor and Ernest Lepore, eds., *Holism: A Consumer Update* (Amsterdam, The Netherlands: Rodopi, 1993).

19 For General Systems Theory, see Donald Polkinghorne, "Systems and Structures," in his *Methodology for the Human Sciences: Systems of Inquiry* (Albany: State University of New York Press, 1983), chapter 4; C. W. Churchman, *The Systems Approach* (New York: Delacorte, 1968); P. B. Checkland, "Science and the Systems Paradigm," *International Journal of General Systems* 3 (1976): 127–34; John P. Van Gigch, *Applied General Systems Theory*, 2nd ed. (New York: Harper and Row, 1978); and Lars Skyttner, *General Systems Theory: Ideas and Applications* (River Edge, NJ: World Scientific, 2001). For the development of general systems theory in the 1930s and 1940s, turn especially to the writings of Ludwig Bertalanffy, *General Systems Theory: Foundations, Development, Applications* (New York: Braziller, 1968). For an explanation of his life and views as well as interpretations by two of his followers, Buckminster Fuller and the economist Kenneth Boulding, see Mark Davidson, *Uncommon Sense: The Life and Thought of Ludwig von Bertalanffy (1901-1972), Father of General Systems Theory* foreword by R. Buckminster Fuller, introduction by Kenneth E. Boulding (Los Angeles: J. P. Tarcher, 1983).

20 Norbert Wiener, *The Human Use of Human Beings: Cybernetics and Society* (Boston: Houghton Mifflin, 1954).

21 Vladimir I. Lenin, "Philosophical Notebooks Summary of Dialectics," in *The Collected Works of Vladimir Lenin*, 2nd English ed. (Moscow: Progress Publishers and Foreign Languages Press, 1965), 38: 221–22; and Stefan T. Possony, ed., *Lenin Reader* (Chicago: Henry Regnery, 1966), 9–10.

22 John Muir, *My First Summer in the Sierra* (Boston: Houghton Mifflin, 1911), 110.

23 James Gilbert, *A Cycle of Outrage: America's Reaction to the Juvenile Delinquent in the 1950s* (New York: Oxford University Press, 1986), 4.

24 This was a common refrain for Martin Luther King, Jr. See, for example, "The Ethical Demands for Integration," *Religion and Labor* 6 (May 1963): 1, 3–4, 7–8, reprinted in *A Testament of Hope: The Essential Writings and Speeches of Martin Luther King, Jr.*, ed. James Melvin Washington (San Francisco: Harper San Francisco, 1986), 122.

25 Taylor Branch, *Parting the Waters: America in the King Years, 1954–63* (New York: Simon and Schuster, 1988); Branch, *Pillar of Fire: America in the King Years, 1963–65* (New York: Simon and Schuster, 1998); Taylor Branch, *At Canaan's Edge: America in the King Years, 1965–68* (New York: Simon and Schuster, 2006); David Garrow,

*Bearing the Cross: Martin Luther King, Jr. and the Southern Christian Leadership Conference* (New York: Morrow, 1986); Coretta Scott King, *My Life with Martin Luther King, Jr.* (New York: Holt, Rinehart and Winston, 1969); and Stephen B. Oates, *Let the Trumpet Sound: The Life of Martin Luther King, Jr.* (New York: Harper and Row, 1982).

26 Teilhard rejected pantheism (all is God) for pantheism; see Pierre Teilhard de Chardin, "Cosmic Life," in *Writings in Time of War*, trans. René Hague (New York: Harper and Row, 1968), 60-61; and Pierre Teilhard de Chardin, *Heart of Matter*, trans. René Hague (New York: Harcourt Brace Jovanovich, 1978), 22–24. For Teilhard's description of the Omega Point, the last phase in his evolutionary schema, and his belief that the ongoing creative hand of God brings all into harmony; see Pierre Teilhard de Chardin, *The Phenomenon of Man*, trans. Bernard Wall (New York: Harper and Row, 1959), 257–72. For a later, and often clearer, translation of Teilhard's most popular work, see *The Human Phenomenon*, trans. Sarah Appleton-Weber (Portland, OR: Sussex Academic Press, 1999). See also Ursula King, *Spirit of Fire: The Life and Vision of Teilhard de Chardin* (New York: Orbis, 1996), 163–64; Mary Lukas and Ellen Lukas, *Teilhard* (Garden City, NY: Doubleday, 1977), 145–46; Robert Speaight, *The Life of Teilhard de Chardin* (New York: Harper and Row, 1967), 230; and Claude Cuénot, *Teilhard de Chardin: A Biographical Study*, trans. Vincent Colimore, ed. René Hague (Baltimore: Helicon Press, 1965), 164–65. Teilhard's religious and scientific writings are many. For a sample of his writings, see Pierre Teilhard de Chardin, *Building the Earth*, trans. Noel Lindsay and Norman Denny (London: Chaplin, 1965); *Christianity and Evolution*, trans. René Hague (New York: Harcourt Brace Jovanovich, 1971); *Divine Milieu*, trans. Bernard Wall (New York: Harper and Row, 1965); *The Future of Man*, trans. Norman Denny (New York: Harper and Row, 1964); *Hymn of the Universe*, trans. Gerald Vann (New York: Harper and Row, 1969); *Science and Christ*, trans. René Hague (New York: Harper and Row, 1968); and *Toward the Future*, trans. René Hague (New York: Harcourt Brace Jovanovich, 1975).

27 Abraham H. Maslow, *Toward a Psychology of Being*, 2nd ed. (Princeton, NJ: D. Van Nostrand, 1968), v.

28 Maslow, *Toward a Psychology of Being*, appendix B, 221.

29 Mary Harrington Hall, "A Conversation with the President of the American Psychological Association Abraham H. Maslow," *Psychology Today* 2 (1968): 54. For Maslow's life, see Edward Hoffman, *The Right to Be Human: A Biography of Abraham Maslow* (Los Angeles: Tarcher, 1988); Willard B. Frick, *Humanistic Psychology: Interviews with Maslow, Murphy, and Rogers* (Columbus, OH: Merrill, 1971); Frank Goble, *The Third Force: The Psychology of Abraham Maslow* (New York: Grossman, 1970); International Study Project and Bertha G. Maslow, comp. *Abraham Maslow: A Memorial Volume* (Monterey, CA: Brooks/Cole, 1972); Richard Lowry, *A. H. Maslow: An Intellectual Portrait* (Monterey, CA: Brooks/Cole, 1973); and Colin Wilson, *New Pathways in Psychology: Maslow and the Post-Freudian Revolution* (New York: Taplinger, 1972), 129–48.

30 Abraham Maslow, "Humanistic Science and Transcendent Experiences," *Journal of Humanistic Psychology*, 5 (Fall 1965), 223.

31 Abraham H. Maslow, *Motivation and Personality*, 1st ed. (New York: Harper and Row, 1954); 2nd ed. (New York: Harper and Row, 1970), preface.

32 Charlotte Buhler, "Human Life as a Whole as a Central Subject of Humanistic Psychology," in *Challenges of Humanistic Psychology*, ed. James F. T. Bugental (New York: McGraw-Hill, 1967), 83–91. Phyllis H. Mattson notes Maslow's contribution to the holistic health movement in *Holistic Health in Perspective* (Palo Alto, CA: Mayfield, 1982), 69, 88–89.

33 I have written about Esalen in *A More Perfect Union* and "Contact, Encounter, and Exchange at Esalen: A Window Onto Late Twentieth-Century American Spirituality," *Pacific Historical Review* 77 (August 2008): 453-87. For Esalen's history, see Marion Goldman, *The American Soul Rush: Esalen and the Rise of Spiritual Privilege*

(New York: New York University Press, 2012); Walter Anderson, *The Upstart Spring: Esalen and the American Awakening* (Reading, Mass.: Addison-Wesley, 1983); Alice Kahn, "Esalen at 25," *Los Angeles Times Magazine*, December 6, 1987; Jeffrey J. Kripal, *Esalen: America and the Religion of No Religion* (Chicago: University of Chicago Press, 2007); Jeffrey J. Kripal and Glenn W. Shuck, eds., *On the Edge of the Future: Esalen and the Evolution of American Culture* (Bloomington: Indiana University Press, 2005); Leonard, "Encounters at the Mind's Edge"; Eugene Taylor, *Shadow Culture: Psychology and Spirituality in America* (Washington, D.C.: Counterpoint, 1999), 235–60; and Calvin Tomkins, "New Paradigms," *New Yorker*, January 5, 1976, 30–51.

34 Stuart Miller, as quoted in Anderson, *Upstart Spring*, 192. See Miller's account in his book *Hot Springs: The True Adventures of the First New York Jewish Literary Intellectual in the Human Potential Movement* (New York: Viking Press, 1971).

# 2
# IRREDUCIBLE RESPONSIBILITY: APPLYING HOLISM TO NAVIGATE THE ANTHROPOCENE

*Andrew Fellows*

## Introduction

The advent of the Anthropocene epoch, in which the great forces of nature are becoming altogether more unpredictable and hostile to life due to human impacts, demands a *metanoia*, to which end I propose a synthesis of Jungian psychology with current approaches to the mind-matter problem, Earth systems science—specifically Gaia theory—and the principles of deep ecology. All of these inputs are essentially holistic.

## Mind and matter

C.G. Jung had explored the mind-matter conundrum through the humanities before beginning his scientific exchanges with Pauli in 1932. In 1954 Jung wrote (CW8: par. 418):

> Since psyche and matter are contained in one and the same world, and moreover are in continuous contact with one another and ultimately rest on irrepresentable, transcendental factors, it is not only possible but fairly probable, even, that psyche and matter are two different aspects of one and the same thing.

A contemporary explication of the Pauli–Jung conjecture by Atmanspacher and Fach (2013: 219–244) has been summarised schematically by Atmanspacher (2014: 253): (Figure 2.1)

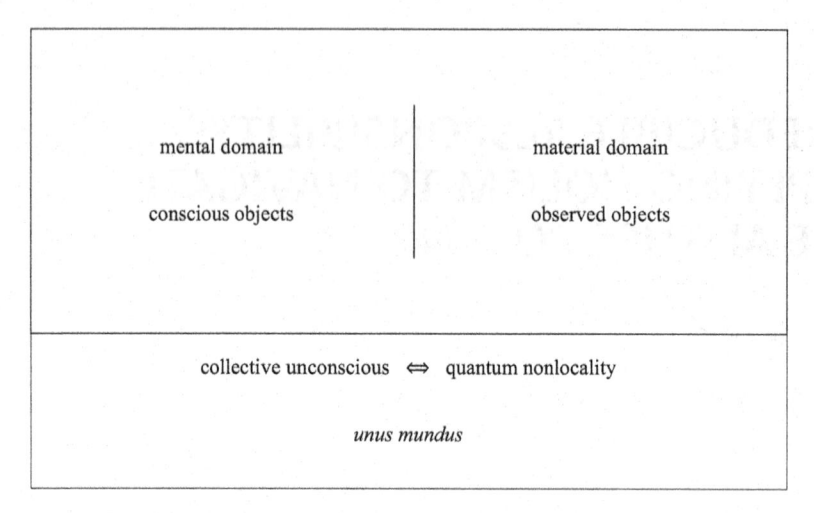

```
┌─────────────────────────────────────────────────────────────┐
│                          │                                  │
│     mental domain        │       material domain            │
│                          │                                  │
│    conscious objects     │      observed objects            │
│                          │                                  │
├─────────────────────────────────────────────────────────────┤
│         collective unconscious  ⇔  quantum nonlocality      │
│                                                             │
│                        unus mundus                          │
└─────────────────────────────────────────────────────────────┘
```

**FIGURE 2.1** Dual-aspect monism according to Pauli and Jung.

The mental and the material are epistemic manifestations of an ontic, psychophysically neutral, holistic reality, called the *unus mundus*, whose symmetry must be broken to yield dual, complementary aspects. Atmanspacher acknowledges (2014: 254) that this is a 'cartoon picture' which 'should be refined by a whole spectrum of boundaries ... each one indicating the transition to a more comprehensive level of wholeness'.

Ongoing research into the mind–brain relationship (Kelly et. al., 2007, 2015) has revisited the 'permission' theories of mind proposed by Myers and James (both known to Jung). According to this research, applying Occam's razor to exceptional experiences and other psychological phenomena suggests, without contradicting neuroscience, that our brains interact with external, nonlocal mind to permit individual consciousness, echoing Jung's concept of the collective unconscious.

## Gaia and psyche

Lovelock defined his Gaia theory (2009: 166) as:

> A view of the Earth introduced in the 1980s that sees it as a self-regulating system made up from the totality of organisms, the surface rocks, the ocean and the atmosphere tightly coupled as an evolving system. The theory sees this system as having a goal—the regulation of surface conditions so as always to be as favourable as possible for contemporary life. It is based on observations and theoretical models; it is fruitful and has made eight successful predictions.

Jung died seven years before Lovelock's first tentative Gaia hypothesis. Their theories are presumably independent, subject to this caveat from von Franz (1992: 15):

> there is not a single important scientific paradigm that is not based on a primal archetypal intuition. An archetypal structure pre-existing ego consciousness has generated the themes of Western natural science.

Moreover, as Korzybski (2000: 58) famously asserted:

> A map *is not* the territory it represents, but, if correct, it has a *similar structure* to the territory, which accounts for its usefulness.

If mind and matter are complementary aspects of the *unus mundus*, then Jung and Lovelock were creating *different maps of ultimately the same territory*, like political and physical maps of the world, so a degree of correlation between them can be expected.

The most significant common properties of Gaia and psyche are apparent teleology, and tensions between homeostasis (self-regulation) and adaptation (self-realisation). Teleology is unprovable, and both domains can alternatively be understood causally as complex adaptive systems—an irreconcilable but complementary perspective (Mackey, 2017). (Table 2.1).

Cybernetics is a crucial element of Gaia theory. Cybernetic systems participate in circular, causal chains that move from action to sensing to comparison with the desired goal, and again to action. Their causality is concealed within their circular logic:

> One of the most characteristic properties of all living organisms, from the smallest to the largest, is their capacity to develop, operate and maintain systems which set a goal and then strive to achieve it through the cybernetic process of trial and error.
>
> *(Lovelock, 2000: 45)*

According to Jungian psychodynamics, self-regulation is achieved, again with causality concealed, through compensation: 'Since the psyche is a self-regulating system, just as the body is, the regulating counteraction will always develop in the unconscious' (CW8: 159).

The goals of self-regulation in Gaia and psyche are to ensure the optimum functioning of the planet or individual respectively under their corresponding current conditions—environmental or psychological.

Gaia theory accommodates evolution but does not specify biodiversity as its goal. Nonetheless, strong correlations between ecological diversity, resilience and productivity are now generally accepted (e.g., Duffy et al., 2017; Monastersky, 2014).

**TABLE 2.1** Dynamical correlations between Gaia and psyche

|  | *Gaia* | *Psyche* |
|---|---|---|
| **Self-regulation:** | Cybernetics | Compensation |
| **Goal of self-regulation:** | Favour contemporary life | Function in the present |
| **Self-realisation:** | Evolution | Individuation |
| **Goal of self-realisation:** | Biodiversity | Wholeness |
| **Pathology:** | Anthropocene | Monotheism of consciousness |

The primacy of self-realisation for Jung is apparent in the opening lines of his autobiography:

> My life is a story of the self-realisation of the unconscious. Everything in the unconscious seeks outward manifestation, and the personality too desires to evolve out of its unconscious conditions and to experience itself as a whole.
>
> *(Jung, 1995: 17)*

This movement towards wholeness—the process of individuation—shifts the midpoint of the personality from the ego towards, and under the influence of, the Self.

Lovelock envisaged a 'doom scenario in which all life on earth down to that last deep-buried spore is annihilated' (2000: 38) due to a genetically engineered bacterium running amok through an unexpected symbiosis with another organism. Within six months

> The near infinity of creatures performing essential cooperative tasks was replaced by a greedy, uniform green scum, knowing nothing but an insatiable urge to feed and grow. ... With Gaia moribund, the cybernetic control of the Earth's surface composition and atmosphere at an optimum value for life had broken down ... this stricken Earth would move slowly but inexorably towards a barren steady state.
>
> *(2000: 40–41)*

This anticipates three major characteristics of the Anthropocene—human agency, monoculture, and tipping points. We comprise some 30% by dry mass of all terrestrial vertebrates, and our domesticated animals another 67%, leaving just 3% for wild animals (Smil, 2011). A conservative analysis (Ceballos, Ehrlich and Dirzo, 2017: E6095, E6089) of 27,600 vertebrate species indicates that

> as much as 50% of the number of animal individuals that once shared Earth with us are already gone, as are billions of populations. ... Beyond global species extinctions Earth is experiencing a huge episode of population

declines and extirpations, which will have negative cascading consequences on ecosystem functioning and services vital to sustaining civilization.

This is 'Earth's ongoing sixth major extinction event ... unparalleled for 65 million years' (Ceballos et. al., 2015: 4). Conversely, the physical 'technosphere' amounts to some 30 trillion tonnes, averaging 50 kg/m$^2$ of the Earth's surface (Zalasiewicz et. al., 2016). The Anthropocene means ever more of us and our stuff, and less other-than-human life—a material correlate of our 'monotheism of consciousness' decried by Jung, who warned that:

> the psyche of civilized man is no longer a self-regulating system but could rather be compared to a machine whose speed-regulation is so insensitive that it can continue to function to the point of self-injury, while on the other hand it is subject to the arbitrary manipulations of a one-sided will.
> *(CW8: 159)*

And again:

> The unconscious ... only becomes dangerous when our conscious attitude to it is hopelessly wrong. To the extent that we repress it, its danger increases.
> *(CW16: 329)*

These coincident pathological dynamics suggest structural correlations between Gaia and psyche. Lovelock and Jung had similar views, albeit expressed very differently, on the role of human consciousness. Lovelock's speculation:

> Do we as a species constitute a Gaian nervous system and a brain which can consciously anticipate environmental changes? ... the evolution of homo sapiens, with his technological inventiveness and his increasingly subtle communications network, has vastly increased Gaia's range of perception. She is now through us awake and aware of herself.
> *(2000: 139–140)*

resembles Jung's epiphany in Kenya decades earlier:

> There the cosmic meaning of consciousness became overwhelmingly clear to me. ... I knew...that man is indispensable for the completion of creation; that, in fact, he himself is the second creator of the world, who alone has given to the world its objective existence ...Human consciousness created objective existence and meaning, and man found his indispensable place in the great process of being.
> *(Jung, 1995: 284–285)*

Understood in the context of the *unus mundus*, these statements and other aspects of Jungian theory suggest the structural correlations in Table 2.2.

Reviewing Jung's 'The Stages of Life', Staude comments:

> Jung…emphasised developing the underdeveloped aspects of the self and maintaining an ongoing dialogue between the ego and non-ego aspects of the self as a total self-regulating developing system.
>
> *(1981: x)*

Jung speculated that individual psychology could be extrapolated to the collective. Self-similarity across scale is characteristic of nonlinear systems, and hence of life:

> Life itself arises at the boundary between order and chaos: it requires both, it is a daughter of both. … It is on the edge between order and chaos that the subtle dance of life takes place.
>
> *(Ritsema and Sabbadini, 2005: 3)*

The Mandelbrot set reveals the infinite complexity of this boundary. Life is fractal in both space and time, so the life cycles of a cell, a person, a civilisation and our species have much in common, from birth and growth to decline and death. Jung's analogy for this process in the individual, which I will now apply collectively, was the sun's diurnal passage across the sky.

Human development has been a hero's journey of separation from the Great Mother, from Gaia. However, as Hopcke (1989: 113, 115) summarised:

> Jung saw … that the Hero could be understood as an archetype within the collective psyche and, moreover, that this archetype was the one most often identified with humanity's emerging ego consciousness. … Jung's deep appreciation for the power and potentiality of the unconscious led him to be suspicious of any overvaluation of heroic ego consciousness.
>
> For Jung, the classical Greek concept of hubris, overweening pride, applies as much to our contemporary faith in our ability to produce, act and achieve as it did in the time of Sophocles or Homer. To identify ourselves with the Hero is to flirt with disaster, psychologically and these days perhaps literally.

**TABLE 2.2** Structural correlations between Gaia and psyche

| *Gaia* | *Psyche* |
|---|---|
| *Homo sapiens* (planetary centre of consciousness) | ego (individual centre of consciousness) |
| anthropogenic impacts (rejected/denied by *H. Sapiens*) | shadow (rejected/denied by ego) |
| *anima mundi* (world soul) | anima/animus (soul) |

This echoes the enantiodromia at the midpoint of 'The Stages of Life':

> The significance of the morning undoubtedly lies in the development of the individual, our entrenchment in the outer world, the propagation of our kind, and the care of our children. This is the obvious purpose of nature. But when this purpose has been attained—and more than attained—shall the earning of money, the extension of conquests, and the expansion of life go steadily on beyond the bounds of all reason and sense? Whoever carries over into the afternoon the law of the morning, or the natural aim, must pay for it with damage to his soul.
>
> *(CW8: 787)*

The hubris that Jung warned against is exemplified by Fukuyama's notorious essay (1989: 4):

> What we may be witnessing is…the end of history as such: that is, the end point of mankind's ideological evolution and the universalization of Western liberal democracy as the final form of human government.

We cannot relinquish the heroic attitude that has brought us unprecedented material comfort and security, but now threatens us with the opposite. Hence the then ExxonMobil CEO, Rex Tillerson, described climate change as 'an engineering problem, and it has engineering solutions' (Daily, 2012).

There is massive inertia in our immense civilisation, but also widespread evidence of our 'cherished convictions and principles' beginning 'to harden and to grow increasingly rigid' leading to 'a period of intolerance and fanaticism' as described by Jung (CW8: 773). His prescience may be summed up (and Tillerson's hubris exposed) in Jung's bleak warning that 'the world today hangs by a thin thread, and that thread is the psyche of man' (Jung, 1977: 303).

We delude ourselves that reason has triumphed, yet our growing population, insatiable consumption, and obsession with economic growth is heating Gaia at a rate equivalent to four Hiroshima atomic bombs every second (Nuccitelli et. al., 2012: 3467). As Capra observed (1983: 25):

> One of the most difficult things for people in our culture to understand is the fact that if you do something that is good, then more of the same will not necessarily be better. This, to me, is the essence of ecological thinking.

The consequences of our hubris will be catastrophic (Ophuls, 2012: n.p.):

> Because our own civilization is global, its collapse will also be global, as well as uniquely devastating owing to the immensity of its population, complexity and consumption. To avoid the common fate of all past

civilizations will require a radical change in our ethos—to wit, the deliberate renunciation of greatness—lest we precipitate a dark age in which the arts and adornments of civilization are partially or completely lost.

Just as in the individual psyche at mid-life, the collective tension between adherents to 'business as usual' and those preparing for a 'deliberate renunciation of greatness', is rising dangerously. Constrained by the immutable laws of nature, the era of heroic development is over, whether we like it or not.

## Sustainable individuation

The 'long-range deep ecology movement', originally proposed in the 1970s by the Norwegian philosopher Arne Næss, offers a 'radical change in our ethos', although 'it can be interpreted as remembering wisdom which men once knew' (Devall and Sessions, 1985: 80). It advocates a psychological rather than moralistic approach to environmentalism by expanding self beyond the boundaries of the narrow ego through the process of caring identification with larger entities such as forests, bioregions and the planet as a whole. Like Jung, Næss formulated a concept of 'Self' inspired by the Upanishads:

> I do not use this expression in any narrow, individualistic sense. I want to give it an expanded meaning based on the distinction between a large comprehensive Self and narrow egoistic self as conceived of in certain Eastern traditions of atman. This large comprehensive Self ... embraces all the life forms on the planet...together with their individual selves ... Viewed systematically, not individually, maximum Self-realization implies maximizing the manifestations of all life.
>
> *(1986: 80)*

Næss's 'Self' is a Gaian complement to the Jungian Self, and both give primacy to Self-realisation. Just as individuation seeks wholeness, Næss advocates diversity: 'Deep cultural diversity is an analogue on the human level to the biological richness and diversity of life-forms' (1986: 73). Like individuation, deep ecology is ordered by something greater and finds unique conscious expression in each individual.

Deep ecology is, above all, *biocentric*, not *anthropocentric*, asserting that ecologically effective ethics can only arise within the context of a cosmology of fundamental interrelatedness. It envisages humane population reduction as compatible with the flourishing of human life and cultures and essential for the biotic community as a whole. Although the alternative looks increasingly dystopian, our cognitive dissonance renders a naturally decreasing population an ecologist's dream and an economist's nightmare.

Deep ecology's outer transition from our anthropocentric *Zeitgeist* towards a biocentric attitude and smaller population correlates with individuation's inner transformation (Table 2.3).

**TABLE 2.3** Correlations between deep ecology and individuation

|  | Deep ecology | Individuation |
|---|---|---|
| **Movement:** | **Of:** worldview/ethos/population | **Of:** midpoint of personality |
|  | **From:** anthropocentric | **From:** ego |
|  | **To:** biocentric | **To:** Self |
| **Goal:** | biotic flourishing and cultural diversity | psychological wholeness |
| **Agent:** | ecological Self | Jungian Self |

The foregoing synergies established between Jungian psychology, Gaia theory and deep ecology offer a robust, non-dogmatic, albeit metaphysical, framework for us to navigate the challenges of the Anthropocene. While the inadequacy of our piecemeal efforts to address well-understood anthropogenic threats such as climate change make such a *metanoia* necessary, it is not alone sufficient. Time is not on our side, and sustainable retreat requires ingenuity as well as, and guided by, insight.[1]

I conclude with inspirations from Jung, Lovelock and Næss:

> **Jungian psychology:** 'The decisive question for man is: Is he related to something infinite or not? That is the telling question of his life.'
> 
> *(Jung, 1995: 357)*

> **Gaia theory:** 'the stable state of our planet includes man as a part of, or partner in, a very democratic entity.'
> 
> *(Lovelock, 2000: 137)*

> **Deep ecology:** 'Part of the joy stems from the consciousness of something bigger than our ego, something which has endured through millions of years and is worth continued life for millions of years. The requisite care flows naturally if the 'self' is widened so that protection of free Nature is felt and conceived as protection of ourselves.'
> 
> *(Næss, 1987: 26)*

Only such holistic awareness can humble us enough to realise and relinquish our suicidal and ecocidal hubris.

## Note

1 The essentially psychological transformation outlined here cannot remain 'merely' academic if it is to inspire, motivate, and support those empowered to make a big enough difference fast enough. My book *Gaia, Psyche and Deep Ecology: Navigating Climate Change in the Anthropocene* (Fellows, 2019) is a response to that challenge.

## References

Atmanspacher, H. (2014) '20th Century Versions of Dual-Aspect Thinking.' *Mind and Matter*, 12(2): 245–69.

Atmanspacher, H. and Fach, W. (2013) 'A Structural-Phenomenological Typology of Mind-Matter Correlations.' *Journal of Analytical Psychology*, 58(2): 219–44.

Capra, F. (1983) *The Turning Point*. London: Fontana.

Ceballos, G. et. al. (2015) 'Accelerated Modern Human-induced Species Losses: Entering the Sixth Mass Extinction.' *Science Advances*, 1(5): e1400253(15).

Ceballos, G., Ehrlich, R. and Dirzo, R. (2017) 'Biological Annihilation via the Ongoing Sixth Mass Extinction Signaled by Vertebrate Population Losses and Declines.' *PNAS*, 114(30): E6089–E6096.

Daily, M. (2012) 'Exxon CEO Calls Climate Change Engineering Problem'. in *Reuters, US Edition*. at www.reuters.com/article/2012/06/27/us-exxon-climate-idUSBRE8 5Q1C820120627 (accessed 22 July 2013).

Devall, B. and Sessions, G. (1985) *Deep Ecology*. Salt Lake City, UT: G.M. Smith.

Duffy, J.E., Godwin, C.M. and Cardinale, B.J. (2017) 'Biodiversity Effects in the Wild Are Common and as Strong as Key Drivers of Productivity.' *Nature*, 549(7671): 261–4.

Fellows, A. (2019) *Gaia, Psyche and Deep Ecology: Navigating Climate Change in the Anthropocene*. London: Routledge.

Fukuyama, F. (1989) 'The End of History?' *The National Interest*, 16, Summer 1989: 3–18.

Hopcke, R.H. (1989) *A Guided Tour of the Collected Works of C.G. Jung*. Boston, MA & Shaftesbury: Shambhala.

Jung, C.G. (1916/1969) 'The Transcendent Function.' in Sir Herbert Read, Michael Fordham, and Gerhard Adler (Eds.); William McGuire (Executive Ed.), *Collected Works Vol. 8: The Structure and Dynamics of the Psyche*. Princeton, NJ: Princeton University Press.

Jung, C.G. (1930/1969) 'The Stages of Life.' in Sir Herbert Read, Michael Fordham, and Gerhard Adler (Eds.); William McGuire (Executive Ed.), *Collected Works Vol. 8: The Structure and Dynamics of the Psyche*. Princeton, NJ: Princeton University Press.

Jung, C.G. (1934/1954) 'The Practical Use of Dream-Analysis.' in Sir Herbert Read, Michael Fordham, and Gerhard Adler (Eds.); William McGuire (Executive Ed.), *Collected Works Vol. 16: The Practice of Psychotherapy*. Princeton, NJ: Princeton University Press.

Jung, C.G. (1946/1969) 'On the Nature of the Psyche.' in Sir Herbert Read, Michael Fordham, and Gerhard Adler (Eds.); William McGuire (Executive Ed.), *Collected Works Vol. 8: The Structure and Dynamics of the Psyche*. Princeton, NJ: Princeton University Press.

Jung, C.G. (1957/1977) 'The Houston Films.' in W. McGuire and R.F.C. Hull (Eds.), *C.G. Jung Speaking: Interviews and Encounters*. Princeton, NJ: Princeton University Press.

Jung, C.G. (1963/1995) *Memories, Dreams, Reflections*. London: Fontana Press.

Kelly, E.F., Crabtree, A. and Marshall, P. (Eds.) (2015) *Beyond Physicalism: Toward Reconciliation of Science and Spirituality*. Lanham, MD: Rowman & Littlefield.

Kelly, E.F., Kelly, E.W. and Crabtree, A. (Eds.) (2007) *Irreducible Mind: Toward a Psychology for the 21st Century*. Lanham, MD: Rowman & Littlefield.

Korzybski, A.H.C. (1931/2000) *Science and Sanity: An Introduction to Non-Aristotelian Systems and General Semantics*. Lancaster, PA: International Non-Aristotelian Library Publishing Co.

Lovelock, J. (1979/2000) *Gaia: A New Look at Life on Earth*. Oxford, New York: Oxford University Press.

Lovelock, J. (2009) *The Vanishing Face of Gaia: A Final Warning*. London, New York: Allen Lane/Penguin Books.

Mackey, J.L. (2017) Personal communication.

Monastersky, R. (2014) 'Biodiversity: Life - a Status Report.' *Nature*, 516(7530): 158–161.

Næss, A. (1986) 'The Deep Ecological Movement: Some Philosophical Aspects.' in G. Sessions (Ed.), 1995. *Deep Ecology for the Twenty-first Century*. Boston, MA, London: Shambhala, 64–84.

Næss, A. (1987) 'Self-Realization: An Ecological Approach to Being in the World.' in A. Drengson and Y. Inoue (Eds.), 1995. *The Deep Ecology Movement: An Introductory Anthology*. Berkeley, CA: North Atlantic Books, 13–30.

Nuccitelli, D. et. al. (2012) 'Comment on Ocean Heat Content and Earth's Radiation Imbalance. II. Relation to Climate Shifts.' *Physics Letters A*, 376(45): 3466–8.

Ophuls, W. (2012) *Immoderate Greatness: Why Civilizations Fail*. North Charleston, SC: CreateSpace Independent Publishing Platform.

Ritsema, R. and Sabbadini, S.A. (2005) *The Original I Ching Oracle: The Pure and Complete Texts with Concordance, Eranos Foundation (SASEF)*. London: Watkins Publishing.

Smil, V. (2011) 'Harvesting the Biosphere: The Human Impact.' *Population and Development Review*, 37(4): 613–36

Staude, J.-R. (1981) *The Adult Development of C.G. Jung*. Boston, MA: Routledge & Kegan Paul.

von Franz, M.-L. (1992/1988) *Psyche and Matter*. Boston, MA; London: Shambhala.

Zalasiewicz, J. et. al. (2016) 'Scale and Diversity of the Physical Technosphere: A Geological Perspective.' *The Anthropocene Review*, 4(1): 9–22.

# 3

# GEORG ERNST STAHL'S HOLISTIC ORGANISM

*Barbara Helen Miller*

A discourse on holism will meet the question: how is life organized? In the context of healing when religious conceptualizations are included, the theme of rebirth appears to be ubiquitous. Pietists based their religious praxis on the experience of rebirth. To safeguard their praxis they made ample use of Georg Ernst Stahl's (1659–1734) doctrine on the holistic organism.

Georg Ernst Stahl's doctrine, holistic organism, attempts to answer the question, 'What organizes life?' He launched his attempt in an environment that was becoming increasingly deist. That is, God was seen as the clock maker: God set the order of the Universe in motion and took no further part in the working. It was all simply and understandably 'mechanistic,' a view which rejects revelation as a source of religious knowledge. For the pietist, who saw that 'God is Love,' this was alarming. Pietists had worked out that they could participate in God's ongoing creativity. Their position was a 'hermeneutics.' This can be succinctly expressed as follows: 'when you read with love what was written with love, you come to know.' Stahl's holistic organism (that gives answer to the question 'what organizes life?') allows for the creativity that flows from emotion. For the pietist 'faith' is *emotional* participation in God, and we *want* to organize ourselves through faith. Such a discourse, taking place in the first decades of the 18th century, allows us to observe the use made of symbols of wholeness at that time. In the following, after introducing Pietism, I shall present Stahl's theory of organism and then discuss the use pietists made of this theory.

## Pietism and hermeneutics

Pietism studies range from a broad view of spiritual renewal movements after the Reformation in several confessional traditions to a narrow view of the pious movement within Lutheranism after 1670. In the broad view Pietism studies include under the umbrella of Pietism the related trends in the 16th and 17th centuries of English Puritanism and Dutch Calvinism and in the 18th century the Herrnhuter or Moravian churches and the Wesleyan movement. When pursuing the broad view one can note that Pietism and, for example, Methodism share in a revived emphasis on conversion, charismatic power, sanctification, and reform through small groups within the church (Brown, 1996, p. 15; Lindberg, 2005, pp. 2–3; see also Stoeffler 1973).

Central to Pietism, whether defined broadly or narrowly, is the subjective experience of God's presence. It was a piety of interiority and introspection and a critique of the externality of worship. Pietism shifted the focus from the theory to the praxis of Christianity. A pietist claim is that the First Reformation initiated in the 16th century was incomplete, for it was only a reform of doctrine. The Second Reformation, which Pietism understood itself to be, was the reform of life (see Strom et al., 2009). The external distinguishing mark of Pietism is the conventicles (ecclesiola in ecclesia), the holding of private meetings alongside public worship. The conventicles brought Luther's understanding of 'the universal priesthood of believers' to the fore (Wallmann, 2005, p. 35), and even took it some steps further. Individual interpretation of the Bible, via the light and grace of the Holy Spirit, was practiced (Stein, 2005, p. 88). Emphasis was upon prayer and hymnody (Lindberg, 2005, p. 1). Pietists were prolific writers-composers of hymns and other devotional literature. Surprising for us today is the explicit sensuality their metaphorical structure depended on. This was the identification of the natural with the spiritual, so that hunger and erotic love could be descriptions of spiritual states. The love of God was expressed in bodily, sensual terms, and religious feeling should be tasted and felt (Geyer-Kordesch 1990, p.79).

Pietism of the late 17th century to mid-18th century, seen as the belief in the power of individual meditation on the divine, emphasised immediate experience as the primary relationship to God's reality. Among the forerunners of Pietism (see Erb, 1979, pp. 1–17) was Johann Arndt (1555–1621), who advocated a mysticism taken from the late Middle Ages, though he reinterpreted ecstatic mystical experience in terms of a developing progression in a believer's love for God. Early pietist proponents were acquainted with and looked positively on the mystical spiritualist Jakob Boehme (1575–1624) (Erb, 1983, p. 4). Boehme combined pansophical, cabbalistic, alchemical, and spiritualist methods and concepts. Both Boehme and Arndt saw the hand of God in the ordering of nature and held rebirth in greater theological regard than justification (Habrich, 2001, pp. 52–53). Boehme is seen as a source of inspiration for the Radical Pietists, which is a term used to designate those who separated themselves from the church and as they did so formed new sectarian bodies. The Radical Pietist Gottfried Arnold (1666–1714) wrote directly defending medieval mysticism. Arnold maintained that theology can be treated as a statement or teaching *concerning* God and such a word or statement *from* God; and that mystical (*from* God) theology *is* proper for the reborn, who are taught and directed by the Spirit in their life and thought (Erb, 2005, p. 182). Later within Pietism, there is emphasis on conversion, a religious attitude fostering change—a sudden or slow creation of a new identity. The conversion experience follows on praxis: the reborn receive inspiration via the Holy Spirit allowing them to interpret the Bible and gain authoritative knowledge (see Swensson, 2011).

There is a strong alchemical/medical line among pietists. Arndt had admiration for the Christian Alchemist Heinrich Khunrath (ca. 1560–1605). Khunrath practiced medicine and was a disciple of Paracelsus (Theophrast Bombast von Hohenheim, ca. 1493–1541). Paracelsus practiced what he called 'Alchemia medica', so named in order to distinguish his practice from 'Alchemia transmutatoria', which was concerned with making gold (Habrich, 2001, p. 48; see also Forshaw, 2008, p. 72). The study of alchemy and chemistry continued in pietist circles. '*Magia naturalis*' and alchemy were not acceptable to the authorities of the Reformation, but during the same period, radical and church pietists were actively positive. Among pietists the later tendency was towards that of medical-pharmaceutical 'Chymie', while the earlier tendency had been towards the hermetic-mystical alchemy and the Boehmist-coloured '*magia naturalis*' (Habrich, 2001, p. 59).

In 1675, the Lutheran minister, Philipp Jakob Spener (1635–1705) published an introduction to the postils of Johann Arndt; the treatise therein was published separately under the title *Pia Desideria: or Heartfelt Desires for a God-pleasing Improvement of the true Protestant Church*. Responding to the disillusionment in the aftermath of the Thirty Years' War, in 1670 Spener introduced to his community, Frankfurt am Main, small prayer and study groups or conventicles of awakened Christians. In his reform efforts Spener advocated and laid emphasis on biblical preaching, as well as on the experience of repentance and the new birth (Spener, 1675/1964; Erb, 1983, p. xiii; see also Stein, 2005).

Following in Spener's footsteps was August Hermann Francke (1663–1727). Through Spener's influence Francke came in 1691 to the newly established Prussian University of Halle. There grew what has come to be known as Halle pietism. Pastoral training and an extensive foreign mission service were central to Francke's concerns. He made a distinction for his students between the 'husks' of external academics and the essential 'kernel', a hermeneutical distinction that on the one hand enabled historical-critical exegesis (outer shell) of Scripture and on the other hand followed an unhistorical-kerygmatic (inner kernel) interpretation (Matthias, 2005, p. 110). Francke conceived that the reborn (the person moved by the Spirit of God), when reading Scripture, will have the capacity to go beyond theoretical knowledge to the *living* knowledge, because Scripture can only be understood by the person who as reader is grasped by the affects that Scripture intends, that is, grasped by that by which the writer of the text was grasped (Matthias, 2005, p. 106; see also Francke, 1692/1983). Francke's hermeneutics was derived from the Strasbourg theologian Johann Conrad Dannhauer[1] (1603–1666) via Spener, a hermeneutics that is under the sign of rebirth and *living* knowledge. Spener had pointed out to Francke and his Leipzig fellow students (gathered for mutual Bible study) that the historical author of the Bible must 'be, so to speak, raised from the dead and presented as living' and that is only possible if 'an image is made of him as a person (emotion, life condition, destiny)' (Spener, cited in Matthias, 2005, p. 105).

We can note the ongoing influence of Jakob Boehme on the innovator of Pietism, the prelate Friedrich Christoph Oetinger (1702–1782). Oetinger studied theology, philosophy, alchemy, medicine, emblem theory, rabbinic and cabbalistic literature, and later the *Arcana Coelestia* (1749) by Emanuel Swedenborg (1688–1772) (Weyer-Menkhoff, 2005, p. 247). From Jakob Boehme he understood a way of thinking about God and the world in terms of their being grasped in a process, in which everything is compounded from dynamic polarities. Oetinger pursued all kinds of engagement with nature, considering that in nature he was close to God's creation, and this led him to assert the primacy of sensation over reflective knowledge. His science of sensory knowledge and of the experience of life led him to formulate the mystical and eschatological '*cognitio centralis*' and '*sensus communis*', the instinct that leads us to the eternal, which also responds to the scream in the street.

## Georg Ernst Stahl and his radical pietist medicine

Georg Ernst Stahl (1659–1734) was a devout pietist. Stahl proposed that the soul and the body are a unity, that life is organic, and that life is the active soul working within the structures and substances of the body. Stahl influenced 18th-century medicine, during dramatic changes in medical thought. In chemistry Stahl proposed the theory of phlogiston as the principle of combustibility. As a philosopher he supported a viewpoint that inspired 18th century vitalism, but is not equivalent to it because he did not centre his theory on the function of specific organs in the body.

Frederick I, King of Brandenburg, Prussia, established the new University at Halle in the 1690s. Stahl was professor at the University of Halle from 1694 to 1715, lecturing on the theory of medicine and on chemistry. Later, in Berlin, he was first court physician to Frederick William I of Prussia.

Stahl proposed a theory of a holistic, self-determined organism. In his definition of organism, he equates 'life' with the ability of the whole organism to organise change. The 'organ' of perception is the sum of all perceptual processes (that includes sensory impressions, mental images and emotions), which he calls the soul or the anima. It is this immaterial vital principle that serves as the differential feature that distinguishes the living from the non-living. Geyer-Kordesch explains: 'When Stahl writes about organism, he does not mean a body "endowed with organs". "Organic" to him means a coordinated and integrated whole, the "organism", adjusting to its environment both on a conscious and unconscious level (sensually, emotionally and mentally) with immediate physiological results. Thus Stahl's medical theory is essentially a theory of a holistic, self-determined "organism"' (Geyer-Kordesch, 1990, p. 69).

For Stahl, a philosopher who tries to describe the phenomena of life must take into account the activity of purpose or goal. There is a striving for particular ends or purposes, which implies a directive agency that guides the goal-seeking effort. The directive agent is, for Stahl, the anima. The directing agent or anima exerts itself and manifests itself through mechanical principles, even as the behaviour is not blind or mechanical. The anima directing the purposive activities of the body acts in an intelligent fashion. The process implies wholes rather than parts. For Stahl, only a false philosophy focuses on the parts, neglecting the whole. Stahl's doctrine of animism involves living creatures and not what is non-living. The non-living is stable over time, not changing, being relatively inert. The living body, living creatures, have a great tendency to decompose and putrefy. This tendency to putrefy is held in check during the limited time that life persists by a conserving agent. This agent that is knowledgeable of the goal preserves the body from corruption, and is the essence of life, the anima. In Stahl's animism, God, as an active principle, as life, is actualized. He writes in his medical doctrine *Theoria Medica vera* (1708), 'Man has been made for the living soul [...], namely for that, that it lives; certainly this expression fits to this acceptance, that the soul, which gives life, has been created as a whole, namely which makes the act of life, and conserves the body, and produces in the body and by the body bodily affections and affections of the divine wisdom [...]' (Stahl quoted in Geyer-Kordesch, 2000, p.172).

The living body depends on motion (obvious in the motion of the heart and circulation of the blood). The control over the body is through the property of motion; and the anima exerts its control by this very property of motion. Stahl denies that this motion is a function of matter, even though material objects do exhibit motion. Through his concept of motion the link is made whereby an immaterial anima can act on the body. For example, motions activate the processes of excretion and secretion, and should the motions be impaired, disease occurs. In health and in disease, the motions of the body follow a certain directing and integrating force, for Stahl, the anima. Stahl emphasises that motion is not life itself but is life's instrument.

Stahl was noting the significant changes in the bodily functions (pulse, perspiration, respiration, digestion) seemingly produced by anger, fear, disgust, hatred, and love. These alterations are obviously quite different from a deliberate exercise of will, seen in voluntary actions. Stahl reasoned that the anima perceived the emotion and induced changes on bodily functions through effecting changes in their motion. But additionally, according to Stahl, voluntary actions are *also* guided by the anima. The anima affects the body at all times, by exerting a regulatory function and giving direction for all bodily activities, so that the functions are at all times with purpose. Purpose, by implying a goal toward which activity is directed, has a forward reference. With this distinction of life imbued with purpose, Stahl shows the difference between mechanism and organism. In an organism, motions are combined towards a specific end, regulated and integrated by a responsible agent, the anima. There is an intent that constitutes the reason for the existence of the organism. A mechanism, while it also has motion, has no such reason for its existence, that is, a mechanism has motion but not for the reason of preserving life (see King 2008).

To maintain health, keep the body free from threatening ailments, and to combat disease, Stahl recommends considering the whole living organism, presided over by the anima, rather than focusing on specific actions of specific parts. He rejected the theory of humours in health or disease due to the lack of confirmation for the various chemical changes that were expected by this explanatory model. He saw that the basic reactions of the body contained nature's own healing power.

There is some similarity between the anima of Stahl and the form of Aristotle, in particular with the Galenists' notion of 'substantial form' (see King 2008). The form of the oak resides in the acorn, which determines that the development is into an oak tree and not into a radish. For Stahl, there must reside in the anima some special knowledge of the bodily organs that regulates the organs growth and function, keeping the organs in proper proportion, thereby achieving appropriate goals. Even as the anima is a conscious agent, many of the activities attributed to its purpose and goal are not perceptible to the individual; we can be aware of bodily sensations, but are not aware of the directional growth of bodily parts. External senses help us to reason and to have memory, but this intelligence differs from that of the anima where there is perception of the guiding principle.

There is also some similarity between the anima of Stahl and the *'archeus'* in alchemy as used by Paracelsus and Jan Baptist van Helmont (1580–1644). *Archeus* was used to refer to the densest aspect of the astral plane, which presides over the growth and continuation of all living beings. In this plane, matter begins to transmute into spiritual energies, in effect being the glue that binds the heavens to the material, and hence the alchemical maxim 'as above so below'. And there is a corollary with 'nature' as used by Thomas Sydenham (1624–1689), sometimes called the Father of English medicine, who said 'nature cures diseases'. But still for Stahl, the anima exists only in the body and is inseparable from it. The anima is dependent upon the body for perception and ideas. It requires sensory organs to aid intellect and carry out purposeful motions.

## Reception

Stahl was in discussion with Leibniz (1646–1716) and Boerhaave (1668–1738), among others. While Stahl took the soul to cause all movements, Hermann Boerhaave and Friedrich Hoffmann (1660–1742) saw all bodily movements resulting from physical causes (Toellner, 1991, p. 250). In 1708 Stahl presented his medical doctrine under the title *Theoria Medica vera*. Leibniz immediately questioned certain points in Stahl's doctrine. Leibniz's own definition of organism was that of 'mixed' and 'living'. Stahl maintained only 'living', asserting that the organism obeys causal laws that are different from laws operating in mechanical nature. Leibniz did not accept this assertion, even as he defended a concept of organism (Carvallo, 2010, p.110).

Christian Thomasius (1655–1728), Professor of Jurisprudence in Halle, engaged Stahlian ideas in his reassessment of Cartsianism (Geyer-Kordesch, 1990, p.83). He additionally showed that medical and judicial reform were linked on a theoretical and practical level (Geyer-Kordesch, 1990, p. 84). The linking of medical and judicial reform would have been helpful in Thomasius' battle against the persecution of witches. Thomasius, a pietist, while engaging positively in Stahl's doctrines, was critical of August Hermann Francke for his educational policies at the University of Halle. In 1699 Thomasius said these policies were producing "uneducated, melancholy, fantastic, obstinate, recalcitrant, and spiteful men" (as quoted by Sassen, 2015).

Christian Wolff (1679–1754), the most eminent German philosopher between Leibniz and Kant, was seen as a threat by the pietist Francke, his fellow lecturer at Halle University. Francke, having the ear of king Frederick William I, had Wolff ousted in 1723, an event which is seen as one of the most celebrated academic dramas of the 18th century, and in the following section their dispute is summarily explicated. Important for pietists was Wolff's distinction that knowledge is arrived at rationally and not through revelation.

## Pietist application

Stahl's doctrines gave credence to the pietist praxis of accessing 'living knowledge.' They reasoned: should the soul carry God's intelligence, then tapping into life's goals and purposes will be fruitful.

Why were Stahl's doctrines so helpful for pietists in legitimising inspirational freedom of the spirit? For pietists, spiritual growth is not possible without mental images. In the *Seelenlehre* (psychology) of Pietism, 'the image, as a sensory composite the product of the imagination, is inseparably linked with the emotions' (Geyer-Kordesch 1990, p. 81). Stahl championed an undivided imagination, in contrast with mechanist and dualist assumptions. For example, Christian Wolff divided the imagination into compartments, one that has the ability to envision abstract concepts and follows reason, and one with images that stir up feelings and follows the passions. Pietists using imagination to tap into God's purpose could resort to Stahl's theory, where the soul integrated perception. Stahl's holistic approach sees the anima's integration of perceptions affecting the mind and the body as a unity. The anima as an intelligence that is the sum of sensory, imaginative, emotive and mental perception had the capacity to form images, incite emotion, formulate an idea, and with these combined processes, effect physiological changes in the body. Both conscious reason and unreasoned emotion are agents that change the vital economy of the individual. Emotion, reason, and imagination are coordinated in the individual organism. Wolff separated reason and emotion, proposing that they were not operating *together* in imagination.

During this period, pietists lived what they called the 'fruits of the belief'. Their conviction was that before the conversion experience it was important for the individual to follow established law; however, after the conversion-rebirth experience, the individual participated in living knowledge. What followed from these ideas was quite unsettling for established society and for orthodox Lutherans.

Challenging the social norms, in pietist families the maidservant was encouraged to read and invited to sit at the family dinner table. Expressive for the unsettling of non-pietists is this statement from an angry slave owner in the Caribbean speaking to a Moravian brother: 'Don't teach my negroes to be Pietists!'(Sensbach 2009). Central for pietists was that everyone should know how to read, and that the Bible be available and open to everyone's interpretation, because the Bible should be available and employed hermeneutically to facilitate conversion.

Conversion is the experienced change from living without knowledge of God's Grace, to the sure knowledge of God's Grace. For pietists ecstatic experience could be the conversion, and the term for ecstasy in some communities was 'motion'. Christian theology posits that with the sure knowledge of God's Grace, one has received the Keys to Heaven. Pietists as the 'regenerated congregation' were sure they had received the Keys to Heaven, which is the authority to forgive sins given by Jesus to Peter. In the Gospel According to St. Mathew 16:18-19 it is written, 'thou art Peter, and upon this rock I will build my church ... . I will give unto thee the keys of the Kingdom of heaven: and whatsoever thou shalt bind on earth shall be bound in heaven: and whatsoever thou shalt loose on earth shall be loosed in heaven.' Note that the regenerated congregation can 'bind and loose'. The ability to bind and loose implies a holistic relationship between parts (earth, the microcosm) and the whole (heaven, the macrocosm), and Pietist healers can make use of their special knowledge of this relationship, including, crucially, when to apply it. Pietists thus took the doctrine of the Keys to Heaven more to heart than did orthodox Christianity, giving them greater independence from Church authority.

So, as we look closely at conversion, what is it that should be achieved? The feeling of being totally alive brings a 'knowing' of the process that brought one to this experience. It was felt that the conversion story should be told to others, that is, one should spread the good news. One such story I heard told of an earthquake that happened at the very moment of conversion. Such simultaneous happenings were noted and appreciated by reference to Christ's death on the cross, when there was also an earthquake. We can keep in mind that in Stahl's formulation the anima fosters renewal through regulation of motion, so that what is bound on earth can be bound in heaven, what is released on earth can be released in heaven. This authoritative knowledge is gained via an independent route free of former authorities. Hence, we see the age-old threat felt by established institutions for authoritative revelations of all kinds. We see, too, that Christian Wolff's description of 'man as either "free", when in use of his reason, or a "slave", when subject to his passions' (Wolff cited in Geyer-Kordesch 1990, p. 82) would make no sense for pietist objectives.

## Concluding remarks

The use pietists made of Stahl's holistic organism was basically to defend pietist hermeneutics. The crux of the issue for pietists can be seen in Oetinger's understanding of what organizes life. Oetinger's notion of God was God as that 'mystery which moves deliberately and constantly toward self-understanding through progressive self-actualization' (Oetinger cited in Stoeffler, 1973, p. 110). Hence, God and man mutually participate in creation by being in a creative process together. What follows from pietist hermeneutical praxis, when done with belief and God's Gift, is renewal, also called 'rebirth' and conversion. Through this experience, one has gained authoritative truths, said to be the gift of discernment conveyed by the Holy Spirit, and this is the inspirational freedom pietists wished to maintain.

Oetinger pointed out the createdness of nature and the limitations of the pure, rational image of the world, which he saw in the Enlightenment's quantification and idea of dominance of nature by humankind. Oetinger's efforts – that find their foundation in a love of God, as revealed in Jesus – was 'to put forth the "phenomenological method" as a politics and science of human love against the "geometric method" of rationalistic abstraction' (Weyer-Menkhoff, 2005, p. 251). He is said to have affected Goethe, Herder, Hölderlin, Hegel, and Schlegel, while the history of his influence is quite hidden (Weyer-Menkhoff, 2005, p. 252). During his lifetime he offered an alternative to the so-called Leibniz-Wolffian tradition that only recognized two faculties, knowledge and will, by adding sensation as man's third faculty.

Pietism studies show that Pietism's abiding concern for free associations and for education, for an 'empiricism' of religious experience and praxis are related to the interests, in their time, of science and nature. Pietists called themselves 'empirics'.

Studies have noted that pietist praxis preceded important achievements credited to the Enlightenment: pietists struggled against dogmatism and via the route of experience surmounted doctrinal differences. And pietists also preceded Enlightenment's concern for self-improvement. Major figures of the 18th- and 19th-century Enlightenment that scholars attest to have come out of Pietism include Lessing, Kant, Schiller, Goethe, Fichte, as well as the 'Father of Protestant Liberalism', Schleiermacher (Lindberg, 2005, p. 13).

A modern theory of religion, such as we find in Tylor (1871), sees religion as science gone wrong, as an error, and religion is stripped of its emotional and transformative aspects (see Droogers, 1994). Adolf Bastian (1860), who is in a line of German philosophers of anthropological thought that goes back to major pietists, insists on the unity of science and faith.[2] Empathy, reciprocal illumination and experience were for Bastian central parts of any empirical research in psychology, culture, and ethnology (Poewe 1994, pp. 236–7).

Pietist hermeneutics has proven to be an integral source of inspiration for subsequent generations. The focus on imagination and the development of personality was taken forward. I hope to have shown the yeasting of praxis and theory set in motion (in part) by pietist involvement with Stahl's medical theory. Stahl's work was reprinted, translated and published far into the 19th century. The organization of life being proposed is one in which there is participation in God's creativity, and participation involves devotional reflection on God's image, which should be seen, felt, and perceived in its entirety/wholeness. Pietist Biblical hermeneutics, as in the citing of the Gospel According to St. John 4:24: 'God is a Spirit: and they that worship him must worship him in spirit and in truth' suggests that to 'worship him in spirit and in truth' is a highly imaginative praxis.

## Notes

1 Dannhauer wrote in 1630 *The Idea of the Good Interpreter*, in which he proposed a *hermeneutica generalis*, which scholars now see makes Schleiermacher's idea of universal hermeneutics not necessarily so new (Bowie, 1998, p. viii).
2 Among those who insisted on the unity of science and faith were 'German philosophers of anthropological thought going back to Johann Arndt (1555–1621), Philipp Jakob Spener (1635–1705), August Hermann Francke (1663–1727), Johann Georg Hamann (1730–1788), Johann Kaspar Lavater (1741–1801), Johann Gottfried Herder (1744–1803), Wilhelm von Humboldt (1767–1835), Adolf Bastian (1826–1905), Theodor Lipps (1851–1914), Leo Frobenius (1873–1939), Wilhelm Schmidt (1868–1954), and Bruno Gutmann (1876–1966), among others' (Poewe, 1994, pp. 236–237).

## References

Bastian, Adolf (1860) *Der Mensch in der Geschichte. Zur Begründung einer psychologischen Weltanschauung.* 3 vols. Leipzig: Otto Wigand.

Bowie, Andrew (1998) Introduction. In F. Schleiermacher, ed, *Hermeneutics and Criticism, And other Writings* (1838/1998, pp. vii–xxxi). Cambridge. UK: Cambridge University Press.

Brown, Dale W. (1996) *Understanding Pietism*, Revised Edition. Nappanee, IN: Evangel Publishing House.

Carvallo, Sarah (2010) Leibniz vs. Stahl. In D. Marcelo, ed, *The Practice of Reason*. (pp. 101–136). Amsterdam: Benjamins Publ. Co.

Droogers, André (1994) The Normalization of Religious Experience: Healing, Prophecy, Dreams, and Visions. In K. Poewe, ed, *Charismatic Christianity as a Global Culture* (pp. 33–49). Columbia, SC: University of South Carolina Press.

Erb, Peter (1979) In *Johann Arndt, True Christianity* [The Classics of Western Spirituality], Mahwah, NJ: Paulist Press.

Erb, Peter (ed.) (1983) *Pietists Selected Writings* [The Classics of Western Spirituality], Mahwah, NJ: Paulist Press.

Erb, Peter (2005) Gottfried Arnold (16661714). In C. Lindberg, ed, *The Pietist Theologians* (pp. 175–189). Malden, MA: Blackwell Publishing.

Forshaw, Peter (2008) "Paradoxes, Absurdities, and Madness": Conflict over Alchemy, Magic and Medicine in the Works of Andreas Libavius and Heinrich Khunrath. *Early Science and Medicine*, 13, 53–81.

Francke, August Hermann (1692/1983) From the Autobiography. In P. Erb, ed, *The Pietists: Selected Writings* (pp. 99–107). New York: Paulist Press.

Geyer-Kordesch, Johanna (1990) Georg Ernst Stahl's radical Pietist medicine and its influence on the German Enlightenment. In A. Cunningham and R. French, eds, *The Medical Enlightenment of the Eighteenth Century* (pp. 67–87). Cambridge, UK: Cambridge University Press

Geyer-Kordesch, Johanna (2000) *Pietismus, Medizin und Aufklärung in Preußen im 18. Jahrhundert*. Hallesche Beiträge zur Europäischen Aufklärung. Berlin: De Gruyter.

Habrich, Christa (2001) Alchemie und Chemie in der pietistischen Tradition. In H.G. Kemper, ed, *Goethe und der Pietismus* [Hallersche Forschungen 6] (pp. 4579). Tübingen: Max-Niemeyer.

King, Lester S. (2008) "Stahl, Georg Ernst." Complete Dictionary of Scientific Biography. Encyclopedia.com. 29 Apr. 2018 http://www.encyclopedia.com.

Lindberg, Carter (2005) Introduction. In C. Lindberg, ed, *The Pietist Theologians* (pp. 1–20). Malden, MA: Blackwell Publishing.

Matthias, Markus (2005) August Hermann Francke (16631727). In C. Lindberg, ed, *The Pietist Theologians* (pp. 100–114). Malden, MA: Blackwell Publishing.

Poewe, Karla (1994) Rethinking the Relationship of Anthropology to Science and Religion. In K. Poewe, ed, *Charismatic Christianity as a Global Culture* (pp. 234–258). Columbia, SC: University of South Carolina Press.

Sassen, Brigitte (2015) 18th Century German Philosophy Prior to Kant. In Edward N. Zalta, ed, *The Stanford Encyclopedia of Philosophy* (Summer 2015 Edition). https://plato.stanford.edu/archives/sum2015/entries/18thGerman-preKant/.

Sensbach, Jon (2009) "Don't Teach My Negroes to Be Pietists:" Pietism and the Roots of the Black Protestant Church. In J. Strom, H. Lehmann and J. Van Horn Melton, eds, *Pietism in Germany and North America 1680–1820* (pp. 183–198). Burlington, VT: Ashgate.

Spener, Philipp Jakob (1675/1964) *Pia Desideria*, Translated and edited by Theodore Tappert. Philadelphia, PA: Fortress Press.

Stein, K. James (2005) Philipp Jakob Spener (1635–1705). In C. Lindberg, ed, *The Pietist Theologians* (pp. 84–99). Malden, MA: Blackwell Publishing.

Stoeffler, Ernest (1973) *German Pietism During the Eighteenth Century*. Leiden: Brill.

Strom, J., Lehmann, H., and Van Horn Melton, J. (2009) *Pietism in Germany and North America* 1680–1820. Burlington, VT: Ashgate.

Swensson, Eric (2011) Reception of the Doctrine of Justification among German Lutheran Pietists. Retrieved 3 July 2011 from http//:www.holytrinitynewrochelle.org/yourti89645.html

Toellner, Richard (1991) Hermann Boerhaave. In D. v. Engelhardt and F. Hartmann, eds, *Klassiker der Medizin* (pp. 245–261). Vol I. München: C.H. Beck.

Tylor, Edward Burnett (1871/1958) *Primitive Culture*. New York: Harper & Row.

Wallmann, Johannes (2005) Johann Arndt (15551621). In C. Lindberg, ed, *The Pietist Theologians* (pp. 21–37). Malden, MA: Blackwell Publishing.

Weyer-Merkhoff, Martin (2005) Friedrich Christoph Oetinger (1702–1782). In C. Lindberg, ed, *The Pietist Theologians* (pp. 239–255). Malden, MA: Blackwell Publishing.

# PART II
# Analytical psychology

# 4

# FROM THE SPLIT TO WHOLENESS: THE *'CONIUNCTIO'* IN C. G. JUNG'S *RED BOOK*

*Alessio De Fiori*

## Introduction

With this essay, I would like to contribute to ongoing reflection on the topic of holism, focusing on the perspective of the concept of *coniunctio oppositorum* elaborated by Jung during the composition period of the *Red Book* (1913–1930), and how from this concept it is possible to see the tendency toward wholeness as the core of psychic life.

As David Henderson wrote: 'In his writings Jung discusses the union of opposites, the coincidence of opposites (*coincidentia oppositorum*), *complexio oppositorum*, conjunction of opposites (*coniunctio oppositorum*), the tension of opposites, compensation, complementarity, *enantiodromia* and psychic balance. He is not systematic in his use of these terms.'[1] Even if from a rigorous philosophical point of view there are some differences between these concepts, Henderson adds that Jung treated them as if they were synonyms. For practical purposes, I refer in this essay to the concepts of the union of the opposites using the term *'coniunctio'* because it represents the culmination of Jung's research on this topic in his late alchemical writings.

## Before the *Red Book* (1901–1912)

First, it is important to understand Jung's view on the psyche before the *Red Book*. Jung's first thinking on the psyche was elaborated jointly with his mentor Eugen Bleuler, the director of the Burghölzli, the famous psychiatric hospital in Zurich where Jung began to work from 1901. Together, the two men developed analyses of mental illness.

In his doctoral dissertation, published in 1901, 'On the psychology and pathology of so-called occult phenomena', Jung studied the case of his cousin, the young medium Helene Preiswerk, who was characterised by him as having a 'split personality'. In his subsequent works, Jung elaborated the concept of the 'complex' through the word association experiment. A 'complex' is a psychical fragment with a strong affective charge and a certain autonomy. Consequently, the personality is seen as the result of numerous complexes, where the neurotic appears as characterized by the prevalence of one complex that escapes the control of consciousness.

In 1908, Bleuler introduced the notion of *schizophrenia* to replace the term '*dementia praecox*'—first put forward by the German psychiatrist Emil Kraeplin in 1896, drawing from collective work undertaken at the Burghölzli Institute, in which the participation of his assistant C. G. Jung was significant.[2] The term *schizophrenia* comes from the ancient Greek 'σχίζειν' (*schizein*), which means 'to divide' and 'φρήν' (*phrén*), that is, 'mind'. In Bleuler's view, the main common characteristic of psychiatric diseases is the division of psychic functions. The definition of 'schizophrenia' is therefore conceived by Bleuler starting from the pathognomical signs of the split (*schize/Spaltung*) of the psyche.

Bleuler published his most important book in 1911, *Dementia Præcox oder Gruppe der Schizophrenien* in which Jung's studies were included and continued. Jung himself largely acknowledged Bleuler's theory.[3] In 1914, Jung wrote that he had retrospectively noticed with satisfaction that in *Dementia Praecox, or the Group of Schizophrenias* Bleuler had taken full advantage of all the essential views of his *Über die Psychologie der Dementia Præcox* published in 1906. As Escamilla has recently suggested, Bleuler and Jung disagreed on the origin of this psychic *Spaltung* and, on the cause of psychosis at this time, Jung was closer to Freud's theory. In any case, from the state of the research in this period it seems possible to say that in general before 1911, even if Jung oscillated between Freud's and Bleuler's theories on the aetiology of psychosis, the two theories still had in common the conception of mental illness as a conflict between opposites.[4]

From 1909, Jung started to study the history of symbolism, hoping, as he wrote to Freud, that this study would enlarge the possibilities to explain the pathology of neurosis from a phylogenic point of view.[5] This research led to the publication in 1911 and 1912 of the work *Wandlungen und Symbole der Libido*, translated in English as *Psychology of the Unconscious: A Study of the Transformations and Symbolisms of the Libido, a Contribution to the History of the Evolution of Thought*.[6] In this work, Jung analysed and compared fantasies and images from the poetry of Miss Frank Miller, a case reported on by Theodore Flournoy.[7] This revealed a collective symbolic heritage from established traditions in religion, mythology, and literature. In particular his analysis focused on the symbols of the hero, the mother, rebirth and sacrifice.

The theoretical premises of this work were for Jung to give value to what he calls '*dream* or *fantasy* thinking', that is, thinking through symbols, rather than via reasoning or reasoned thought ('directed thinking'). If reasoned thought is specific to science, '*dream* or *fantasy* thinking' could be seen as the proper language of the unconscious.

Based on these premises Jung introduces a new conception of libido, which is characterized not only sexually but with an energetic value that it expresses in the production of symbols. In this book, consequently, Jung relativized the importance of the Oedipus complex, rendering it not as a dominant psychic process but as one symbol among others, a view that led to his definitive break with Sigmund Freud. As such, the symbol became at this point the path that brought Jung to seek other perspectives on the aetiology of mental illness.

## The *Red Book* (1913–1930)

After the publication of *Psychology of the Unconscious* (first published in 1912), Jung experienced a period of disorientation, caused by the schism with Freud, the loss of his theoretical bearings, and the premonition of war in Europe, which came to him in frightful dreams and visions at the end of 1913. In the advent of the First World War, he saw the symptoms of the end of an epoch, characterized by a crisis in the traditional values of Europe, an end to the symbols and rituals that constituted the Christian myth, and the death of God. In this context, he came to ask himself which myth he inhabited, and which was his personal myth, as he revealed in the 1925 lecture *Introduction to Analytical Psychology*, collected by his secretary in his putative autobiography.[8] *Liber Novus* or *The Red Book* was Jung's attempt to find an answer to this question. As Romano Màdera wrote recently, starting with the *Red Book*, the *coniunctio* appeared as 'the myth that defines Jung's biography and constitutes the core of his thought'.[9]

From 1913, through the experience of creating the *Red Book,* Jung tried to study associative thinking, starting with the symbolic content of his own unconscious. In this way, he made himself the laboratory of what he had theorized in *Psychology of the Unconscious*, and plunged himself into the deepest waters of his psychic life searching for new meaning and orientation. This experience brought him to postulate within the unconscious a function that could repair the psychic split through the principle of compensation (*Kompensation*). The expression of the psychic function is the 'symbol' (from ancient Greek συμβάλλω: 'throw together'), which shows, in its genesis as in its dynamics, a dialectical union of opposites. The *Red Book* appears, therefore, as the theoretical laboratory that allowed Jung to consider the unconscious psychic process from the dialectics of symbols as a *coniunctio oppositorum*.

While in *Wandlungen und Symbole der Libido* Jung analysed the role of symbols in the development of the libido, in the *Red Book* he analysed their genealogy from the point of view of the subject, namely, from his psychic life. It is for this reason that the *Red Book* remained unpublished for almost 50 years. In this book, every character presented him- or herself as a symbol of a psychic complex, and in the development of the text we often find the opposition between two symbols leading to a new symbol after unification. This represents the resolution of the first conflict, which allows a new state.

## Liber Primus

These dynamics are theoretically explained in the beginning of the *Liber Primus*, in the chapter 'The Way of What is to Come', with the dialectic between the *Sinn*, the *Widersinn* and the *Übersinn*. *Sinn* and *Widersinn* (sense and non-sense) are the two terms of the opposition and the *Übersinn* (the supreme meaning) the term of their union and overcoming. The three take the shape of the philosophical *coniunctio oppositorum*:

> But the supreme meaning is the path, the way and the bridge to what is to come. That is the God yet to come. It is not the coming God himself but his image which appears in the supreme meaning. God is an image and those who worship him must worship him in the images of the supreme meaning.
>
> The supreme meaning is not a meaning and not an absurdity, it is image and force in one, magnificence and force together.
>
> The supreme meaning is the beginning and the end. It is the bridge of going across and fulfilment.[10]

The "supreme meaning" presents itself paradoxically as a notion joining opposites: it is "the beginning and the end," "shadow and light." The "God yet to come" announced by these prophetic words heralds itself therefore as a God reuniting a quality with its contrary, reuniting good and evil, shadow and light. The "supreme meaning" as a conjunction of "sense" and "non-sense" appears in this excerpt at the same time as a "bridge of going," from an object to its opposite, and as a "fulfilment," which gives the sense of the conflict between the opposites.

The dialectic between sense and counter-sense at work in the first chapter of *Liber Primus* gives form to what we could call an "ontological *coniunctio*" because it concerns the heart of the dynamic specific to the psychical process. At the same time the prophecy of the "God yet to come" is announced here, which will be fulfilled at the end of *Liber Primus*. In the third chapter of "On the service of the Soul," the birth of the "God yet to come" is announced in the features of a child, who appears as a kind of "incarnation" of the "supreme meaning."

But before looking at the realization of the vision of the "God yet to come," it seems important to linger over Chapter 6, entitled "Splitting of the Spirit," where it is possible to distinguish the outline of the path which leads from the period of Jung's psychiatric research to the period of his intellectual maturity that begins with the *Red Book* and can be summarized with the formula: from the *Spaltung* to the *coniunctio*. This road presents itself as a descent into oneself, in the image of the descent into hell. The "Split" is that which characterizes the depth of the soul. The division of the spirit here takes the form of the opposition between "the spirit of this time" and "the spirit of the depths." Its condition is represented by the dying God.[11]

But the overtaking of the separation and thus the passage from the *Spaltung* to the *coniunctio* can only be produced by that which comes in the following chapter: "Murder of the Hero." Jung transcribes the dream which he probably had the night between 17 and 18 December 1913, where, with a "savage" he ambushed Siegfried, the Germanic hero, who was announced by the sound of his horn, "coming high across the mountains on a chariot made of the bones of the dead".[12] When Siegfried finds himself in front of the two men, they fire and the hero "fell slain".[13] The murder of the hero is the condition of the passage toward the emergence of the re-composition. It symbolizes the end of the model, the end of the conscious attitude, or to employ a concept that Jung would develop later, it represents the end of the identification with the *persona*, which permits the emergence of the contents of the unconscious repressed personality.

This dialectic of the *coniunctio oppositorum* appears already in its symbolical representation with the first characters of the *Red Book* that come into view in the chapter "Mysterium. Encounter". They are Elijah, the prophet of the Old Testament, and Salomé, the daughter of Herod, who asked for the head of John the Baptist, the last prophet. Taking into account Jung's psychological types, which he was elaborating in the same period, Elijah could symbolise the thinking function. He has great wisdom, which, however, is cold and sterile. Salomé may symbolise the feeling function. She is blind, and could represent feeling with its irrational power, pure wildness without any morality. Both move forward holding hands, while a snake, symbol of the metamorphic power of libido, follows them between their feet. This image announces the reconciliation of 'thinking' and 'feeling'. The 'I' of the *Red Book* at first looks at Salomé with contempt, but when she says she loves him, he understands that she represents a part of his soul that was repressed and is asking to be recognized and brought to light. Then, the 'I' looks at Salomé affectionately, and the truth of the symbol of *coniunctio* appears at the end of the *Liber Primus* ('Resolution'): 'If you go to thinking, take your heart with you. If you go to love, take your head with you. Love is empty without thinking, thinking hollow without love.'[14]

Jung's discovery through his *Red Book* experience of a part of the unconscious that is not just limited to individual history but also shared by all humanity made it possible for him also to find a reconciliation of the opposition between the individual and the collective. The echoes of the First World War brought Jung to realize that what happens in an individual history is a reflection of what happens in collective history:

> As a man you are part of mankind, and therefore you have a share in the whole of mankind, as if you were the whole of mankind. If you overpower and kill your fellow man who is contrary to you, then you also kill that person in yourself and have murdered a part of your life. The spirit of this dead man follows you and does not let your life become joyful. You need your wholeness to live onward.[15]

This realisation led Jung to understand a dialectical process between the individual subject and the collective, and therefore in this quotation we find the concept of 'wholeness' as *coniunctio* between the singular and the universal, the one and the all.

In the penultimate chapter of the *Liber Primus*, titled 'Instruction', Jung describes the awareness of the eminently symbolic psychic process. This is also where he postulates a psychic function that plays the role of re-composing the split and that preserves psychic equilibrium. In this way, Jung recognizes the process of the symbol's creation as the core of the dynamics of the psyche and the development of the libido, and in this we can see the core of what he will later call the 'individuation process':

> The binding and loosing take place in me. But insofar as it takes place in me, and I am a part of the world, it also takes place through me in the world, and no one can hinder it. It doesn't take place according to the way of my will but in the way of unavoidable effect. [...] You see how incredible it was to believe such of oneself. It applies not to me, but to the symbol. The symbol becomes my lord and unfailing commander.[16]

In the last chapter of *Liber Primus*, 'Resolution', we find the culmination and apotheosis of the entire process he has set in motion in this first section of the *Red Book*. Here we find the image of the 'divine child' (*das göttliche Kind*) as a symbol of the union of opposites. The divine child, like an apocalyptic apparition on Golgotha, lies with a white serpent in his left hand and a black serpent in his right hand on 'the green mountain' where he sees the 'Christ on it in his last hour and torment'. This image is presaged in the third chapter 'On the Service of the Soul', where the birth of the new God is as a child, as a realisation, or maybe it would be more correct to say as the 'incarnation' of the 'supreme meaning'.

> Your God is a child, so long as you are not childlike. Is the child order, meaning? Or disorder, caprice? Disorder and meaninglessness are the mother of order and meaning. Order and meaning are things that have become and are no longer becoming.
>
> You open the gates of the soul to let the dark flood of chaos flow into your order and meaning. If you marry the ordered to the chaos you produce the divine child, the supreme meaning beyond meaning and meaninglessness.[17]

The 'divine child' represents the realisation of the way to come that, as Bernardo Nante writes, could be seen as 'a young redeemer, a Christ that, like Heracles as a child in his famous trials, defeats the snakes, namely the opposites, with his hands'.[18] In this way, *Liber Primus* begins with what could be called an image of 'ontological *coniunctio*', that is the *Übersinn*, to announce the way that is to come. And it ends with the image of 'eschatological *coniunctio*', that is the 'divine child'.

## Liber Secundus

*Liber Secundus* proceeds with a similar dialectical process, represented by the 'I's encounters with the different characters, following the dynamics of moving from a symbol to its opposite and their integration. A clear and beautiful example is found in the second chapter, 'The castle in the forest', with the encounter between the 'I' and the old scholar, who lives in the castle, in a room full of books, where the air is 'heavy' and he seems 'careworn'. Jung writes: 'He has that modest-fearful look of scholarly men who have long since been squashed to nothing by the abundance of knowledge.'[19] The old scholar is so immersed in his books as to forget the presence of the 'I' in the room. He is the symbol of the scholar totally absorbed in research and no longer able to live in reality, far from human warmth and from simplicity. Meanwhile, the 'I' will find warmth and simplicity in the daughter of the old man that he encounters later in the castle. In a short dialogue she says to him: 'The more uncommon these highest truths are, the more inhuman must they be and the less they speak to you as something valuable or meaningful concerning human essence and being.'[20] Then the 'I' says to her that he loves her, before she dissolves into the darkness leaving behind her 'a profusion of red roses' in the room.[21] In this case, the first symbol of the old scholar represents the eminent attitude of the 'I', while the second symbol of the daughter represents his opposite, and in this passage from a symbol to its opposite, he finds their integration.

The encounter with Philemon 'the magician' at the end of the *Liber Secundus* leads the 'I' to his self (*Selbst*) and the contact with the self brings the gift of magic: 'Magic is a way of living. If one has done one's best to steer the chariot, and one then notices that a greater other is actually steering it, then magical operation takes place.'[22]

The image of the chariot, that recalls the myth of Plato's *Phaedrus*, could be seen as an image where the driver represents the 'I' that holds in his hands the bridles of the horses that, in turn, represent the opposites. So magic is when the individual could hold the opposites. Later in the same chapter, which closes *Liber Secundus*, the art of living is explained by the character of the serpent as resulting from the equilibrium of the opposites.

At the end of *Liber Secundus* is the encounter with the self that leads the 'I' to reach God. And the self appears as the psychic function of the conjunction of the opposites. It is interesting in this regard to report that Jung added to the last edition of *Psychology of the Unconscious*, retitled *Symbole der Wandlung* in 1952, the sentence: 'The archetype of the self has, functionally, the significance of a ruler of the inner world, i.e., of the collective unconscious. The self, as a symbol of wholeness, is a *coincidentia oppositorum*, and therefore contains light and darkness simultaneously'.[23] That means, on the one hand, that when he wrote the first version of *Psychology of the Unconscious* he did not yet have the named philosophical concept of 'coniunctio',[24] but did understand the dynamics of the psychic process in terms of the union of opposites; on the other hand, it indicates that the *coniunctio* in the *Red Book* represents the culmination of research which began with the publication of *Psychology of the Unconscious*.

## Scrutinies

The third and last part of the *Red Book* is called *Scrutinies* (*Prügunfen*) and contains the speech of Philemon to the spirits of the afterlife that came back from Jerusalem looking for an answer to religious and eschatological questions: the *Seven Sermons to the Dead* (*Septem Sermones ad Mortuos*).

The first Sermon introduces the pairs of opposites of *Nothingness* and *Fullness*: 'Nothingness is the same as fullness. In infinity full is as good as empty. Nothingness is empty and full.'[25] The conjunction between these opposites is called the *Pleroma*: 'We call this nothingness or fullness the *Pleroma*.'[26] The *Pleroma*, a notion of gnostic origins, appears as the supreme conjunction of all opposites, for instance, light and darkness, hot and cold, force and matter, time and space, good and evil, the beautiful and the ugly, etc.[27] In this understanding, the *Pleroma* is the supreme conjunction of all the opposites in a sort of cosmological totality, of the kind which could be called the 'cosmological *coniunctio*' of the *Red Book*.

In Sermon II we find Abraxas, a divinity of gnostic inspiration, as the conjunction of God and the Devil. In Sermon III we find the pair of opposites of the Sun as '*summum bonum*' and the devil as '*infimum malum*.'[28] Man draws from the Sun 'the highest good' and from the Devil 'the minimal evil' and Abraxas represents the middle way between good and evil.

In Sermon IV we find the pairs of opposites 'one is the *Burning One*, the other the *Growing One*,' which are symbolized respectively by *Eros* and the *Tree of Life*. In this Sermon, we find for the first time a symbol of quaternity, represented by a cross at the extremes of which is found, on the horizontal, the opposition between *Eros* and the *Tree of Life* and, on the vertical, the opposition of God and Devil. In this same sermon we find again the opposition between 'The bright Gods form the heavenly world' and 'The dark Gods form the earthly world.'[29]

In Sermon V we find the pairs of opposites spirituality/sexuality and *Mater Cœlestis/Phallos*. Spirituality and sexuality appear as two demons which hold man in their power. To man goes the task to succeed and differentiate himself from them, to not allow himself to be dominated by these pairs of opposites. To sexuality correspond the earth and the symbol of the phallos. To spirituality correspond the heavens and the symbol of the *Mater Cœlestis*. In this Sermon is also prefigured a symbol of quaternity in the form of a cross where the meridian is composed by the pair of opposites spirituality and sexuality, and the parallel by the pair of opposites 'terrestrial' and 'celestial'.

In Sermon VI we find the pair of opposites serpent/white bird. The serpent is the demon of sexuality, while the white bird is that of spirituality. About the image of the complementary movement, Christine Maillard writes: 'the Serpent and the Bird are presented in their respective movements: crawling and flying.

They are the movement of the universes of the low and of the high toward the soul, where their *coniunctio* will occur.'[30]

In the *Seven Sermons to the Dead* is unveiled the realisation of the *coniunctio* that can be found throughout the *Red Book* from the beginning to the end. The *coniunctio* appears in the shape of the quaternity as the opposition of two complementary pairs of opposites, a *complexio oppositorum* of four terms.

Finally, in Sermon VII we find not pairs of opposites but the revelation of the star, which it seems possible to read as the supreme conjunction of the opposites in the human and as that which brings union between the human and God: 'This star is the God and the goal of man.'[31] In this sense the star could be seen as a symbol of the notion of self. If in the first sermon the *Pleroma* appears like the supreme *coniunctio* of the double pairs of opposites from the perspective of the macrocosm, the star in the seventh sermon could be seen as the supreme *coniunctio* within the individual, from the perspective of the microcosm.

All these symbols find their figural representation in the mandala *Systema mundi totius*,[32] showing a cosmological picture of wholeness that embraces all the figures of the *Seven Sermons to the Dead* in a great symbolic synthesis. The mandala is structured as different concentric circles, with symbols on each of the four poles.

In the first circle, toward the exterior, we find the vertical pair of opposites *Abraxas/Erikapaios* or *Phanès* and the horizontal pair of opposites *Inans/Plenum*; in the second circle, toward the interior, we find again the vertical pair of opposites *Ignis* (Fire) and *Ero/Tree of Life*; and the horizontal pair of opposites *Dea luna Satanas/Deus sol*. Further toward the interior is found the pair Serpent (wrapped around a phallus)/*White bird* or *Spiritus sanctus*; and the star is at the centre of the mandala, in the place where normally, in Tibetan Buddhist mandalas, the Buddha is found. Buddha, like Christ, is for Jung a symbol of the self.[33]

## Conclusion

In Philemon's speech in the *Seven Sermons*, we find the *coniunctio* of a double pair of opposites, which appears as the solution to the question at the origin of the *Red Book*. The quaternity will become the structure for all of Jung's scientific work to follow, from *Psychological Types* (1921)[34] to his last book, *Mysterium Coniunctionis*, published in two volumes in 1955 and 1956, which appears as the definitive achievement of almost 50 years of research.

At this point, we can better understand Romano Màdera's phrase that I quoted earlier, about the importance of the elaboration of the *coniunctio* during the period of the *Red Book*, where it appears as the means of liberation from Jung's period of disorientation, as a new horizon of meaning: on one hand, the answer to Jung's question about his personal myth, and on the other hand, one of the key concepts of his subsequent work.

As such, the *coniunctio* seems to be the key concept of the psychic process seen as a natural tendency of the psyche to develop, in the phrase of my title, from the split to wholeness. At the same time, the *coniunctio* becomes also a key concept for Jung's psychotherapeutic approach. It is interesting in this regard that in 1946, in his essay 'On the nature of the psyche', Jung wrote that the emergence in dreams of symbols of the union of opposites (*complexio oppositorum*) could foretell the maximum therapeutic effect.[35] In this sense, as Antony Stevens writes, the individuation process allows us to think that 'the goal of personal development is wholeness,'[36] for which Jung's psychotherapeutic approach is intended to act as a support. And it was possibly the elaboration of the notion of *coniunctio* that brought Jung, as Sonu Shamdasani writes, to shift 'the aims of psychotherapy from being solely the cure of pathology to one of higher psychological and spiritual development'.[37] But in this *notion* it is also possible to discover the answer found by Jung to epochal religious questions, such as the crisis of Christianity and the death of God. In this regard, as Christine Maillard notices with an interesting etymological analysis, it is possible to see in the *Red Book* a passage from the idea of 'perfection' in Christianity (*Vollkommenheit*) to the concept of 'completeness' (*Vollständigkeit*) at the core of the Jungian psychological approach.[38]

To summarise and conclude, with this study we have found in the notion of *coniunctio* the most important discovery that Jung achieved with the experience of the *Red Book* during the 1910s, which would be at the core of his subsequent work. We have also found three forms of *coniunctio* in the *Red Book*, like the different concentric circles of a mandala: 'ontological *coniunctio*', 'eschatological *coniunctio*' and 'cosmological *coniunctio*'. This notion can lead to the re-conception of a holistic vision of psychic development, between the different parts of personality and the self, between the One and the All, between human and God.

## Notes

1 D. Henderson, 'The Coincidence of opposites. C.G. Jung's Reception of Nicholas of Cusa', in *Studies in Spirituality*, n° 20, 2010, p. 101.
2 Eugen Bleuler, 'Die schizophrenen Geistesstörungen im Lichte langjähriger Kranken-und Familiengeschichten', in *Thieme*, 1908.
3 Jung refused to consider himself as 'from the Freudian school in order to recognize himself as a student of Bleuler'. P. Roazen, *Freud and his followers* (1975) [P. Roazen, *La saga freudienne*, Paris, Puf, 1986, p. 221].
4 See. the theory of "ambitendency" or "ambivalency" in M. Escamilla, *Bleuler, Jung, and the Creation of the Schizophrenias*, Einsiedeln, Daimon Verlag, 2016.
5 Letter from Jung to Freud of 8 November 1909 (159 J).
6 Definitive version of 1952: *Symbols of Transformation*, C.G. Jung, *Collected Works*, vol. 5.
7 F. Miller, "Quelques faits d'imagination créatrice subconscients", in *Archives de psychologie*, V, n° 17, 1905, pp. 36–51.
8 'I had explained the myths of peoples of the past; I had written a book about the hero, the myth in which man has always lived. But in what myth does man live nowadays? In the Christian myth, the answer might be. "Do you live in it?" I asked myself. To be honest, the answer was no. For me, it is not what I live by." "Then do we no longer have any myth?" "No, evidently we no longer have any myth." "But then what is your myth, the myth in which you do live?"' C.G. Jung, *Memories,*

*Dreams, Reflections*, recorded and edited by A. Jaffé, translated from the German by R. and C. Winston, Toronto, Random House, 1961 [1989], p.171. On the genesis and the controversies related to this book see S. Shamdasani, "Memories, Dreams, Omissions", in *Spring,* 57, 1995.
9 '[...] il mito che regge la biografia di Jung e che costituisce il midollo del suo pensiero'. R. Màdera, *Carl Gustav Jung. L'opera al rosso*, Milan, Feltrinelli, 2016, p. 89.
10 C. G. Jung, *The Red Book*, edited by S. Shamdasani, translated by M. Kyburz, J. Peck, S. Shamdasani, New York, Philemon Foundation and W.W. Norton & Co., 2009, pp. 229–230.
11 'The God becomes sick if he oversteps the height of the zenith. That is why the spirit of the depths took me when the spirit of this time had led me to the summit.' *Ibid.*, p. 241.
12 *Ibid.*
13 *Ibid.*, p. 242.
14 C. G. Jung, *The Red Book*, p. 253.
15 Ibid.
16 *Ibid.*, p. 250.
17 *Ibid.*, p. 235.
18 B. Nante, *El Libro Rojo de Jung*, Siruela, Buenos Aires, 2010 (p. 245 of the Italian edition: *Guida alla lettura del Libro Rosso di C.G. Jung*, Turin, Bollati Boringhieri, 2012).
19 C. G. Jung, *The Red Book*, p. 261.
20 *Ibid.*, p. 62.
21 Ibidem.
22 *Ibid.*, p. 314.
23 C. G. Jung, *Collected Works*, vol. 5, p. 576.
24 The terms "*coniunctio*" and "*coincidentia oppositorum*" do not appear in the *Red Book*.
25 C. G. Jung, *The Red Book*, p. 346.
26 *Ibid.*, p. 347.
27 *Ibid.*
28 *Ibid.*, p. 350.
29 *Ibid.*, p. 351.
30 C. Maillard, *Au cœur du Livre Rouge. Les sept sermons aux morts de Carl Gustav Jung*, Paris, Imago, 2017; p. 272. "[...] Le Serpent et l'Oiseau sont présentés dans leurs mouvements respectifs: la reptation, le vol. Ils sont le mouvement des univers d'en bas et d'en haut vers l'âme, où s'opérera leur *coniunctio*".
31 C. G. Jung, *The Red Book*, p. 354.
32 The dating of the mandala is uncertain, but Jung starts to paint mandalas from 1916. The *Systema mundi totius* will later be published anonymously in the journal "Du" in 1955.
33 "The paradoxical qualities of the term reflect the fact that wholeness consists partly of the conscious man and partly of the unconscious man. But we cannot define the latter or indicate his boundaries. Hence in its scientific usage the term 'self' refers neither to Christ nor to the Buddha but to the totality of the figures that are its equivalent, and each of these figures is a symbol of the self." C. G. Jung, *Collected Works*, vol. 12, p. 20.
34 The quaternity in *Psychological Types* take the shape of the pairs of opposites: thinking – feeling and intuition – sensation.
35 C. G. Jung, 'On the nature of the psyche' in *Collected Works,* vol. 8, p. 401.
36 A. Stevens, *Jung: A very short introduction*, Oxford: Oxford University Press, 2001; p. 14.
37 S. Shamdasani, 'Des névroses à une nouvelle cure des âmes. C. G. Jung et la refonte du patient thérapeutique', in *Cahiers jungiens de psychanalyse*, n°146, 2017/2.
38 C. Maillard, *Au cœur du Livre Rouge*, p. 277.

## References

Bleuler, E. (1911) *Dementia Præcox oder Gruppe der Schizophrenien*, Leipzig, Franz Deuticke.
Escamilla, M. (2016) *Bleuler, Jung, and the Creation of the Schizophrenias*, Einsiedeln, Daimon Verlag.
Henderson, D. (2010) 'The Coincidence of Opposites: C.G. Jung's Reception of Nicholas of Cusa', *Studies in Spirituality*, n° 20: 101–113.
Jung, C. G. (1954 [1979]) *The Collected Works of C.G. Jung*, edited by H. Read, M. Fordham, G. Adler, W. McGuire, translated by R.F.C. Hull, London, Routledge and Kegan Paul, Princeton, Princeton University Press.
Jung, C. G. (1961 [1989]) *Memories, Dreams, Reflections*, recorded and edited by A. Jaffé, translated from the German by R. and C. Winston, Toronto, Random House.
Jung, C. G. (2009) *The Red Book*, edited by S. Shamdasani, translated by M. Kyburz, J. Peck, and S. Shamdasani, New York, Philemon Foundation and W.W. Norton & Co.
Màdera, R. (2016) *Carl Gustav Jung. L'opera al rosso*, Milan, Feltrinelli.
Maillard, C. (2017) *Au cœur du Livre Rouge. Les sept sermons aux morts de Carl Gustav Jung*, Paris, Imago.
Miller, F. (1905) 'Quelques faits d'imagination créatrice subconscients', in *Archives de psychologie*, V, n° 17: 36–51.
Nante, B. (2010) *El Libro Rojo de Jung*, Siruela, Buenos Aires.
Roazen, P. (1975) *Freud and his Followers*, New York, Knopf.
Shamdasani, S. (1995) 'Memories, Dreams, Omissions', in *Spring*, 57: 115–137.
Shamdasani, S. (2017) 'Des névroses à une nouvelle cure des âmes. C. G. Jung et la refonte du patient thérapeutique', in *Cahiers jungiens de psychanalyse*, 146/2: 7–28.
Stevens, A. (2001) *Jung: A Very Short Introduction*, Oxford, Oxford University Press.

# 5
# SCIENCE AS A SYSTEM: CONNECTIONS BETWEEN CARL GUSTAV JUNG'S HOLISTIC THOUGHTS ABOUT SCIENCE AND HIS *RED BOOK* EXPERIENCE

*Armelle Line Peltier*

## Introduction

Carl Gustav Jung was a Swiss psychiatrist who demonstrated remarkable reflexivity concerning his theories and his therapeutic practices. One can identify many examples of epistemological reflection from across Jung's *Collected Works*, and these cannot be set apart from the rest of his psychological studies: this underscores the idea that practice and thinking are connected in psychology in order to produce knowledge. An important moment of Jung's career—but not representative of its entirety—was his *Red Book* experience, which was a turning point in his intellectual development.[1] Jung gives testimony to this moment both in his pseudo-autobiography *Memories, Dreams, Reflections* (1961), and in *The Red Book*. In the following oft-quoted passage he writes:

> The years when I was pursuing my inner images were the most important in my life – in them everything essential was decided. It all began then; the later details are only supplements and clarifications of the material that burst forth from the unconscious, and at first swamped me. It was the *prima materia* for a lifetime's work.
>
> (Jung, 1967/1979, p. 225)

This enigmatic moment led Jung to elaborate the method of *active imagination* that he used with some patients.[2] This allows us to interrogate this particular experience as a *practice of science* and to compare this to Jung's *thoughts* about science as psychology.

A considerable amount of secondary literature has interrogated Jung's career from psychological, historical and philosophical perspectives—less from an epistemological perspective. Since the publication of *The Red Book* in 2009, many of its commentators have tried to explain how the book was constructed and what the experiences contained within it meant to Jung.[3] But none of them have identified parallels between Jung's practice during his *Red Book* experience and his general thoughts about science. This research is relevant to any examination of the relations and connections between Jung's scientific systems. Firstly I shall describe the *Red Book* experience as a global practice of science and then I shall present Jung's thoughts about the structure of science. Following from this, I shall reveal connections between 'doing' and 'thinking' and finally I will clarify the type of holistic systems that Jung created in order to construct knowledge about psyche.

## Jung's practice of science through the *Red Book* experience

Studying Jung's *Red Book* experience allows us to understand how Jung's science changed during the 1910s. At that time, he was in a situation of "disorientation" in which he felt lost psychologically and intellectually (Jung, 1967/1979, p. 174). Among other things, this period coincided with the end of his collaboration with Sigmund Freud and the psychoanalytic movement, and the completion of his work at the Burghölzli in Zurich. Jung found himself in a strange position: he was a young, gifted psychiatrist who knew little about how to relate to himself. In 1913, he began to experience some visions and hallucinations, which he allowed to continue until 1916. Between 1913 and 1930, he documented these experiences in drafts, and then transcribed them into a beautiful medieval codex he called *Liber Novus*— known to us as *The Red Book*. Of significant interest is the way Jung experienced himself— his psyche, in other words, the object of study—in visions. It means that in the same movement, Jung experienced himself, created ideas and developed a practice. Jung explains this moment of his life in his pseudo-autobiography in the chapter 'Confrontation with the Unconscious' (1967/1979, pp. 195–225). He used methods from different fields of knowledge in order to continue to engage with his experiences. For example, in order to stay calm and concentrate he used yoga or "childish" games involving sand and little stones (building little villages). And to make visions appear he used introspection or imagination.

We can define the methodology used by Jung during the *Red Book* experience as a transdisciplinary methodology. Not only did Jung want to incorporate aspects of other disciplines into his psychology, he wanted to create a new system for studying the psyche in its complexity and to survive the disorder of his own psyche. Thus, we can observe here that he was an eclectic and syncretic scientist, an approach that tends to be associated with a holistic attitude towards science. This methodology can be characterised as a process of trial and error. Jung tended not to observe the classical steps involved in a 'scientific experiment', preferring to work out a dialectic between the steps in the absence of any specific order.[4]

## The structure of science as a living organism
### Structure of science and psychology

Perhaps Jung used a transdisciplinary practice because it was required by his object of study (his psyche). The psyche forms a bond between the structure of the practice and the structure of the object of study. As the founder of analytical psychology, he developed a theoretical system about psyche as a whole comprising: "(1) consciousness, (2) the personal unconscious, and (3) the collective unconscious" (1931/1975, pars. 283–342). In his mind, science does not work as a single entity but as an assembly of different disciplines. In 1946, he stated: "Science *qua* science has no boundaries, and there is no speciality whatever that can boast of complete self-sufficiency. Any speciality is bound to spill over its borders and to encroach on adjoining territory if it is to lay serious claim to the status of a science" (1946/1985, par. 212). This quotation underlines his scientific opinions: (1) science is not a single entity but an assembly of different fields and disciplines; (2) these different fields have to work together and to establish a dialectic in order to build the most efficient ways of knowing; (3) there does not exist a single or a better way of knowing the world, contrary to claims made by logical positivists and presented in their models of physics; (4) the goal of science is not to find the truth but to build knowledge of an object of study; and (5) progress in science must be understood in terms of increase of knowledge. This corresponds with Jung's opinions about psychology: for him science needed to be larger than a defined paradigm.

Psychology must work on a transdisciplinary level. To complete the previous quotation: "Even so highly specialized a technique as Freudian psychoanalysis was unable, at the very outset, to avoid poaching on other, and sometimes exceedingly remote, scientific preserves. It is, in fact, impossible to treat the psyche, and human personality in general, sectionally" (1946/1985, par. 212). Elsewhere Jung writes: "The psyche, as a reflection of the world and man, is a thing of such infinite complexity that it can be observed and studied from a great many sides" (1931/1975, par. 283). It presents the fact that some phenomena—specifically those in the human sciences—need to be studied from a holistic point of view because their objects of study work on an organic level.

> That this is so is immediately understandable when we consider that the unconscious, as the totality of all archetypes, is the deposit of all human experience right back to its remotest beginnings. Not, indeed, a dead deposit, a sort of abandoned rubbish-heap, but a living system of reactions and aptitudes that determine the individual's life in invisible ways—all the more effective because invisible.
>
> *(Jung, 1931/1975, par. 339)*

For Jung, psychology is a flexible science, adaptive to the study of the psyche because psyche is always an object in movement, changing all the time and related to many so-called "factors."

## Discourses in *The Red Book*

If we write about Jung's practice during his *Red Book* experience, it is crucial to discover what epistemological perspectives are implicit within this practice. Indeed, throughout the text one can identify discourses about knowledge and ways of knowing which reveal Jung's reflections on his work. In the book, the word 'science' is not so important when he writes about *magic, reason, knowledge*, even *poison*. Jung's approach is highly flexible because during his journey through his own psyche he does not look for an exact definition of its structure and dynamics, but for a way to continue to learn and produce knowledge and technique.

Moreover, we learn in the text that there is not one and only one way to produce knowledge and technique but rather a multitude of ways.[5] Jung searches for meaning, and signification, understanding the psyche with his eyes wide open. About this research, he writes: "The spirit of the depths took my understanding and all my knowledge and placed them at the service of the inexplicable and the paradoxical. He robbed me of speech and writing for everything that was not in his service, namely the melting together of sense and nonsense, which produces the supreme meaning" (Jung, 2009, pp. 229). Jung tries to integrate what is significant for him—sense and nonsense—adopting an open attitude of integration towards the contents of his unconscious and eschewing that of resistance. This can be compared with his dialogue throughout the book where he draws attention to several dualities: *reason* and *unreason*, *spirit of this time* and *spirit of the depths*, *science* and *magic*. But in the end there is nothing to throw away, and we are left with complementarities in which each pole of the binary cannot subsist independently of the other. By their dialectics and their relations they can produce what Jung called "the supreme meaning". This meaning can be understood as a global and holistic vision of the object of study, potentially leading to the construction of a more efficient way of studying it.

The "nonsense" that Jung refers to can be understood as another way to proceed, one which appears to be embodied in the chapter he called "The magician". There, the "I" meets Philemon who teaches him some lessons about other ways of learning: there exist many more ways of learning than the ones we know because we still don't know a lot of things about the world. In this chapter, Jung writes: "The practice of magic consists in making what is not understood understandable in an incomprehensible manner. [...] The magical way arises by itself. If one opens up chaos, magic also arises" (Jung, 2009, p. 314). And: "The magical always surrounds me, always involves me. It opens spaces that have no doors and leads out into the open where there is no exit. The magical is good and evil and neither good nor evil" (Jung, 2009, p. 314). It appears here that magic is an attitude that "has no doors," it opens up possibilities of doing and thinking. It means that it is another way of knowing, a form of "aptitude". In the book it constitutes a "way of living" characteristic of an open-minded attitude towards searching and learning, an unfolding of knowledge which has not been subordinated to the form of the way. From this dialogue we also learn that magic is not a classical discipline, and unlike science it is not to be found exclusively in universities but also inside each human: a universal attitude or method of humankind (Jung, 2009, p. 314). Jung tends to create a microsystem in the psyche with consciousness, unconsciousness, and the collective unconsciousness correlated to a macrosystem, thereby linking humans through their ability to understand and know what they all have in common: psyche.

## Experience is inherent to elaboration of thoughts

Scientists do not respect the hypothetical classical steps that logical positivism wanted science to be based upon. Indeed, science is constructed by errors, mistakes, *ad hoc* hypotheses, and so on. Everything is mixed depending on the object of study and what it is possible for the scientist to do (see Feyerabend, 1975/1993). This was also the case for Jung during his career, specifically during his *Red Book* experience, because some possibilities seemed to be better in terms of producing therapeutic practices, ideas, or hypotheses. The philosopher of science Paul Karl Feyerabend writes:

> Creation of a *thing*, and creation plus full understanding of a *correct idea* of the thing, *are very often parts of one and the same indivisible process* and cannot be separated without bringing the process to a stop. The process itself is not guided by a well-defined programme, and cannot be guided by such a programme, for it contains the conditions for the realization of all possible programmes.
>
> *(1975/1993, p. 17; emphasis added)*

Based on this, we can conclude that it was necessary for Jung to mix scientific steps and scientific ways of producing ideas and practice. These two kinds of systems—the methodological and the theoretical—cannot be separated and the construction of one is dependent on the other because they appear together.

The creation of a kind of holistic system of ideas depends on, and is the mirror of, the system of practice used to build it. Ludwig von Bertalanffy, founder of the *General System Theory*, writes:

> We realize, however, that all scientific laws merely represent abstractions and idealizations expressing certain aspects of reality. Every science means a schematized picture of reality, in the sense that a certain conceptual construct is unequivocally related to certain features of order in reality; just as the blueprint of a building isn't the building itself and by no means represents it in every detail such as the arrangement of bricks and the forces keeping them together, but nevertheless an unequivocal correspondence exists between the design on paper and the real construction of stone, iron and wood.
>
> *(1968/2015, p. 83)*

This underscores the idea that science is constructed on the basis of the chosen object of study and it works as a system because it depends on everything in it: nothing could exist without the rest. This is how Jung constructs his system of ideas and practice, by building every level depending on the others and starting from the microcosm of the collective unconsciousness and then moving to the macrocosm of science.

## Creation of holistic systems of doing and thinking

### System of methods

Feyerabend explains that scientific progress (increase of knowledge) is a result of a removal of reason and arguably this is also the case for Jung, as the *Red Book* experience appears to attest.[6] This allows Jung to build a holistic methodology producing at the end a kind of knowledge. His "whole" of methods is holistic because of its transdisciplinary nature and its constant dialectic between practice and its effects. It works as an organism—in the same way the process of thinking cannot work without the practice.

### System of ideas

Bertalanffy developed General System Theory, which is a transdisciplinary theory in which science is viewed as an organic system or a symbolic one that corresponds to reality. In his view, science is a system composed of other systems corresponding to different disciplines. These parts are different but not totally separable, and they share a structure in common. We find affinities in Jung's approach to science via the parallel between the micro-system and the macro-system. In this context Jung writes:

> This whole psychic organism corresponds exactly to the body, which, though individually varied, is in all essential features the specifically human body which all men have. In its development and structure, it still preserves elements that connect it with the invertebrates and ultimately with the protozoa. Theoretically it should be possible to "peel" the collective unconscious, layer by layer, until we came to the psychology of the worm, and even of the amoeba. We are all agreed that it would be quite impossible to understand the living organism apart from its relation to the environment.
>
> *(1931/1975, par. 322)*

In Bertalanffy's theory, science is seen as a totality that works as a living organism and not as a dead object. In consequence, relations between the parts are complex and not only viewed as cause and effect, or stimulus and reaction. For example, Freud developed a mechanist view of the mind in which symptoms are a reaction to a drive. On the contrary, for Jung the human organism is not only dependant on some effects but on a multiplicity of events which integrate the human in his environment, history and a constellation of so called "events" or "reasons".

*The Red Book*'s discourse is holistic because it speaks about all the aspects of life— including science—and these occur together as parts of a "whole" system. One can discern features of this holistic approach at the end of *The Red Book* and in *Septem Sermones ad Mortuos* in which the mind—the object of study—is presented with a specific frame influencing the building of science's structure. Jung's microcosm and macrocosm are related, and the following quotation by Bertalanffy captures the essence of this relation and its exploration: "Unity of Science is granted, not by a utopian reduction of all sciences to physics and chemistry, but by the structural uniformities of the different levels of reality" (1968/2015, p. 87).

## Conclusion

Throughout the *Red Book* Jung's experience indicates two organic systems, one composed by ideas (hypotheses, knowledge, suppositions, etc.) and one of methods. These two systems are complemented by the relation between the microcosm of the psyche and the macrocosm of the universe and both are always connected to the environment. These two systems work in parallel as they are constructed through a dialectic—one in comparison to the other—the psyche in comparison to the practice used to cure it. Summarising Leibniz as one of the forerunners of his idea of synchronicity, Jung writes: "Not only is man a microcosm enclosing the whole in himself, but every entelechy or monad is in effect such a microcosm. Each 'simple substance' has connections 'which express all the others'" (1952/1975, par. 937). For him, the psyche and the human as living organism work according to a holistic dynamic and this is why he created a holistic methodology that would facilitate its study. Moreover, through the specific example of the *Red Book* experience, Jung demonstrates a high degree of consistency regarding his unique approach to science.

This specific way of doing science was not consistent with science and psychology at the beginning of the twentieth century and this may be one of several reasons that led Jung not to publish the *Red Book*. On the contrary, Jung built a holistic science based on a holistic point of view about humankind and the psyche in which both are respected as living systems.

## Notes

1 I use the term "experience" rather than "experiences" when referring to Jung's *Red Book* experience because it is a global experience not several experiences.
2 This therapeutic method should help the patient to bring unconscious contents to consciousness. See Jung, 1916/1958, pars. 129–193, (translated from "Die Transzendente Funktion", *Geist und Werke,* Zurich: Rhein-Verlag), par. 130.

3 E.g. Drob, 2012; Jones, 2014; Kirsch & Hogenson, 2014; Maillard, 2011; Maillard and Liard, 2014; Shamdasani, 2009.
4 For further information, see Armelle Line Peltier, 2019, *Une pensée créatrice en science. L'élaboration de la connaissance chez Carl Gustav Jung (1875–1961) à travers l'étude du Livre Rouge (1913–1930)*, thèse d'épistémologie et d'histoire des sciences et des techniques, sous la direction de Bernard Ancori et Christine Maillard, Strasbourg, Université de Strasbourg.
5 For example in "On the Service of the Soul" from the *Red Book* Jung comments: "Must I also learn to do without meaning? [...] What is there, where there is no meaning? Only nonsense, or madness, it seems to me. Is there also a supreme meaning? Is that your meaning, my soul?" (2009, p. 235).
6 Feyerabend writes that: "Without 'chaos', no knowledge. Without a frequent dismissal of reason, no progress" (1975/1995, p. 158).

## References

Bertalanffy, L. (1968/2015). *General System Theory: Foundations, Development, Applications*. New York: George Braziller.
Drob, S. L. (2012). *Reading the Red Book, An Interpretive Guide to C. G. Jung's Liber Novus*. New Orleans: Spring Journal Books.
Feyerabend, P. K. (1975/1993). *Against Method*. London: Verso.
Jones, R. A. (2014). *Jung and the Question of Science*. London: Routledge.
Jung, C. G. (1916/1958). "The Transcendent Function", *The Structure and Dynamics of the Psyche. Collected Works 8*. Princeton: Princeton University Press, pars. 129–193, (translated from "Die Transzendente Funktion", *Geist und Werke*, Zurich: Rhein-Verlag).
Jung, C. G. (1931/1975). "The Structure of the Psyche", *The Structure and Dynamics of the Psyche. Collected Works 8*. Princeton: Princeton University Press, pars. 283–342, (translated from "Die Struktur der Seele", *Seelenprobleme der Gegenwart*. Zurich: Rascher).
Jung, C. G. (1946/1985), "Psychotherapy Today", *Practice of Psychotherapy: Essays on the Psychology of the Transference and Other Subjects. Collected Works 16*. Princeton: Princeton University Press, pars. 212–229, (translated from "Die Psychotherapie in der Gegenwart", *Aufsätze zur Zeitgeschichte*. Zurich: Rascher).
Jung, C. G. (1952/1975). "Synchronicity: An Acausal Connecting Principle", *The Structure and Dynamics of the Psyche, Collected Works 8*. Princeton: Princeton University Press, pars. 815–968, (translated from "Synchronizität als ein Prinzip akausaler Zusammenhänge", *Naturerklärung und Psyche*. Zurich: Rascher).
Jung, C. G. (1967/1979). *Memories, Dreams, Reflections*. London: Fount Paperbacks, (*Erinnerungen, Träume, Gedanken*, translated from the German by Winston R. and C.).
Jung, C. G. (2009). *The Red Book*. London: Philemon Foundation and W. W. Norton & Co.
Kirsch, T. and Hogenson, G. (ed.), (2014). *The Red Book: Reflections on C. G. Jung's Liber Novus*. London: Routledge.
Maillard, C. (dir.), (2011). "Art, sciences et psychologie. Autour du *Livre Rouge* de Carl Gustav Jung (1914/1930)", *Recherches Germaniques*. Special edition no. 8, Strasbourg: Presses Universitaires de Strasbourg.
Maillard, C. and Liard, V. (dir.), (2014). "Carl Gustav Jung (1875–1961). Pour une réévaluation de l'œuvre", *Recherches Germaniques*. Special edition no. 9, Strasbourg: Presses Universitaires de Strasbourg.
Shamdasani, S. (2009). "Introduction", *Liber Novus: The "Red Book" of C. G. Jung*. New York: Norton and Company.

# 6

# THE HOLISTIC WISH: MIGRATION OF FEELING, THOUGHT AND EXPERIENCE

*Phil Goss*

### Introduction: Wishing and psychic self-regulation

Wishing, wish fulfilment and the disappointment of un-fulfilled wishes are undisputedly part of the experience of being human. To make a wish, or two, or classically *three*, is a ubiquitous hallmark of childhood's awakening to life's possibilities and the power of imagining what could be, even when we know logically that (for example), being able to fly, or to multiply a 1p coin into a million pounds is beyond possibility (after all, hundreds, if not thousands of years of alchemical practices are based around this human wish for the impossible).

Likewise, the need, and the mechanisms in our dream life, for some wishes to be safely fulfilled (Freud, 1900) rather than dangerously acted out has been an established maxim of psychoanalytic thinking since its inception. In broader cultural exchange, the saying *Be careful what you wish for* speaks to the *shadow* (Jung, 1968) danger of wishing – as if the sheer power of our drive to wish for something might well unconsciously steer us towards being bitten rather than nourished by what we thought we wanted.

As highlighted, the roots of psychology are intimately entangled with the notion of *wishing*. Freud (1900) made a claim for its fundamental importance, writing: "Nothing but a wish can set our mental apparatus working" (p. 567). While of course his situating of the wish as pivotal to how we think and feel revolved around the notion of wish *fulfilment* as the key function of dreaming, there has been less focus on the importance or otherwise of wishing in our waking lives. As Schonbachler et al. (2016) observe, little thought has been given to the significance of the *conscious* wish in psychoanalysis, not to mention neuroscience, despite the conscious wish seeming to have an important compensatory function in sustaining our sense of balance in day-to-day life.

Where this is deployed within healthy parameters, Schonbachler et al. 2016 give the example of someone sustaining themselves to complete a tough work schedule by wishing for the holiday they have booked (and daydreaming they were on it), the wish assumes an important role in psychic regulation. This contrasts with being stuck in a wishful state about something we cannot have in the present and becoming helplessly lost in it. The trick with a wish seems to be to allow ourselves to wish for something unattainable in the present, but to use the daydream/fantasy that arises from the wish to nourish us in the face of pressure, boredom, or disappointment and to get us through, or to successfully complete, difficult tasks and episodes in life.

So, how might we see wishing as informing notions of holism, and our understanding of holistic influences and tendencies in the human psyche, not to mention across the many and complex levels of organic and inorganic life on this planet? A wish operates as an intuitive and instinctually based thought that operates around the *fringes* of psychic processes—not what I can/cannot do or I will/will not do (i.e., within ego control), but what I long to happen even though it probably, or even certainly, *won't* come to pass, and I have no real control over making it happen. The ideal of a fulfilled wish is akin to the idealism that can underlie holism, and in both cases, I argue, this idealism and the imaginative ideation that results can be helpful in our struggle for fulfilment, or even just survival, where this is bounded by a suitably developed grasp of reality and necessity.

Of course, even a fulfilled wish can be as likely to lead to disintegrative and deconstructive developments in our experiencing and identity, as it is to integrating and confirmative outcomes in our lives and sense of self. If any of us wish for a new job or relationship, while the wish may have a 'growthful' basis (though this is by no means certain in all cases), the outcome is as likely to turn out negative as positive, or it may bifurcate into a mixture of the two (perhaps the most likely outcome). This point is made to both counter the risk of over-idealising the act of wishing, and to emphasise the elusive, self-determining quality of this process. Fulfilled wishes often have a life of their own.

## The holistic wish: Principles and theory

It is from this starting point that I want to speculate about what I see as the tendency in the human psyche to migrate towards a more holistically informed state. By a 'holistically informed state', I am trying to name an experience of living that more or less consistently provides a feeling of well-being and integration but which may oscillate considerably depending on life's vagaries and uncertainties; but to some degree is there, if not *all* the time, at least for *most* of the time. I want to argue that this is something human beings tend to wish for, a kind of 'good enough' steady state in life, rather than the idealised 'good life'. In this respect, the holistic wish may appear as a reaction to unhappiness or adversity in childhood, in exaggerated, idealised, form, as a compensation for such circumstances, but this might be the facilitating factor in bringing the individual to a 'good enough' sense of wholeness.

A holistic wish may take many forms, from a fleeting moment of felt and sensed integration which gives birth to a wish for something more long-lasting, through to a mentalised commitment to adopting attitudes and disciplines which aim at fostering a sustained sense of this. However, I want to make a distinction between the holistic wish and Jung's classic formulation for individuation (1962). While there is obvious overlap between the two - in terms of an identified archetypal movement in the human psyche towards fuller integration of all aspects of self, and a shared sense of 'becoming' (which also maps across to Rogers' actualising tendency [1959]) – the holistic wish, I propose, suggests itself more as an important starting point for these processes, rather than as a term which describes the process itself, and this bears closer examination.

I am applying a phenomenological lens to this pursuit of the holistic wish and the underlying migratory tendencies in the psyche, with reference to Brooke's (2015) application of phenomenology to the Jungian conceptual framework as it gets actualised both moment by moment, and also across a lifetime, as well as Craig's (2012) existential modelling of profound processes in the human endeavour.

The root of the holistic wish in the human psyche has a dual aspect—relational and developmental, more like two stems arising from the roots of a plant—their pattern of growth and fate clearly interlinked, and yet distinctive in their origin and purpose: one (relational) originating in an archetypal need for relationship and connection to other(s), the other (developmental), directing its energy towards a physiological and psychological becoming, which is equally inherent in the organism.

The Greek term φυτόν (*phyton*) (meaning plant) refers to the living plant that grows and may be applied colloquially to the collective experiencing of shared life, or the individual, distinctive grasping for individual meaning and experiencing, separated out from the crowd. An example would be where a group of people are walking in the countryside, talking and laughing together—as a collective experience of *phyton,* and one where the effect is rhizomatic, to borrow from the lexicon of Deleuze and Guattari (1972); i.e. the 'growth', the shared embrace of life, moves laterally around the group of walkers, and its root, its *phyton*, germinates and springs from individual pockets of animated or reflective conversation around the group, while creating an overall shared vibe or feel which all in the group experience some sense of being part of, however fleeting. On the other hand—or maybe as a further off-shoot of this bubbling dynamic—one individual in the group feels a strong need to break off from the group and walk by themselves, choosing to leap from the shared fishbowl into one of their own, a more individualistic *phyton*, feeling a sense of freed growth and distinctiveness.

Altogether, this is a moving patchwork of *relational* holistic activity, a state of collective (and individual) migration towards a shared state of meaningful and satisfying 'mind' and in both cases seem to parallel aspects of Fordham's ideas (1985) about how the human psyche, including ego-formation, develops through firstly *de-integrating* (i.e., allowing itself to reach out and let go of its self-containment, in order to phenomenologically *experience* contact—with other(s) or environment, new phenomena, old phenomena again or the absence of something—and then *reintegrate* this into their sense of self and of reality, in an ongoing, constant experiential learning process); a developmental, but non-linear, reaching-outside-the-box movement beginning in early childhood and remaining as a psychological routine beyond that.

As Fordham (1985) also observes it is quite possible and not uncommon for this process to misfire so that the mind becomes overwhelmed by stimuli, or becomes under-stimulated, in line with thinking and research on attachment patterns. Here the risk of mental *disintegration* can come into play, and this also speaks to the messy, destructive and deadening *shadow* side of thinking on holism, as highlighted by Andrew Culp in *Dark Deleuze* (2016) to helpfully counter tendencies to portray the work of Deleuze and others as entirely constructive and meaningful.

## The holistic wish: A clinical example

To illustrate these themes, I want to supply a brief clinical vignette, to highlight how a holistic wish was germinated for a client who had long experienced most contact with others as difficult: at worst threatening, at best unsatisfying; a dynamic arising from a, by turn, isolating and persecutory set of childhood experiences which led to an idealising of an isolated way of life as the only true source of nourishment. As a consequence, this woman chose to live in a remote area, travelling into the nearest village, only for basic provisions, once or twice a week, and relying on a dialogue she generated with the countryside around her—speaking to the landscape and familiar natural objects within it—the trees, the animals in the fields she walked and drove by, as if they were her closest family members and friends. She would then listen and "hear" responses from these familiar others and sometimes write down the dialogues she had had with them.

At this point I want to apply my way of working with Jung's (1968) formula for contra-sexual influences in the human psyche, *anima* and *animus*. Classically *anima* is the feminine influence in the male psyche and *animus* the masculine influence in the female psyche. In post-Jungian thinking both influences are often recognised to be at work in any of us, irrespective of our gender. I combine this dyadic influence with Freud's use of *Eros* and *Thanatos* (Mitchell and Black, 2016) as life and death instincts to help me make sense of what might be going on for those I am working with—and also for me (Goss 2010).

The client was referred to me by an old friend of hers who had visited her and was worried because she seemed to be hearing voices. I had a strong sense of the death instinct at work drawing her away from relational contact with others in life. At the same time, there was something at work in her, seeking out there, every day, in the natural world, *relationship,* via her rhizomatic contacts with living things. In contra-sexual terms, it was as if her *thanimus* (closed down, deathly masculine) aspects which had seemingly closed her off from conventional human contact, was being challenged and countered by an *erosima* tendency (fluid, feminine, relationally seeking) which moved her towards the relational, via the natural world. Here the holistic wish migrated her psyche towards a better balance of being, and although our work may have helped, it was this contact with nature that was germinal to the process. In addition, the acquisition of a pet dog acted as an invaluable bridge for her to begin to make meaningful contact and relationship with other people.

Within the scope of the above example, the visual or otherwise sensorial encounter with landscape and environment, whatever the context (rural or urban, however despoiled), is fertile territory for germination of the holistic wish, as evidenced in Romantic and post-Romantic writing (Vine, 2014). This suggests that the workings of *anima* and *animus* might inform our engagement with the holistic wish, feeding the migratory yearnings of the human soul.

## The holistic wish and the human psyche

To further develop this idea of the subtle importance of the capacity to wish—in fostering a healthy relationship to life, which allows for a holistic undercurrent to our journey through it to emerge while moving in and out of different experiences, episodes, and encounters—I will speculate how and where in the human psyche it operates, with reference to neuroscientific readings of how the workings of the brain may reflect this. This speculation reflects a position which argues that as well as powerful relationally/socially constructivist influences shaping our development, there are also dimensions of psychic development and experiencing which have an archetypal dimension. In this context, the chapter posits that the wish (per se) has a commonly shared as well as personally unique dimension, and that the holistic wish lies in potential in all of us, in the same way that a more destructive wish (to be fragmented, or even dissolved) awaits constellation in us. Here *Eros* and *Thanatos* vie to generate wishes that can be consciously recognised and even acted on.

But, within the psyche how and where this potential lies in wait and then gets activated in relation to other influences is not easy to pin down, and nor should it be considering its elusive mercurial quality. It is also important to bear in mind that we are not envisaging a map of the psyche which can be physically located within the human organism, but rather something that is generated by the interaction of body and mind, takes a virtual form and is a combination of instinctual, mental and imaginal influences.

One metaphor I find useful in this regard is of intra-psychic activity as a weather system, creating effects consciously and unconsciously. Within that system, a kind of condensation arises from the body and mind, producing clouds of influence on and in us. Where the imaginal in the psyche influences the formation of these clouds then the right condition can arise for a unique manifestation of a wish (holistic or otherwise). Here, Corbin's (1972) concept of the *mundus imaginalis* comes into play, as an image-making function in the human psyche which operates in between the reception of sense impressions and the creation of an image that the mind can recognise and be affected by. This is what enables the sunlight, warmth, rain or storm inside us to be noticed by the mind, in image form; or in classical Jungian terms, how the idea of something that is wished for from deep in the unconscious gets turned into a symbol which the conscious mind can notice and do something (or nothing) with. Panskepp (1998) posited that alongside a more appetitive, desiring system within the circuits in the human brain, which corresponds (Schonbachler et al. 2016) more readily to the wish-fulfilling features of neurobiological reward systems as prioritised for its significance by psychoanalysis (Freud 1911), there is another system. This is hallmarked by *seeking* and is anticipatory in its nature. It looks for resources in the outside world so as to meet biological needs, while also mediating appetitive learning so there is an eagerness, a wish, to explore the environment, rather than just sate appetite. So, this dimension of dopamine activation motivates us to seek understanding and meaning alongside fulfilling survival needs.

Schonbachler et al. (2016) argue that this seeking function in the brain applies more of a subtle tonic (Schonbachler et al., p. 171) influence on mental activity rather than generating the bodily based reach for satisfaction associated with wish fulfilment. If, they further argue, the seeking function does not get satisfaction in the external world, then a displaced wish (Schonbachler et al., p. 171) becomes conscious (affectively charged and experienced) to compensate for this dissatisfaction at an unconscious level. I suggest that this helpful psychoanalytic-neuroscientific formulation provides the seeking arena in which a distinctively holistic wish bursts like a shooting star in the night sky of our inner world, at key moments in life (early childhood, pre-puberty and adolescence in particular) and when these conditions are in place. What makes the holistic wish distinctive, like Jung's distinction between a big and an ordinary dream, is that the holistic wish draws on an archetypal potentiality to seize its opportunity to appear and then lodge itself as deeply important to the individual.

## Concluding comments: The road as the engine of holistic migration of psyche

I want to conclude by pondering the relevance of the image of the *road* as speaking to the connection between a holistic version of psychic life, and the possibilities inherent in a teleological view of the human condition—where we move towards something in front of us as well as well as away from something. On the surface, not least because it is laid down as a surface on top of what was naturally there before, the notion of a road—especially where it cuts its way in a straight, linear form, laid down by the human hand and mind, through the natural environment, could appear contradictory to holistically lateral, multi-directional or circumambulatory notions of growth. Here the *rhizome* dynamic, which sprouts new and different versions of plant life or of human experience and insight, can do its work anywhere within the field of phenomenological experiencing, including where the linear forwards can be seen as unhelpfully perpetuating patriarchal myopia about the nature of human and natural movements of growth and change.

I want to suggest the road as symbol of the migratory tendency in the human psyche, which takes the lateral along the road with us. Like a walking combine harvester, consuming everything in its path, we scan with all of our senses the images of abundance (or absence) along the roadside, both in rural and urban contexts, taking it all in laterally as we move forward through life. This speaks to the value of seeing movement through life as forward reaching, and enabling clarity of insight to emerge as well as organic messiness and *shadow* to play its part.

In this respect, I suggest, the holistic wish operates in the psyche broadly in a kind of pincer movement to subtly, generally unconsciously influence our direction of travel. There is first a barely noticeable draw towards wishing, which, as suggested, colours childhood and remains a feature of adult becoming. It moves inwardly, in a spiral motion from the fringes of psyche, maybe as a wish sent from the deeper self to attract ego healthily towards expansion and deepening, however holistically messy this may be. Second, our natural developmental and relational inclinations, however stymied or warped by the vagaries of upbringing, personality and whatever else falls across our path, lead us to migrate towards where the holistic wish seems to be taking us, however unclear any sense of "destination" is.

This latter dimension, with reference again to the darkness in Deleuze and certainly in the occasionally uncomfortably dark Jung, implies a collective dimension at least. A post-religious, and in the recent history of the UK in particular, a post-Christian holistic wish emerges: a migration towards facing difficult, darker and less virtuous (*shadow*) aspects of who we are as a route towards a more complete sense of self, as a partially conscious migration towards spiritual insight and a 'new settlement' in the relationship between the human, nature, and the divine and sublime.

Finally, on a country lane I am familiar with in the north of England, there are steps in the side of a stone wall, leading to a path across a rising hill. The sign next to it reads "Please clean up after your dog". Next to this request to clean up the mess (made by our instinctual natures?), is a proclamation: "There is no such thing as the dog-poo fairy", along with the illustration of a fairy, the granter of wishes. I beg to differ: I think there is a wish fairy inside us, but we cannot predict if or when our wishes will be granted or what the consequences will be, and how much poo we'll have to clear up as a result, as we walk forwards through the fog towards the hazy holistic horizon.

## References

Brooke, R. (2015). *Jung and Phenomenology*. London: Routledge.

Corbin, H. (1972). Mundus imaginalis, the imaginary and the imaginal. *Spring Publications*. James Hillman (ed.). New York: Analytical Psychology Club of New York, Inc. pp. 1–19.

Craig, E. (2012). Human existence (Cún Zài): What is it? What's in it for us as existential psychotherapists? *The Humanistic Psychologist*, 40: 1–22. London: Routledge.

Culp, A. (2016). *Dark Deleuze*. Minneapolis: University of Minnesota Press.

Deleuze, G. and Guattari, F. (1972). *Anti-Oedipus*. Trans. (2004) Robert Hurley, Mark Seem and Helen R. Lane. London and New York: Continuum, 2004.

Fonagy, P., Gergely, G. and Target, M. (2008). Psychoanalytic constructs and attachment theory and research. In Cassidy, J., Shaver, P. *Handbook of Attachment: Theory, Research and Clinical Applications*. New York and London: Guilford Press. pp. 783–810.

Fordham, M. (1985) *Explorations into the Self*. London: Academic Press.

Freud, S. (1900). *The Interpretation of Dreams*. Standard Edition, 4/5.

Freud, S. (1911). *Formulations on Two Principles of Mental Functioning*. Standard Edition (volume 12).

Goss, P. (2010). *Men, Women and Relationships: A Post-Jungian Approach. Gender Electrics and Magic Beans*. Hove, UK: Routledge.

Jung, C. G. (1962). *Symbols of Transformation: An Analysis of the Prelude to a Case of Schizophrenia* (CW Vol. 2). London: Routledge

Jung. C. G. (1968). Anima and Animus. In Sir Herbert Read, Michael Fordham and Gerhard Adler (eds.), William McGuire (Executive ed.), R.F.C Hull (Trans.), *Two Essays in Analytical Psychology*. London: Routledge.

Jung, C. G. (1968). The Shadow. In Sir Herbert Read, Michael Fordham and Gerhard Adler (eds.), William McGuire (Executive ed.), R.F.C Hull (Trans.), *Archetypes of the Collective Unconscious*. London: Routledge.

Mitchell, S. and Black. M. (2016). *Freud and Beyond: A History of Modern Psychoanalytic Thought* (Updated Edition). New York: Basic Books/Hachette Books.

Panksepp, J. (1998). *Affective Neuroscience, the Foundations of Human and Animal Emotions*. New York: Oxford University Press.

Rogers, C. (1961). *On Becoming a Person*. Boston: Houghton Mifflin.

Schonbachler, G., Stogkovic, D., and Boothe, B. (2016). Mapping a gap: the concepts of the wish and wishing in psychoanalysis and the neurosciences. *Neuropsychoanalysis*, 18(2): pp. 163–177. New York: Routledge.

Vine, S. (2014). *Reinventing the Sublime*. Eastbourne, UK: Sussex Academic Press.

# 7

# HOLISTIC EDUCATION: THE JUNGIAN DILEMMA

*Robert Mitchell*

## Introduction

We may take it for granted that seeking holism means working toward individuation, as Jung intended. Yet, even for Jung, education of the young was to be focused on developing ego-centered, mental consciousness rather than the whole personality of the child. Jung said: "It is not the child, but only the adult, who can achieve personality as the fruit of a full life directed to this end" (Jung, 1981, p. 171). Thus, Jung equated the development of "personality" with the individuation process in the second half of life. However, as with many of Jung's statements regarding the psychology of children, his full intent is ambiguous and even contradictory as, for example, in his reference to individuation as a two-part process. Clarifying Jung's ambiguity, Jolande Jacobi writes:

> Although the whole process [of individuation] plots the course of conscious realization, the first phase aims at the crystallization of a stable ego, and the second at the achievement of a permanent relationship between the ego and the Self.
>
> *(Jacobi, 1965, p. 64)*

Jacobi views child development as a part of the individuation process. It is *not* exclusive to the adult in the second half of life. Thus, she legitimizes the term, *Developmental Individuation*.

In *Ego and Archetype*, Edward Edinger discusses individuation and the stages of development. He illuminates what Jungians have taken as the current working formula, "first half of life: ego-Self separation; second half of life: ego-Self reunion" (Edinger, 1972, p. 5). Edinger goes on to say:

> This formula ... neglects many empirical observations made in child psychology and in the psychotherapy of adults. According to these observations, a more nearly correct formula would be a circular one ... The process of alternation between ego-Self union and ego-Self separation seems to occur repeatedly throughout the life of the individual both in childhood and maturity.
>
> *(Edinger, 1972, p. 5)*

This is a revision of Jung's perspective on personality, which he equates to the ego-Self relationship. The key word in the first phase of the Jungian formula is ego-Self "separation." Edinger's formula of developmental differentiation does not mean separation. In respect to this, Jacobi says:

> When the occupant of the psychic centre is smaller than the God-image, or when this centre is still walled in by convention or petrified beliefs, void within, and ruled by fear, the relationship to the God-image is at an end, the ego-Self axis is broken ... The growing number of people who have lost their relation to the Self provides a shattering object lesson as to where such a separation may lead.
>
> *(Jacobi, 1965, p. 55)*

Thus Jacobi implies that a developing ego that becomes separated from the Self is an incomplete, or not fully developed, personality.

Herein lies the Jungian dilemma—a concession or compromise with Freud, allowing that an incomplete, not fully developed, or repressed personality should be subordinate, in the first half of life, to ego development. Yet, the observations of both Jacobi and Edinger suggest a lifelong interactive ego–Self relationship that emphasizes both the personality of the child and the development of the ego. Thus, *Developmental Individuation* pays specific attention to preserving the ego–Self axis. In contrast, the clinician can only try to repair the damage when the ego–Self axis is weakened to the breaking point.

Still, there are many factors outside of the child's education and home that affect the repression of the personality, the development of the ego, and the breaking of the ego–Self axis: for example, peer pressure and social and cultural factors that emphasize technology, economic opportunity, and career placement over a holistic development. These influences greatly exacerbate the split between ego and Self. The objective of holistic education is to mitigate these outside factors and develop an ego that is differentiated (crystalized and stabilized) yet preserves the integrity of the ego–Self axis. Thus, holistic education depends on two things: (1) the teacher's nurturing relationship with the students in the class and (2) a curriculum that relates child development to the human cultural continuum.

## The concept of holism in education

What are the aims of education? From a classical perspective, there are three aims: personal, civic, and occupational. The personal aim is developmental. Holistic development of the child's personality means developing the child's highest potential. The civic aim is both social and cultural in scope. The occupational aim means acquiring utilitarian skills and knowledge so the adult can contribute to the welfare of the social economy.

The concept of holistic education arose as a reaction against a narrow emphasis on only one of these aims, throwing the child's development out of balance. Aristotle introduced the concept of educational holism in *The Politics:* "nor yet is it clear whether … education ought to be conducted with more concern for the intellect than for the character of the soul" (Sinclair 1962, p. 453). The modern concept of holistic education arose with the European Enlightenment and addressed the same concern over too much emphasis on intellectual development and not enough emphasis on metaphysics to nurture the soul. The concept of holistic education that evolved in the 1970s, however, was a "child-centered" concept that distorted the theory of holism espoused 250 years ago by Jean Jacques Rousseau. On child-centered education in his definitive book on holistic education, author Scott Forbes writes, citing Rousseau, "What must be avoided is 'an excess of rigor and an excess of indulgence.' This is what Rousseau called 'well-regulated freedom'" (Forbes 2003, p. 94). Furthermore Allan Bloom, in his introduction to Rousseau's *Emile* writes, "The child must always do what he wants to do. This, we recognize, is the dictum of modern-day progressive education, and Rousseau is rightly seen as its source. What is forgotten is that Rousseau's full formula is that … the child … should want to do only what the tutor wants him to do" (Bloom 1979, p. 13). The holistic teacher's developmental objective is to bring the four aims of education—occupational, social, cultural, and developmental—into balance.

Paul Tillich's term "ultimacy" gives a sense of that balance. Ultimacy means the highest state one can aspire to; reaching one's highest potential; and engaging in the service of something sacred. (Forbes 2003, p. 17) This last part implies not only finding one's highest potential but using that potential in service to the culture in terms of an occupation: a *calling* that engages one in service to that which is sacred in the culture. Thus, holism defined as ultimacy brings together the occupational, social, cultural, and developmental aims of education.

In the 18th and 19th centuries three figures emerged to define the modern concept of holistic education: Jean Jacques Rousseau's theoretical book, *Emile: on Education* (1762), remains a significant influence on the modern holistic concept of child development. Johann Heinrich Pestalozzi and Friedrich Froebel put Rousseau's theories into practice and contributed to the cultural aspect of holism.

## Jean Jacques Rousseau (1712–1778)

Rousseau speaks directly in outlining three masters of the child's developing personality: *nature, education,* and *experience* (Rousseau 1762, pp. 38–39). Within these masters we find two specific objectives of the educational process. The first is to produce an individual that retains a connection to nature. In holistic education, the child is not burdened with the yoke of a cultural complex that shapes the personality. Rather, the child embraces nature, specifically her own human nature, as a fundamental building block of personality. This leads to the second master, education, which guides the child toward conscious recognition of a transcendent or spiritual aspect to the personality. Thus, holism in education means drawing together, through worldly experience and the acquisition of knowledge, human nature and human spirit into a holistic personality.

On acquiring knowledge, Rousseau says that before adolescence, knowledge is primarily derived from non-intellectual experiences—impulse, instinct, sensation, and image. We can observe directly the instinctive, sentient, and imaginal nature of the child. These aspects of the psyche, which Jungian psychology relegates to the unconscious, are what cultural philosopher Jean Gebser called the archaic, magical and mythic *structures of consciousness* (1985, pp. 36–73).

Rousseau outlines a specific order of acquiring knowledge (Rousseau 1762, p. 203; Forbes 2003, p. 65). The *natural order* is that the senses—sentience, or the "magical" structure of consciousness—awaken, through education, conscious ideas that can be compared and judged. When individual experiences acquire a repertoire of images associated with sensations, these are further refined into more complex ideas. This developmental evolution conforms to Gebser's phylogenic evolution from archaic (instinctive), to magical (sentient), to mythic (imaginal), to mental (ideational) consciousness (1985, pp. 36–97).

Rousseau compares this natural order to the *corrupted order* of acquiring knowledge (Rousseau 1762, p. 215; Forbes 2003, p. 73). Rather than the senses awakening images that lead to ideas, the ideas are simply learned and the student is measured by performance, not competence. This corrupted devolution of consciousness is evident, for example, when ideas are configured into slogans that evoke images that are used to invoke sensations. This corrupted order is often used as an oratory technique in which the objective is to lead the audience not from image to idea but, rather, from image to emotion through which ideas can then be manipulated.

## Johann Heinrich Pestalozzi (1746–1827)

Pestalozzi put many of Rousseau's theoretical ideas into practice, and he was an important influence on Jung. Pestalozzi says, "to elevate human nature to its highest, its noblest" expression requires stimulating the spiritual power that makes the individual whole (Pestalozzi, in Forbes 2003, p. 110). Here, again, is an image of a nurtured ego–Self axis that draws together human nature and human spirit and holds them in dynamic tension and balance as the personality evolves. That spiritual power, says Pestalozzi, is not found in religion but, rather, in "the innermost sanctuary of his being" (Pestalozzi, in Forbes 2003, p. 111). This goes by many different names. We might call it the "Spark of Divinity" within. Jung called it the Self. Jean Gebser called it the "Ever-Present Origin" (1985, p. xxvii, pp. 397–399). In holistic education, this inner spirit of the student is recognized and acknowledged by the teacher through transpersonal relationships that nurture the ego–Self axis.

On the acquisition of knowledge, Pestalozzi says that knowledge comes through direct, face-to-face experience of the reality of the world using the non-conceptual or pre-conceptual faculties of sensation, intuition, and imagination to interact with nature. He continues to say that all these faculties are innate to human nature, and should be properly developed (Forbes 2003, pp. 111–112). Education is largely responsible for that development.

Pestalozzi put Rousseau's theoretical ideas on child development into practice in a functioning school (Forbes 2003, p. 111). However, Pestalozzi's greatest contribution to the holistic paradigm comes from the juncture of education and culture. On that point, Jung has taken note of Pestalozzi.

Pestalozzi attributed the purpose of education to acquiring (to use Tillich's term) ultimacy as a personality objective. That is, the goal of ultimacy is "the elevation of man to the dignity of a spiritual being" (Pestalozzi, in Forbes 2003, p. 128) within the context of an earthly culture. In a modern sense, we might refer to this objective as the sanctification of the individual personality, which then seeks a calling that contributes to the sociocultural environment.

It is this concept that most impressed Jung. In a lecture entitled "Psychotherapy Today" (1941), Jung addressed the interface between the individuating personality and the sociocultural environment. Jung wrote:

> [T]he natural process of individuation brings to birth a consciousness of human community precisely because it makes us aware of the unconscious, which unites and is common to all mankind. Individuation is an at-one-ment with oneself and at the same time with humanity ... Once the individual is thus secured in himself, there is some guarantee that the organized accumulation of individuals in the State ... will result in the formation no longer of an anonymous mass but of a conscious community.
>
> *(Jung 1985, p. 108)*

Jung's footnotes quote Pestalozzi: "None of the institutions, measures, and means of education established for the masses and the needs of men in the aggregate ... serve to advance human culture. ... Our race develops its human qualities in essence only from face to face, from heart to heart" (Jung 1985, p. 106, n. 8)—that is, from the soul-nurturing quality of the teacher's personality.

Thus, both Pestalozzi's interpretation of the holistic paradigm and a Jungian interpretation of *Developmental Individuation* strive toward achieving ultimacy, spiritual maturity: a personality that contributes to the culture through an occupation, or vocation, that is engaged in the service of something sacred.

## Friedrich Froebel (1782–1852)

Froebel says that the holistic paradigm, ultimacy, is "the goal of all human history, individual and collective" (Froebel, in Forbes 2003, p. 133) That is, Froebel suggests a holistic cultural curriculum based on *recapitulation theory:* a study of the human cultural continuum that, like the personality of the child, evolves out of the Self, or Ever-Present Origin. Thus, it transcends the restraints of cultural complexes that are subordinate to the cultural super-ego.

In summation, Jung's multiple references to the individuation imperative and recapitulation theory address both the developmental and curricular goals of holistic education. Developmentally, holism is stimulated by the relationship between the teacher and her students. Jung said, "[T]he real psychological education [of the child is] made possible through the personality of the teacher" (Jung 1981, p. 56). Holistic education is based on "guided" experiential learning that brings together the instinctive, sentient, and imaginative nature of the child with emerging mental consciousness. The non-rational nature of the child, as the source of knowledge, is nurtured in the trans-personal relationship between the teacher and her students.

This soul nurturing aspect of *Developmental Individuation* progressively sublimates, without weakening, the ego–Self axis. The ego emerges, differentiated and crystalized, without breaking its connection to the Self. This concept has the support of Jacobi, Edinger, and Jung's best acknowledgments of the developmental aspect of individuation. It is also explicitly defined in Jean Gebser's concept of integrality, where the archaic (instinctive), magical (sentient) and mythic (imaginal) structures of consciousness are *not* replaced by, but subliminally integrated with, the emerging mental structure of consciousness (see 1985, pp. 97–102). The concept of ultimacy can thus be further examined in the light of both Jung's individuation and Gebser's integrality.

The second aspect that brings Jung and holistic education together is a cultural curriculum. A holistic cultural curriculum correlates the students' stages of development with the evolution of the human cultural continuum. Jung said, "Important as it is to pay attention to what is practical and useful, and to consider the future, that backward glance at the past is just as important. Culture means continuity, not a tearing up of roots through 'progress' … How should we lay hold of the future … unless we are possessed of the human experience which the past has bequeathed to us?" (Jung, 1981, pp. 144–145).

## The psychology of holistic education

In addition to these three educational authors, the 20th century has produced three significant psychological perspectives on holistic education. In addition to Carl Jung, there are the holistic perspectives of Abraham Maslow (1908–1970) and Carl Rogers (1902–1987).

In Maslow's terminology, ultimacy and Edinger's model of retaining the ego–Self axis are expressed in the concept of "self-actualization" through "peak experiences." We seek out the peak experiences that, accumulatively, lead to self-actualization—the all-pervasive motivation in life (Maslow, in Forbes 2003, p. 173). This, too, can be equated to Jung's individuation-imperative and Gebser's concept of integrality.

Rogers equates the concept of ultimacy to the human capacity to function in harmony and find universal, objective, cross-cultural values "based squarely upon knowledge of the nature of man" (Rogers, in Forbes 2003, p. 199). This alludes to a holistic cultural curriculum based on the human cultural continuum.

## The Jungian dilemma

As a lifelong, two-part process, Jungian individuation is thoroughly integrated with the holistic concept of achieving ultimacy in both its educative and psychological definitions. However, when current Jungian orthodoxy constricts the individuation process to the second half of life, it would appear to contradict any application to the child's education. This dilemma is mitigated by Jacobi's and Edinger's implications of a concept of *Developmental Individuation* that is separate from individuation in the second half of life.

*Developmental Individuation* is adaptation to outer reality, leading to the crystallization and stabilization of the ego, but without breaking the ego-Self axis. It is based on Rousseau's three foundations for the acquisition of knowledge: nature, education and experience. The ego is differentiated from the Self, though the connection is retained through the process of sublimating the archaic, magical and mythic structures of consciousness. This process is the concern of parents and teachers, not clinicians. The second phase is a concrete adaptation to those sublimated structures of consciousness from the perspective of mental consciousness.

## Conclusion

The current educational emphasis on practical utilitarianism and technological competency—the contra-holistic perspective—is too easily supported by Jungian orthodoxy. There are two processes that mitigate this influence and draw upon this new concept of *Developmental Individuation*. In the holistic classroom, the instinctive, sentient, and imaginal structures of the child's consciousness are guided toward awakening in mental consciousness by a teacher who is deeply engaged in her own individuation process—that is, she has retained the link to her imaginal, sentient, and instinctive nature leading back to the Self. This creates the subliminal, transpersonal bond between teacher and student that is, advantageously for the child, one step removed from the parents. This connection to the child's nature mitigates the collective influences of the cultural superego on the developing psyche and shields the developing ego from separation from the Self. Here, we are again reminded of Jacobi's warning that there are far too many people in whom the ego–Self axis has been broken. This may, indeed, have serious consequences for the continuity of the human continuum.

The second process lies in the development of a holistic cultural curriculum that teaches the cultural continuum of humanity. This concept transcends the cultural superego that sustains cultural complexes. Wrote Jung: "the school curriculum should … never wander too far from the humanities into overspecialized fields … The man who is unconscious of the historical context and lets slip his link with the past is in constant danger of succumbing to the crazes and delusions engendered by all novelties" (Jung 1981, pp. 144–145). And again: "Attainment of consciousness is culture in its broadest sense, and self-knowledge is therefore the heart and essence of this process" (Jung 1989, pp. 324–325).

## References

Bloom, Allan. 1979. "Introduction" in *Emile or On Education* (1762), Trans. Bloom, Allan. Basic Books: New York.
Edinger, Edward F. 1972. *Ego and Archetype*. Shambhala: Boston.
Forbes, Scott. 2003. *Holistic Education: An Analysis of Its Ideas and Nature*. Foundation for Educational Renewal: Brandon, VT.
Gebser, Jean. 1985. *The Ever-Present Origin*. Trans. Barstad, Noel. Ohio University Press: Athens, OH.
Jacobi, Jolande. 1965. *The Way of Individuation: The Indispensable Key to Understanding Jungian Psychology*. Trans. R.F.C. Hull. Harcourt, Brace, Jovanovich: New York.
Jung, Carl. 1981. *CW 17, The Development of Personality*. Princeton University Press, Princeton, NJ.
Jung, Carl. 1985. *CW 16, The Practice of Psychotherapy*, Princeton University Press, Princeton, NJ.
Jung, Carl. 1989, with Aniela Jaffé, *Memories, Dreams, Reflections*. Vintage Books: New York.
Rousseau, Jean Jacques, 1979. *Emile, or On Education* (1762), Trans. Bloom, Allan. Basic Books: New York.
Sinclair, T.A., 1962, trans. *Aristotle the Politics*. Penguin Books: New York.

# 8

# SIMONDON AND JUNG: RE-THINKING INDIVIDUATION

*Mark Saban*

My aim in this chapter is to examine Gilbert Simondon's philosophy of individuation from a very partial perspective: that of Jung's psychology. Simondon has, I think, some things to say that might enrich the ways in which we might approach key aspects of analytical psychology.

I am a Jungian analyst and not a philosopher. I am very aware that this means I am in danger of doing what Jungians (and Jung himself) have historically been very good at doing: colonising alien disciplines, appropriating (and thereby distorting) the fruits of those disciplines, and forcing the whole into service for the greater good of Jungian psychology. The pages of Jungian journals are littered with half-digested, half-thought neuroscience, quantum physics, post-modern philosophy—in much the same way they used to be strewn with barely understood ideas from anthropology, ethology, and theology.

In this case, however, I am encouraged by the important fact that Simondon is a member of a very select group: important modern thinkers who have not only read Jung, but quote him, and not only quote him but quote him approvingly, and not only quote him approvingly but incorporate and develop his ideas within their philosophy.

Simondon is then capable of thinking forward—rigorously and critically—what Jung describes as the "central concept of [his] psychology" (Jung and Jaffé 1989, p. 209): the "individuation process". One might suggest that he is capable of individuating individuation.

Jungians will not be surprised to note that Simondon's Jung-connection gets him into trouble with otherwise supportive critics. David Scott, in his important English-language commentary on Simondon's magnum opus, suggests that "Simondon's preference for Jung over Freud is both illuminating and, from our contemporary perspective, perhaps a bit odd. Still, we must remember that

Deleuze and Guattari likewise speak admiringly of Jung" (Scott 2014, pp. 91–92, note 9).

Bernard Stiegler is less generous:

> In my opinion Simondon understands nothing about psychoanalysis, because what he writes about it is so poor and even hostile. I believe it is because he started out with Jung toward individuation, that he understands nothing Freud says.
>
> *(Stiegler 2012, p. 164)*

However, although his commentators are bemused and embarrassed by Simondon's interest in Jung, they are unable to ignore it, or indeed his critical attitude toward Freud and psychoanalysis.

## Who was Simondon?

Born in 1924, Gilbert Simondon was early influenced by the pre-Socratic philosophers, by Friedrich Nietzsche, and by Henri Bergson. He pursued his philosophical studies under the supervision of, among others, phenomenologist Maurice Merleau-Ponty, and philosophers of science Gaston Bachelard (another philosopher sympathetic to Jung), and his pupil, Georges Canghuilem. Though refusing to categorise his thinking as either phenomenology or philosophy of science, Simondon maintained a close interest in science, and particularly what the French call *la technique*: which we might approximately translate as technology. Indeed, it was Simondon's secondary thesis, *Du mode d'existence des objets techniques* (On the mode of existence of technical objects) (Simondon 2012), first published in 1958, that made his name in philosophy, so that for many years, especially in the English-speaking world, Simondon was wrongly identified as primarily a philosopher of technology. Simondon's main thesis, *L'individuation à la lumière des notions de Forme et d'Information* (Individuation in the light of the notions of form and information) (Simondon 2005), was only published in its entirety in the year of his death, 1989. However, Gilles Deleuze glowingly reviewed a section of this work, entitled *L'individu et sa génèse physico-biologique* (Individuation and its physical-biological genesis) (Simondon 1995) in 1966 (Deleuze 2001). In several of Deleuze's writings he refers to Simondon's ideas on individuation as an important influence on his own philosophy. It seems likely that Deleuze's own Jungian influence predisposed him in favour of a thinker who overtly espoused aspects of Jung's psychology.[1]

However, it is only in recent years that Simondon has begun to receive serious attention as an important thinker in his own right, even in his native country. His reception in the English-speaking world has been severely hampered by the fact that many of his most important works remain untranslated. Despite this, interest in Simondon seems to be rapidly gathering steam. The appeal of his philosophy of individuation is its breadth: it is applied to the inorganic realm, to the realm of living beings, and, as the second part of his thesis puts it, to the psychic and collective. It is this last arena of individuation that is of particular interest in the context of Jung's psychology.

Simondon has much to say about psychic individuation (i.e., the individuation of the individual psyche) and much to say about the individuation of the collective, but what is perhaps most interesting and most important about Simondon's thought is that it has things to say about the ways in which the psychic and collective are necessarily interwoven—a field he calls the *transindividual*.

## Simondon's individuation

For Simondon the attempt to think the world starting with individuals, objects, or substances is already misguided. What matters is not entities but *process* and *relation*. He therefore focuses primarily upon *genesis*: the way in which things, persons, collectives, become what they now are and indeed continue to become until death. This process of becoming he calls, after Jung, individuation (Simondon 2005, 1995).

One problem with thinking in terms of entities, Simondon claims, is that it assumes that there is only one kind of equilibrium—stable equilibrium—in which all potential transformation has been already exhausted. However, when we think in terms of individuation, he suggests, we are acknowledging another kind of equilibrium: *metastable* equilibrium. By metastability Simondon means a tense balance—beyond stability—that holds a high energy potential. A metastable system is always *more than itself*, because it contains not only its present capacities but also an ongoing potential for self-transformation or mutation. This potential can only be tapped to the extent that it can be actualized, structured, or positioned *at another level*. Metastable systems contain contrary potentials, potentials that are incompatible and therefore require resolution through the creation of a new structure, form, phase, or level to express them. The metastable system presupposes the existence of what he calls a *disparation* [disparity] between "two disparate scales of reality between which there is as yet no interactive communication" (Deleuze 2004, p. 87).

For Simondon, individuation is thus always in a sense a resolution to the problem of *disparation*. In the case of crystallisation the *disparation* occurs between the singularity of the seed crystal and the preindividual system in a metastable state (the super-cooled liquid). The result is the individuation of the ice crystal within the mother liquid. The crystal will continue to individuate so long as it is within the metastable mother liquid.

So much for individuation on the physical level. There is however a kind of step change when we move on to what Simondon calls the *vital* level (i.e., the realm of living things), because the individuation of living beings can never be completed in the way that a crystal can. This is because on the vital level a truly stable equilibrium is never reached. It is also the case that the disparation from which the individuation of *living* beings proceeds exists not only, as in the case of the crystal, between internal and external milieus but also through *internal resonance*.

The living being integrates elements of the external milieu into its internal organisation and the resultant internal metastability means that the ongoing individuation of a living being is one of interminable development. This means that, as Simondon puts it: "The living individual is a system of individuation, an individuating system and a system individuating itself" (2009, p. 7).

## The preindividual

At any moment in the process of individuation, the regime of metastability presents itself as a disparation between the subject as individual (the product of previous individuations) and another dimension which Simondon calls "the preindividual". The preindividual reality is never exhausted but is carried forward within it, so that the constituted individual transports within itself a charge of preindividual reality, which means that it is animated by, and rich in, potentials.

If we translate this insight into depth psychological terms, when he refers to the preindividual Simondon seems to be pointing to a factor that is close to what Jung articulates as the collective unconscious, a resource of "archetypal" potential that is available to every human subject, especially at moments of problematic transition—puberty for example, often experienced by the ego (in projection) as an outer threat or problem, but which ultimately enables individual transformation. It is the ongoing encounter between the subject ego and the collective unconscious that constitutes, for Jung, the process of psychological individuation.

For both Simondon and Jung the ongoing phases of individuation show up as attempts to resolve the tense character of the metastable state, which is experienced by the subject as a problematic conflict. In Jungian terms we might see this as the difficult encounter between ego and unconscious.

Where, however, Simondon goes further than Jung is in his concept of the transindividual, which is that central aspect of psychic individuation which engages with the psychosocial.

## The transindividual

Simondon argues that a purely sociological approach, which seeks to explain human behaviour while starting from the assumption of an entity entitled "society", provides just as partial an account as a purely psychological approach, which, starting from the other pole, seeks to explain human behaviour starting with the assumption of the psychological individual as primary. By placing the emphasis upon individuation *processes*, rather than upon entities (individuals or societies) that may or may not emerge from those processes, and upon the *relations* which emerge between these processes, Simondon requires us to take seriously both individual and collective individuation—processes which are, for him, intimately connected: as he says, "The two individuations, psychic and collective …

allow us to define a category of transindividual that tries to take into account their systematic unity" (Simondon 2005, p. 29).

For Simondon the transindividual is not a unifying of individual and society. It is rather a relation of two relations: the relation that is interior to the individual (the psychic) and the relation which is exterior to the individual (the collective). Psyche, which is neither an enclosed interior nor a pure exteriority, is therefore situated at the intersection of a double polarity, between the relation to the world and others and the relation to self (Combes 2013, p. 30).

Now, Simondon makes an important move here (and one which places him squarely in the company of Frosh and others who have recently attempted to think the psychosocial (Frosh, 2014, 2016, 2018; Frosh and Baraitser, 2008)—he situates affectivity and the emotions at the centre of individuality, since they mediate between these two relations—individual/self and individual/world. There is something paradoxical here: affectivity includes a relation between the constituted individual (ego) and that not-yet-individuated (preindividual) reality that, as we have seen, any living individuating being carries with it. This is because it is our affective life that reminds us that we are not only individual egos. It does so by presenting us with the problem of what Simondon describes as "the heterogeneity between perceptual worlds [the world of observing subject and observed object] and the affective world, between the individual and the preindividual" (Simondon 2005, p. 253).

For Simondon, the subject is then always both "individual and more-than-individual; it is incompatible with itself" (Simondon 2005, p. 253). For Simondon this tension cannot be resolved solely within the subject (any attempt to do so induces neurosis), but only in relation with others. It is only within the unity of the collective—as a milieu in which perception and emotion can be unified—that a subject can bring together these two sides of its psychic activity and to some degree coincide with itself. As Simondon puts it:

> Relation to others puts us into question as individuated being; it situates us, making us face others as being young or old, sick or healthy, strong or weak, man or woman: yet we are not young or old absolutely in this relation; we are younger or older than another; we are stronger or weaker as well.
>
> *(Simondon 2005, p. 266)*

His point is that in relationship with others it is the affective: that by which we are always already engaged with others, that comes into play alongside and in tension with what he calls the perceptual dimension: that which brings into play a sense of separation between subject and object.

However, in normal life our interaction with others is intersubjective—ego interacts with ego. The transindividual is only achieved when we move beyond this horizontal engagement into one that enables the subject to interact with the collective that, as it were, lies beneath or beyond. The transindividual requires the obliteration of interindividual (ego/ego) relations with others because access to the true nature of "collective" can only occur through the preindividual zone, which is outside of functional relations between individuals.

What gets loosened through this encounter with the preindividual is the constitution of the ego; the ego needs to be, as it were, dis-individuated in order that a new individuation can occur. This is experienced as a profound challenge to those everyday aspects of community that normally disguise the preindividual. It is this encounter, articulated as the relativisation of the ego in the face of the collective unconscious, that plays such an important part in Jungian individuation, though on an emphatically intrapsychic level.

Simondon says that such an event cannot be brought about by voluntary decision: it requires an unforeseeable event. The other must cease to be merely part of a functioning intersubjective system and becomes *that which puts me in question*. We begin to attain to psychological individuation through the transindividual, but it gets experienced as dis-individuation.

As Muriel Combes puts it, Simondon's claim that psychological individuality "is elaborated in elaborating transindividuality," "indicates that the aptitude for the collective, that is, the presence of the collective within the subject in the form of an unstructured preindividual potential, constitutes a condition for the relation of the subject to itself" (Simondon 1995, 2005 ). This would suggest that we can only have a relationship to ourselves (to our "inside") when we are turned toward the outside.

Combes continues:

> It is not relation to self [ego] that comes first and makes the collective possible, but relation to what, in the [wider] self, surpasses the individual, communicating without mediation with a nonindividual share in the other. What gives consistency to relation to self, what gives consistency to the psychological dimension of the individual, is something in the individual surpassing the individual, turning it toward the collective; what is real in the psychological is transindividual.
>
> *(Combes 2013, pp. 40–41)*

In this way, Simondon posits a conception of a subject who is in effect "nothing more than the operation of relating two individuations, psychic and collective, reciprocally determined and, as such, in time and of time, conditioned and conditioning" (Scott 2014, p. 127).

By rethinking individuation in this way Simondon frees up depth psychology's potential to find a creative engagement with the psychosocial. He moves beyond Jung who by identifying psyche with interiority gets trapped within an individualistic model whereby society is seen as at best an outer obstacle to the freedom of the subject to achieve the inner journey of individuation. However, Simondon is, in my view, making available a potential that is already, in an unthematized state, present within Jung's ideas. So it is that Jung's collective unconscious can be re-visioned in the form of a preindividual that enables a deep engagement with both inner and outer collective.

Psychological individuality, then, is never merely the product of psychic individuation, but rather the result of what in this individuation is directed toward the collective. "Psychological individuality is necessarily constituted at the very center of the constitution of the collective" (Combes 2013, p. 39).

## Simondon and Jung

I hope this brief introduction has, albeit sketchily, pointed to the potential that Simondon's thinking has to loosen up certain problems within Jungian studies: such as Jung's tendency to psychologise, his tendency to favour an atomised vision of society as a collection of psychological individuals, and his tendency to represent the interior of the individual as of central importance, and to downplay the exterior—the outer other—as trivial.

In fact, the sophistication of Simondon's philosophical approach to individuation-as-process offers a way to move beyond simplistic binaries like inner/outer, and individual/collective. And yet, there remain important resonances between Simondon's vision and that of Jung. Simondon's preindividual opens up the possibility of a re-thinking of the collective unconscious/archetypal realm, which in Jung's writings and in the writings of his successors can become limited to static reified places in some inner topology, such that some Jungian writing becomes not much more than a highly reductive inventory of archetypes. Simondon's emphasis upon the ontological primacy of *process*, enables us to re-vision this dimension as the metastable preindividual, always exceeding the ego and always carried forward from one phase of individuation to the next, constantly challenging the constituted individual (by which it is experienced as "other") to new individuations. This enables us to concentrate upon the way this *disparation* is occurring here and now, how this tension, this conflict has the capacity to disindividuate the ego and push us toward the transindividual. Here, in the political psychosocial realm lies the greatest contrast with Jung, and the greatest opportunity.

## Note

1 See Christian Kerslake's *Deleuze and the Unconscious* (Kerslake, 2007).

## References

Combes, M., 2013. *Gilbert Simondon and the Philosophy of the Transindividual*. MIT Press: Cambridge, MA.
Deleuze, G., 2001. Review of Gilbert Simondon's L'individu et sa genese physico-biologique (1966). *Pli Warwick J. Philos.* 12, 43–49.

Deleuze, G., 2004. *Desert Islands: and Other Texts, 1953–1974*. Semiotexte: Los Angeles, CA, Cambridge, MA.
Frosh, S., 2014. The nature of the psychosocial: debates from studies in the psychosocial. *J. Psycho-Soc. Stud.* 8, 159–169.
Frosh, S., 2016. Towards a psychosocial psychoanalysis. *Am. Imago* 73, 469–482.
Frosh, S., 2018. Rethinking psychoanalysis in the psychosocial. *Psychoanal. Cult. Soc.* 23, 5–14.
Frosh, S., Baraitser, L., 2008. Psychoanalysis and psychosocial studies. *Psychoanal. Cult. Soc.* 13, 346–365.
Jung, C.G., and Jaffé, A., 1989. *Memories, Dreams, Reflections*. Vintage Books: New York.
Kerslake, C., 2007. *Deleuze and the Unconscious*. Continuum: London & New York.
Scott, D., 2014. *Gilbert Simondon's Psychic and Collective Individuation: A Critical Introduction and Guide*. Edinburgh University Press: Edinburgh.
Simondon, G., 1995. *L'individu et sa genèse physico-biologique*. Editions Jérôme Millon: Grenoble.
Simondon, G., 2005. *L'individuation à la lumière des notions de forme et d'information*. Editions Jérôme Millon: Grenoble.
Simondon, G., 2009. The position of the problem of ontogenesis. *Parrhesia*. 7, 4–16.
Simondon, G., 2012. *Du mode d'existence des objets techniques*. Editions Aubier: Paris.
Stiegler, B., 2012. A rational theory of miracles: on pharmacology and transindividuation. *New Form.* 77, 164–184.

# PART III
# Philosophy

# 9

# A WHOLE MADE OF HOLES: INTERROGATING HOLISM VIA JUNG AND SCHELLING

*Gordon Barentsen*

## Introduction

In this paper, I cast a critical eye on the idea of holism as a system wherein the whole predominates over the sum of its parts. What happens to holism when the whole is ultimately indistinguishable from its parts? When the whole folds back into its parts at every moment of its unfolding? When the whole is revealed as a circle without circumference whose completion is always promissory? And what are the *ethical* implications of such a critique for holism? While C.G. Jung's alchemical work and therapeutics often reflect a drive toward unity and non-difference, particularly in reference to the *unus mundus* as a "unitary world", this idealist drive is profoundly troubled by an archetypal metapsychology, which persists as an indeterminate remainder in his thought and which ultimately troubles the idea of holism in analytical psychology. To explore this tension between therapeutics and metapsychology in Jung's thought, I put analytical psychology into dialogue with the *Naturphilosophie* of German philosopher Friedrich Schelling, who is perhaps the most protean philosopher of the 19th century.[1] Medical historian Werner Leibbrand provocatively states that "Jung's system cannot be conceived without Schelling's philosophy" (cited in Ellenberger 1970, p. 728), and indeed the intellectual countertransference between analytical psychology and Schelling's *Naturphilosophie* gives us crucial insight into Jung's embattled attempts to differentiate psyche from Nature. It also sheds light on a metapsychology which resists what I call (following Derrida) Jung's *therapeutics of presence* – his tendency to reify archetypes into relatively coherent, self-present wholes in the interests of a teleologised therapy. To critique the idea of a Jungian holism, then, I will focus on one specific aspect of the Schelling–Jung intellectual partnership, one which arguably makes Schelling more important to Jung's intellectual history than Kant, Nietzsche, or Schopenhauer: the remarkable isomorphism between Schelling's conception of the *actant* in his *Naturphilosophie* and Jung's mature formulation of the *archetype*.[2] Both actant and archetype articulate an open energic economy which resists encapsulation within the completion of a holistic system that projects the image of a whole over the domain of its parts. As such, both represent a self-organising purposiveness that cannot be reined in by a teleological unity. I conclude by briefly touching on the significant problems this shared economy poses for the ethical presuppositions represented by holism. Let us now turn to Schelling's *Naturphilosophie* to understand how he conceives Nature dynamically, and in a way which analytical psychology ultimately recasts as psyche.

## Schelling's *Naturphilosophie*: Inhibition, actants, derangement

Schelling's *First Outline of a System of the Philosophy of Nature* (1798) is part of the broader field of German *Naturphilosophie* which emerged at the turn of the 18th century. This tradition includes Immanuel Kant, whose *Naturphilosophie* conceived the archetypes of species as transcendental entities of an ideal existence. But contrary to Kant, Schelling's *First Outline* is a *speculative* metaphysics which attempts to think the dynamic forces behind Nature's infinite productivity. Thus Schelling writes in the *First Outline* that "Nature *is* a priori," and this Nature is a whole which "is not merely a product, but at the same time productive" (2004, p. 197). Like Nature, the organism self-organises according to principles irreducible to a logical system, and in this sense the *Naturphilosophie* is a crucial part of Schelling's goal to think a Nature commensurate with the idea of human freedom. Indeed, the *First Outline* offers us a glimpse of what later becomes the Schellingian unconscious, and Jason Wirth suggests that while the *Naturphilosophie* is not psychology, it *proceeds* psychologically as "doing philosophy in accordance with nature" and "a gateway into the originating experience of philosophizing" (2015, p. 17). But for Schelling this freedom is always attended by anxiety, and in the *Naturphilosophie* this anxiety is reflected in Nature's ambivalence toward its products.

To answer the question of how natural products emerge from Nature's primordial, undifferentiated fluidity, what he calls the "absolute noncomposite" (Schelling 2004, p. 6), Schelling develops *inhibition* as a primal limiting force intrinsic to Nature—in a word, the force of Nature's auto-alterity. Within the homogeneous "universal organism" of Nature, inhibition is "an *original diremption in Nature itself*, [an] original antithesis in the heart of Nature, *which does not ... itself appear*" (ibid., p. 205), but nevertheless constitutes Nature as an object to itself. That is, Nature as whole is always already inhibited into its parts in what Schelling calls "the drama of a struggle between form and the formless" (ibid., p. 28). This drama, this inhibition of Nature's dynamism into concrete products, is performed by what Schelling calls *actants* [*Aktionen*]—hypothetical points of intensity which articulate what he calls "the original multiplicity of individual principles in Nature" (ibid., p. 21 n. 1). The actant is "a seed around which Nature can begin to form itself" (ibid.), and as such it is a necessary postulate in order to think Nature's dynamism at all. Already using quasi-psychological language, Schelling writes that the actant is caught in a drama of freedom and compulsion: the actant follows its own drive to "free transformation" to produce according to its nature. But in combination with *other* actants, each individual actant is *compelled* [*Zwang*] by its connections with the others (ibid., p. 33). In Jungian terms, we might call this an enantiodromia whereby freedom always already runs into compulsion and vice versa. Moreover, Schelling's language for this drama is that of derangement [*Störung*]; actants "mutually derange" each other (ibid., p. 26), and this is precisely the language that Jung uses to describe the system of the drives in his later metapsychology—a system in which drives "derange and repress" [*stört und verdrängt*] each other (Jung, 1947, para. 378, trans. mod.).

But Nature's auto-alterity involves it in a paradox from which it cannot escape. Schelling conceives Nature's productivity as a graduated series of stages [*Stufenfolge*], increasing in complexity, which culminates in an *absolute organism* that "*lives in all products, that always* becomes *and never is, and in which the absolute activity* [of Nature] *exhausts itself*" (Schelling 2004, pp. 16, 43n). This absolute organism is the goal of Nature's productivity. Schelling further writes: "Nature contests the Individual; it longs for the Absolute and continually endeavors to represent it. ... Individual products, therefore, in which Nature's activity is at a standstill, can only be seen as *misbegotten attempts* to achieve such a proportion" (ibid., p. 35). This is to say that the sexual proliferation of beings, each of which recapitulates Nature's dynamism, signifies a self-organising *purposiveness* which unworks the *Stufenfolge*'s teleological desire to move forward to the absolute product. Schelling states the matter bluntly: "Nature hates sex ... it arises against the will of Nature. The separation into sexes is an inevitable fate, with which, after Nature is once organic ... it can never overcome. By this very hatred of separation it finds itself involved in a contradiction, inasmuch as what is odious to Nature it is compelled to develop in the most careful manner, ... as if it did so on purpose" (ibid., p. 231n). To sum up: Nature's original diremption compels it to produce the individual through the combinatory drama of the actants. This purposive, self-organising production dooms Nature's nostalgic yearning to return to stasis just as it empowers Nature's forward desire for wholeness as absolute product. But this wholeness remains promissory, a horizon of totality; always and everywhere, Nature's whole is plagued by the tumescence of its productivity. Nature's products are *pharmaka* – both toxins and cures for Nature's longing for the absolute.

Schelling's deranged Nature is remarkably prescient of Jung's post-1940 thinking and his move away from Kant. Turning to Jung, then, I begin with his highly problematic project of differentiating mind from Nature, which anticipates his later refinement of the psychoid archetype as a point of intensity which, like the actant, marks the ultimate dissolution of the boundary between mind and Nature in an unbound metapsychological economy.

## Jung: Analytical psychology as ungrounded science

Holism figures in Jung's alchemical researches as the *unus mundus*, the "unitary world" toward which both psychology and physics strive as, ostensibly, a domain of unification and synthesis (Jung, 1958, para. 852). In *Mysterium Coniunctionis* he calls the *unus mundus* "the original, non-differentiated unity of the world or of Being" (Jung, 1955, para. 660) and equates it with the collective unconscious[3] as the "inter-connection or unity of causally unrelated events" underlying synchronicity (ibid., para. 662). But this analogy is charged with a differential that casts doubt on what Jung calls the "non-differentiated" nature of this Being. The *unus mundus*, Jung says, is metaphysical speculation where the collective unconscious can be "indirectly experienced" (ibid., para. 660). But the archetypal economy of the collective unconscious is far from non-differentiated—indeed, it is a differential dynamism which allows us to conceive of archetypes at all, and it is Jungian metapsychology's isomorphism with Schelling's deranged Nature which, *if* we think a totality in Jung, insists that we think it away from a synthetic holism.

The psyche is the fundamental problem of Jung's 1934 essay "The Fundamental Problem of Contemporary Psychology."[4] Here, Jung attempts to define psychic reality as a domain of mental "psychic images" which wrap around us to such an extent that "we cannot penetrate at all to the essence of things external to ourselves" (Jung 1934, para. 680). And although he tries to dissect this psychic reality into "material" and "spiritual" dimensions, Jung finally admits that one must contradict oneself to do justice to an indeterminate X that he calls psyche, but which unworks his attempts to properly *psychologise* this psyche (ibid.). But Jung still invokes the sole validity of this indeterminate psyche to "end the conflict between mind and matter, spirit and nature, as *contradictory* explanatory principles" (ibid., para. 681, my italics) so as to posit psychic reality as a whole which in his words "still exists in its original oneness, and awaits man's advance to a level of consciousness where he … recognizes both as constituent elements of one psyche" (ibid., para. 682). But what is the nature of this "one psyche"? Jung's idealist narrative of recognition, and the psychic wholeness it steadfastly implies, nevertheless cannot dispel what lies *beyond* psychic reality—which is in Jung's words, "*physical process[es] whose nature[s] [are] ultimately unknown*" (ibid., para. 681, my italics). Thus, we see that Nature flows both inside and outside the psyche. But as we turn to Jung's mature formulation of the archetype, its affinity with the actantial dynamics of Schelling's *Naturphilosophie* offers a way of thinking psyche and Nature otherwise. This mature formulation opens up the psyche encrypted in the Nature of Schelling's *First Outline*, one which ultimately corroborates Jung's assertion in *Symbols of Transformation* that "the unconscious *is* nature" (Jung 1952, p. 62).

Jung first describes the archetype in 1919 as "instinct's perception of itself" (Jung 1919, para. 277), moving to a more Kantian framework in 1921 when he describes it as "the noumenon of the image which intuition perceives and, in perceiving, creates" (Jung 1921, p. 401). But Jung's thinking about the archetype ultimately moves away from this Kantian influence in a shift which culminates in certain key works of the 1940s. This shift moves Jung much closer to Schelling: where Schelling had maintained in the *First Outline* that Nature *itself* is a priori, Jung's *On the Psychology of the Unconscious* (1943) casts the archetypes as "*deposits of the constantly repeated experiences of humanity* … subjective fantasy-ideas *aroused by the physical process*" (Jung 1943, para. 109), imbricating mind and Nature in a manner disallowed by Kant's architectonic.[5] And in a footnote marking the return of his oft-repressed metaphysics, Jung makes the point more directly: the archetypes are "the effect and deposit of experiences that have already taken place, *but equally they appear as the factors which cause such experiences*" (ibid., para. 151 n. 3, my italics). The archetypes now mark a paradoxical, uncontainable fluidity tied to the materiality of Being. The linear model of Jung's therapeutics of presence, which privileges archetypes "which stand for the goal of the developmental process" (ibid., para. 185) strains and fractures under what he now sees as "an indefinite number of archetypes representative of situations" (ibid.). *Teleological* development is imperilled by the unruly *purposiveness* of the individuation process, whose drive does not conform to any holistic economy.

Consummating the break with Kantian thought, "On the Nature of the Psyche" (Jung 1947) reveals a profound nonhumanism at the heart of analytical psychology, reflected in Jung's supplementation of the archetype's "merely psychic" operations with "a further degree of conceptual differentiation" – the archetype's *psychoid* nature which, he emphasises, "cannot with certainty be designated as psychic" (Jung 1947, pars. 419, 439). To this end, Jung's well-known description of the archetype's "spectrum" establishes a "psychic infra-red" pole where the archetype recedes into physiology and "chemical and physical conditions," as well as a "psychic ultra-violet" pole which is neither psychic nor physiological (ibid., para. 420). Indeed there is a strange chiasmus, a crossover in the Schelling–Jung intellectual partnership here: where Schelling's actant is driven, *compelled* by the quasi-psychic drive to combine and decombine, the Jungian archetype is now a similar organisational point of intensity in Nature, likened to "the axial structure of a crystal which, as it were, preforms the crystalline structure in the mother liquid" (Jung 1954, para. 155). Just as Schelling's actant is the seed around which Nature forms, the archetype is the nonmolar intensity which organises Nature according to its inscrutable force. And Jung goes further, extending this fluidity and materiality to the project of analytical psychology itself. Writing that "no explanation of the psychic can be anything other than the living process of the psyche itself," and that "psychology is doomed to cancel itself out as a science and therein precisely it reaches its scientific goal" (Jung 1947, para. 429), Jung casts analytical psychology not as an encyclopedic science which seeks to complete the circle of its own knowledge, but instead as a disciplinary individuation process, a "science" which becomes its own subject by paradoxically becoming its own object of knowledge. In other words, analytical psychology as a unitary science is always already implicated in the natural dynamism which creates it.

## Conclusion: The darkness of obligation

We have seen that for Schelling and Jung, Nature is an unruly pulsion of intangible intensities; we might call it a "whole made of holes," a unity which at every moment collapses back into its ungrounded nonmolar forces. Schelling's Nature finds no rest in its productivity, no completion in its compulsion. The teleological contract of Jung's therapeutics of presence is underwritten by a profoundly nonhumanist archetypal economy far from the "non-differentiated unity" of Jung's *unus mundus*. How does this sit with the twenty-first century holistic phantasy of a "globalised" world and its recycled Kantian morality which sees Nature as an object of human consumption? I suggest that what John Caputo calls a *poetics of obligation*, a deconstruction of ethics which preserves the connectedness between beings, might be the Derridean dangerous supplement to ethics we need to do justice to Nature's purposive valency. Caputo describes this poetics of obligation as "the feeling that comes over us when others need our help, when they call out for help, or support, or freedom, or whatever they need, a feeling that grows in strength directly in proportion to the desperateness of the situation of the other. The power of obligation varies directly with the powerlessness of the one who calls for help, which is the power of powerlessness" (Caputo, 1993, p. 5). But because this "spontaneous causality" (ibid., p. 12) of obligation is unbound by the ethical, it always carries the risk of obscenity: the dark realisation that Yahweh's command that Abraham sacrifice Isaac is on the same footing as the command given to Nazi soldiers to kill Jews. Thus, the risk of obligation does not cancel the ethical, but rather challenges its claims to absolute sovereignty; it risks the condemnation of moral discourse to open the ethical to the indeterminacy of Nature which both imperils the ethical and powers its evolution. It is a chemical binding, a magnetic pull between self and Other which may at times run in tandem with the ethical, but which also shows the ethical the impossible fantasy of its universality and the need to rethink itself, to rewrite or perhaps even jettison cherished beliefs in order to survive as part of the purposive materiality of the Nature in which it exists.

## Notes

1 Where necessary, I reference Schelling's original German from Schelling, F. (auth.), Schröter, M. (ed.) (1927–1959), *Schellings Werke*. (13 vols). München: C.H. Beck'sche Verlagsbuchhandlerung. Shamdasani (2005) has documented many of the serious translation issues with Jung's *Collected Works*; thus, I modify translations and provide German terms from Jung, C. (auth.), Hurwitz-Eisner, L., Jung-Merker, L., Niehus-Jung, M., Riklin, F., Rüf, E., Zander, L. (eds.) (2011) *Gesammelte Werke*. (24 vols). Ostfildern: Patmos Verlag.

2 Jung had little to no firsthand knowledge of Schelling. His *Bibliothek-Katalog*, the record of his library contents at the time of his death in 1961, shows that Jung owned two volumes of Schelling's philosophy of mythology and his *Treatise on the Deities of Samothrace*, but the degree to which he studied these volumes is unknown. The brief references to Schelling scattered throughout his work are almost certainly informed by Eduard von Hartmann's *Philosophy of the Unconscious* (1869), which profoundly influenced both Jung and Freud. All the more significant that Jung's metapsychology is so closely aligned to the *Naturphilosophie* at the core of Schelling's thought. I am grateful to Andreas Jung, Jung's grandson, for lending me his personal copy of the *Katalog*.
3 Jung continues: "It is clear from the empirical material at our disposal today that the contents of the unconscious, unlike conscious contents, are mutually contaminated to such a degree that they cannot be distinguished from one another and can therefore easily take one another's place, as can be seen most clearly in dreams. The indistinguishableness of its contents gives one the impression that everything is connected with everything else and therefore, despite their multifarious modes of manifestation, that they are at bottom a unity." But this seems to ignore the dynamism of this interchangeability without which this unity would be static, meaningless and indiscernible. As a play of *differences*, this dynamism always already undercuts the simple concept of non-differentiation and is necessary to conceive this "mutual contamination" at all.
4 Hull translates the German title (*Das Grundproblem der Gegenwärtigen Psychologie*) as "Basic Postulates of Analytical Psychology." However, I retranslate this as "Fundamental Problem" as Hull's translation captures nothing of the essay's tenor, which is that of wrestling with the psyche as the fundamental *problem* [*Grundproblem*] (and not "basic postulate") of contemporary psychology.
5 Absent from the original (1916) edition and relegated to a footnote in the extensively revised third edition of 1926 (1926, pp. 71–72), this crucial idea of mind-Nature imbrication is fully incorporated into Jung's thinking only in the fifth edition of 1943.

## References

Caputo, J. (1993). *Against Ethics*. Bloomington and Indianapolis: Indiana University Press.
Ellenberger, H. (1970). *The Discovery of the Unconscious: The History and Development of Dynamic Psychiatry*. New York: Basic Books.
Jung, C. (1919). 'Instinct and the Unconscious', in *The Structure and Dynamics of the Psyche*, 2nd ed. Translated by R. Hull (pp. 129–138). *Collected Works of C.G. Jung*, Vol. 8. Princeton: Princeton University Press, 1969.
Jung, C. (1921). *Psychological Types*, 2nd ed. Translated by R. Hull. *Collected Works of C.G. Jung*, Vol. 6. Princeton: Princeton University Press, 1971.
Jung, C. (1926). 'The Unconscious in the Normal and Pathological Mind', in *Two Essays on Analytical Psychology*, Translated by H. and C. Baynes (pp. 1–121). London: Baillière, Tyndall and Cox, 1928.
Jung, C. (1934). 'Basic Postulates of Analytical Psychology', in *The Structure and Dynamics of the Psyche*, 2nd ed. Translated by R. Hull (pp. 338–357). *Collected Works of C.G. Jung*, Vol. 8. Princeton: Princeton University Press, 1969.
Jung, C. (1943). *On the Psychology of the Unconscious*, in *Two Essays on Analytical Psychology*, 2nd ed. Translated by R. Hull (pp. 1–119). *Collected Works of C.G. Jung*, Vol. 7. Princeton: Princeton University Press, 1966.
Jung, C. (1947). 'On the Nature of the Psyche', in *The Structure and Dynamics of the Psyche*, 2nd ed. Translated by R. Hull (pp. 159–234). *Collected Works of C.G. Jung*, Vol. 8. Princeton: Princeton University Press, 1969.

Jung, C. (1952). *Symbols of Transformation*, 2nd ed. Translated by R. Hull. *Collected Works of C.G. Jung*, Vol. 5. Princeton: Princeton University Press, 1967.

Jung, C. (1954). 'Psychological Aspects of the Mother Archetype', in *The Archetypes and the Collective Unconscious*, 2nd ed. Translated by R. Hull (pp. 73–110). *Collected Works of C.G. Jung*, Vol. 9, Part I. Princeton: Princeton University Press, 1968.

Jung, C. (1955). *Mysterium Coniunctionis*, 2nd ed. Translated by R. Hull. *Collected Works of C.G. Jung*, Vol. 14. Princeton: Princeton University Press, 1970.

Jung, C. (1958). 'A Psychological View of Conscience', in *Civilization in Transition*, 2nd ed. Translated by R. Hull (pp. 437–455). *Collected Works of C.G. Jung*, Vol. 10. Princeton: Princeton University Press, 1970.

Schelling, F. (2004). *First Outline of a System of the Philosophy of Nature*. Translated by K. Peterson. Albany: State University of New York Press.

Shamdasani, S. (2005). *Jung Stripped Bare By His Biographers, Even*. London and New York: Karnac Books.

Wirth, J. (2015). *Schelling's Practice of the Wild: Time, Art, Imagination*. Albany: State University of New York Press.

# 10

# JUNG, SPINOZA, DELEUZE: A MOVE TOWARDS REALISM

*Robert Langan*

## Introduction

During a period of collaboration that lasted from 1932 until 1958, the Swiss psychiatrist C.G. Jung's (1875–1961) and the quantum physicist Wolfgang Pauli (1900–1958) developed a dual-aspect monism in which mind and matter are taken to be complementary aspects of an ontic whole. The Jungian scholar and theoretical physicist Harald Atmanspacher describes these aspects as 'local', 'epistemic' parts of an ontic whole, and states that Jungian archetypes can be thought of as ordering factors of both aspects. Awareness of the complementarity between these two aspects occurs during synchronistic experiences, or 'meaningful coincidences' (Atmanspacher, 2012).

Atmanspacher notes that the closest historical precursor for Jung's monism is the metaphysics of the 17th-century Dutch philosopher Baruch Spinoza (1632–1677) (2014, p. 1). Yet Jung scarcely cites Spinoza in his entire *Collected Works*, and on the few occasions he does, he tends to dismiss Spinoza as an overt rationalist (Jung, 1919/1969, par. 276; 1945/1948/1969, pars. 385, 390). That Spinoza greatly influenced German Romantics such as Johann Wolfgang von Goethe (1749–1832), to whom Jung's entire project was hugely indebted, also goes unheeded by Jung. If Spinoza influenced Jung, Jung seems largely unaware of it. Jungian analyst Joseph Cambray has suggested a number of reasons as to why Jung seems to misunderstand and dismiss Spinoza, speculating that Jung may have had some sort of complex against Spinoza that prevented him from acknowledging any similarity or debt he owed to the philosopher (Cambray, 2014, pp. 45–49). It is possible, however, that Jung's cool reception of Spinoza is in fact a matter of theory. If so, this may reflect that the respective metaphysics of both men are not so closely aligned after all.

## Realism vs. anti-realism

The Jung–Pauli model emphasizes the idea that consciousness is the catalyst that actualizes the dual aspects of mind and matter out of the ontic domain. In a letter written in December 1956, Jung tells Pauli that the individuated person realizes "both aspects of the world objectively", and that the balanced individual "must discriminate this one world", that he calls the *unus mundus*, "in order to be able of conceiving it, but he must not forget that what he discriminates is always the one world, and discrimination is a presupposition of consciousness" (Meier, 2001, pp. 156–157). This implies that the "decay" of aspects from the *unus mundus* is dependent on the interjection of consciousness—it also suggests some link between the underlying ontic domain and the archetypal Self.

This view is echoed throughout Jung's work. When Jung writes on the mandala as a symbol of individuation in both Indian and Western cultures, he notes that no distinction is made between the human essence and the Divine, that the God-image unfolds both in the world and in man (1955a/1969, par. 717). In *Mysterium Coniunctionis*, Jung references the mandala when he describes the metaphysical nature of the *unus mundus* as "the ultimate unity of all the archetypes as well as of the multiplicity of the phenomenal world", a restoration "of the original state of the cosmos and the divine unconsciousness of the world" (1955b/1970 pars. 660–661).

Pauli, who was wary of Jung's tendency to explain everything in terms of projection of the psyche and who urged Jung to conceive of the archetypes as psychophysically neutral, nonetheless proposed to Jung that the Self could be conceived of as the "superordinate organizing principle overarching psyche and world" beyond space time (Gieser, 2005, pp. 177–178, 281–281). Pauli was impelled to make this point due to the problems of observation in quantum mechanics, where the measuring device itself affects what is studied. Pauli thought this problem went further than issues with instrumentation, that the internal state of the observer, their psychic state, had to be accounted for as well (Atmanspacher and Fach, 2013, p. 224). This sensitivity to human observation was characteristic of the Copenhagen school of quantum mechanics, of which Pauli was a key figure (Gieser, 2005, p. 71). Various theories that grant reality no autonomy from the human mind have been derived from the Copenhagen interpretation—such as the agential realism of theoretical physicist and feminist philosopher Karen Barad (2007). What all these models have in common is that consciousness acts as the catalyst for the emergence of reality out of a monist whole.

Such versions of reality are *mind-dependent*; that is to say, they refer to an ontology where the world is dependent upon the mind. The speculative realist philosophers Manuel DeLanda and Graham Harman call this kind of philosophy *anti-realism*. Anti-realism dominates much of continental philosophy, where the relation of a human subject with the world is considered a "privileged relation" (2017, pp. 37–39). DeLanda and Harman note that anti-realism can apply to different forms of idealism, such as in the phenomenologies of Edmund Husserl and

Martin Heidegger, or the poststructuralism of Jacques Derrida; yet it can also apply to materialism without realism, such as in the agential realism of Barad or the mathematical philosophies of Alain Badiou or Quintein Meillasoux (ibid., chs. 1–4). What DeLanda and Harman take issue with in anti-realist philosophy is how it appoints the human mind as the supreme mediator for all events in the world. This, they argue, is a sort of occasionalism that was once ascribed to God but which was restricted to the human mind in the critical philosophy of Immanuel Kant (1724–1804) and the empiricism of David Hume (1711–1776):

> The real problem with occasionalism was not that *God* was the sole causal mediator, but that *any* one entity was given a causal monopoly. And that's precisely what Hume and Kant are doing, simply transferring the monopoly from God to the human mind. And unlike the religious occasionalists, they have succeeded in persuading modern Western intellectuals.
> 
> *(Ibid, p. 47)*[1]

Because of this commitment to a privileged relationship between the human mind and the rest of the world, anti-realism treats the cosmos as if it can be neatly and evenly partitioned between the human and the nonhuman, rather than treating subjective relations as no more important than interactions between the *nonhuman and the nonhuman*. In contradistinction, a *realist philosophy* grants the world an existence *independent* of the human mind.

DeLanda's neo-materialist philosophy rejects the idea that form is imposed on "dead matter" by the human mind. Instead, all matter is capable of self-organization—life and consciousness merely being one such emergent property (DeLanda, 2016). DeLanda's philosophy is strongly influenced by the work of French philosopher Gilles Deleuze (1925–1995). Deleuze was partly impelled towards a realist position in order to escape the limits imposed on all possible experience and knowledge by a priori structures of cognition, as Kant had established in his critical philosophy. The speculative realist Levi Bryant notes that among other things Deleuze criticizes Kant for deriving the categories of understanding by reifying what is known from experience, and thus valorizing the appearance of an object while "ignoring the productive processes through which the object came to be" (2009, pp. 31–38). This critique can be applied to any philosophy that makes reality dependent on the human mind. Deleuze wishes to explore the genesis of any entity—human, rock, or otherwise—and he sees the human mind as just one of many individuals in a flat ontology, which makes his philosophy *immanent* (ibid., p. 45; DeLanda, 2016, pp. 15–16). A major influence on Deleuze's realist ontology and his commitment to immanence was Spinoza.

## Spinoza, attributes, and absolute parity

A key difference between Spinoza's monism and that of Jung's concerns how Spinoza treats the attribute of thought, and how Jung tends to misread Spinoza on at least two occasions with respect to this point. In *Instinct and the Unconscious* (1919), Jung includes Spinoza in a line of philosophers who have diminished the archetype from a metaphysical construct into a mere act of cognition. He cites Spinoza's famous work, the *Ethics* (1677), and laments that over time, "the metaphysical value of the 'idea' or archetype steadily deteriorated. It became a "thought", an internal condition of cognition, as clearly formulated by Spinoza: "By 'idea' I understand a conception of the mind which the mind forms by reason of its being a thinking thing'" (Jung, 1919/1969, par. 276).

However, Spinoza argues that it is not only the human mind that forms conceptions of things, but all thinking things—most of all God, who has absolute powers of thinking and comprehending (E IP31). Deleuze notes that when reading Spinoza, one must distinguish "the ideas that we have" in our own minds from a different kind of idea, "the idea that we are," or the mind as the idea of the body (1970/1988, p. 73). Spinoza takes the notion that mind and matter are parallel aspects of the same substance to the utmost extreme: everything that exists has an idea of itself; everything, whether human or a blade of grass, has a mind of its own; and the idea of each thing is conceived in the mind of God, what Spinoza calls God's Infinite Intellect (E IIP4; IIP8–9; IIP11C). This has been described by some Spinoza scholars as comparable to the laws of logic or psychology (Nadler, 2006, p. 94). There is nothing that Spinoza's God does not conceive that He does not also create, and vice versa. "The order and connection of ideas is the same as the order and connection of things," and "God's power of thinking is equal to his realized power of action" (E IIP7, IIP7C).[2]

Spinoza decouples thought from the human mind, while at the same time he gives thought a power absolutely equal to that of matter (Deleuze, 1970/1988, pp. 51–52). Thus, Jung has criticized Spinoza for diminishing the metaphysical value of the archetype, but only because he seemingly assumed that Spinoza's definition of an idea applied merely to rote human cognition. Instead, Spinoza presaged the concept that Jung ultimately arrives at: the collective unconscious as the mental aspect of a monist whole (Atmanspacher, 2012, p. 12).

In *The Phenomenology of the Spirit in Fairy Tales*, Jung takes Spinoza to task for allegedly reducing spirit to matter, for making spirit merely a surface feature of the One Substance (1945/1948/1969, pars. 385, 390). As Cambray observes, this seems to be another incorrect reading, as Jung misunderstands a crucial aspect of Spinoza's monism: namely, the irreducible nature of Spinoza's attributes (Cambray, 2014, p. 47). Yet it is not just the noncausal overlap between thought and extension that makes Spinoza's psychoparallelism unique. Deleuze notes that similar theories existed in Spinoza's day: the Cartesians, for instance, could deny a real causality between mind and matter while affirming "an ideal correspondence" between them that maintained the divine nature of the mind or soul. Furthermore, Gottfried Wilhelm Leibniz (1646–1716) affirms "an identity of order between" mind and matter—however, he does this without granting matter "the same 'dignity' or perfection" that the mind possesses (Deleuze, 1970/1988, pp. 87–88). In Leibniz's ontology, the simple substances or monads that constitute a living being are organized in a hierarchy, where the monad of the mind contains within its reasons the actions of all the other monads that compose the body (Leibniz, 1714/2017, pars. 49–51). What makes Spinoza's theory original is that he rejects any hierarchy or means of assuring that the mind still has a privileged place above matter. Instead he endorses an identity of connection between the two aspects, an equal valance "between what occurs in one and the other." Spinoza's metaphysical project was devoted to conceiving God as completely immanent to all things, and part of the way he did this was to establish *absolute parity* between the attributes, so that neither is "superior to one another, none is reserved for the creator, none is relegated to the created beings and their imperfection" (Deleuze, 1970/1988, pp. 87–88).

This strict equality between the attributes may be the cause for Jung's accusation that Spinoza has allegedly devalued the nature of the archetype, or that Spinoza has supposedly reduced spirit to matter. For while Jung may share Spinoza's dual-aspect parallelism, he also places a premium on the psyche in his model, a premium that Spinoza's realism would likely reject. In his essay *Synchronicity: An Acausal Connecting Principle* (1952), Jung cites Leibniz's monadology as a forerunner to his theory of synchronicity. The monad is a microcosm of the entire world, and the monad of the human soul is capable of unconscious perceptions that represent the external state of things. This complements Jung's connection of the Self with the monist whole. Jung credits Leibniz for understanding that internal knowledge, a knowledge from within the mind, can apprehend the nature of the world itself (1952/1969, par. 937).

The example of Leibniz is useful, since it further articulates problems in the idea of the Self as "a microcosm enclosing the whole in itself" (ibid.). The radical way in which Leibniz arrives at the conclusion that the monad contains all of existence is via the principle of sufficient reason, where every true proposition is analytical—anything that can be said about a thing, must inhere within it (Deleuze, 1969/1990, pp. 113–121). If the entire world is predicated within each of Leibniz's monads, this suggests two things. First, the structure of the monad must rely heavily on relations of *interiority*. DeLanda, following Deleuze, distinguishes between "relations of *interiority*, in which the very identity of the terms is constituted in their relation, from relations of *exteriority*, in which the terms maintain their autonomy despite the fact their relation may have properties of its own" (DeLanda and Harman, 2017, pp. 30–31). Relations of interiority are common to anti-realism, where the components of the whole are inextricably fused. Secondly, in order to explain how all these monads, closed wholes each containing all the world within them, do not contradict one another, Leibniz must evoke a "pre-established harmony" of all things, and so he requires a grand mediator to grant passage to all existence. In this case, the role falls back to a transcendent God, who chooses the best of "compossible" worlds for the monads to coexist (Deleuze, 1968/1990, pp. 78–79). This preserves all the problems of a transcendent arbitrator of existence, whether that arbitrator is God or the human mind.

## A move towards realism

Jung's dual-aspect monism places a premium on consciousness as the catalyst for the world to exist, and where the Self is a microcosm of the monist whole. Despite the fact that both Jung and Spinoza deploy a dual-aspect monism, Jung's anti-realism differs critically from Spinoza's metaphysics, and in turn it leaves Jung exposed to the criticisms of the anti-realist positions raised above.

One might suggest that it is best to simply restrict Jung to the bounds of phenomenology (Brooke, 1991). However, this would merely transfer the problems of a *mind-dependent* holism into human experience alone and would thus maintain the issues of anti-realism that are, in any event, already inherent in phenomenology (DeLanda and Harman, 2017). Such a move would not eliminate issues of interiority, and it certainly would not offer a genetic account of the human and nonhuman. What may be preferable going forward is to ascertain if there are resources embedded in Jung's writing that move him closer towards a realist position. Simply put, can we move Jung's ontology closer towards that of Deleuze and Spinoza? Is there a common ground between them that would allow us to rethink the Self as a microcosm of the whole?

Interestingly, elsewhere in *Synchronicity* Jung dismisses any need for the pre-established harmony or the compossibility organized by Leibniz's God (1952/1969, par. 948). Earlier in the essay, Jung criticizes the idea derived from Schopenhauer that synchronicity could simply be simultaneous points in causal series that radiate from a first cause as being well beyond provable bounds. "It would only hold water," he writes, "if the first cause really were a unity. But if it were a multiplicity, which is just as likely, then [this] whole explanation collapses." The first cause, states Jung, is only plausible in the form of "unity and multiplicity at once" (ibid., par. 828). Now Deleuze's maneuver with Leibniz's philosophy is to remove God as regulator and essentially permit the *incompossible* by allowing for synthetic relations to develop between monads (1968/1990, pp. 328–330; 1969/1990, pp. 113–121). Something similar that Deleuze valued so highly in Spinoza's philosophy is how relations are purely *extrinsic* to the terms involved (Ramey, 2012, p. 35). Components are independent of the whole and in fact can be subsumed by other things, or conversely, they can bridge new connections. Realism values extrinsic relations between things, not just intrinsic relations between the human mind and the world. This is why Spinoza insists that it is much more important to know what a thing can do than what a thing is, to explore one's capacity to affect and be affected (E IIP4).

Cambray notes that Spinoza's theory of affects accords nicely with Jung's theory of psychic energy (Cambray, 2014, p. 45). Because of this, Spinoza's theory of knowledge is in fact closer to Jung's theory of psychic development than Jung ever seemed to realize, since Spinoza's theory of knowledge is intrinsically tied with his theory of affects. Far from being the champion of pure, reified rationalism, Spinoza considers abstract thought the result of an individual who, rather than having comprehended what he has the capacity to affect and be affected by, instead "retains only an extrinsic sign, a variable perceptible characteristic" of what he comes into contact with, reifying them into classifications, quantities, and transcendental forces (Deleuze, 1970/1988, pp. 44–48). Adequate ideas can only be formed when we understand how our emotions our influenced by our capacity to affect and be affected by other modes of substance. When we understand something that is common between ourselves and another thing, we adequately comprehend how our intrinsic composition is compounded by another body. Spinoza calls these adequate ideas the common notions. He emphasizes that common notions are not universals, which he considers generalized abstractions and thus inadequate ideas. Instead they are knowledge gained a posteriori, *knowledge that is gleaned internally through the mind's own resources* (Nadler, 2006, p. 176; E IIP40, IIP40S).

Therefore, the internal apprehension of things that Jung credited Leibniz for can also be found in Spinoza—but it is an intensive knowledge, not gleaned through a pre-established harmony or causal mediator, but rather through the collisions and interactions of different bodies. Perhaps Jung *was* at least partly aware of this nuance in Spinoza's thought, for when Jung defines his own intuition in *Psychological Types*, he cites two philosophers who developed a similar concept: Henri Bergson and Spinoza (Jung, 1921/1971, par. 770). Bergson's method of intuition was a method to glean the *intensive, qualitative* nature of things (Deleuze, 1966/1988). Similarly, Spinoza sees intuition, the *scientia intuitiva*, as the highest kind of knowledge, an understanding that allows one to know things as they are in God (E IIP45-47). The intuition, Deleuze writes, is when Spinoza goes beyond reason to a place "where ideas are redoubled and reflected in us as they are in God, giving us the experience of being eternal" (1970/1988, p. 58).

On the basis of these findings one may endeavor to reframe the Jungian Self from a closed whole to what Spinoza and Deleuze speak of: an individual that fully realizes God's immanent power. Indeed, the ultimate goals of Jung's project—individuation and knowledge of the *unus mundus* through knowledge of the Self—may ironically not be tenable given the privileged role accorded to consciousness in the Jung–Pauli model if it remains hindered by anti-realism, whereas the resources for such Divine knowledge are abundant in Spinoza's realist philosophy. Therefore a reconciliation between Jung and Spinoza is not only agreeable, but perhaps long overdue.

## Notes

1 Harman notes that Kant, strictly speaking, is something of a realist in the respect that he treats the thing-in-itself as existing beyond the mind. However, his privileging of thought-world relations as the root of all other relations makes him, at best, a realist nonetheless "who sees no possibility of discussing any relation that does not involve human beings" (2017, p. 29). This opens the door for complete anti-realism where the thing-in-itself is eliminated entirely, like in Hegel's philosophy (ibid., pp. 45–46).
2 It is worth noting that Spinoza's realism was at one point a matter of dispute. A debate within Spinoza scholarship known as 'the problem of the attributes' is concerned with

whether or not the attributes are what the human intellect project onto God, or if they are indeed objective expressions of God's essence. Most contemporary scholarship tends in the latter direction (Lloyd, 1996, pp. 42–48). There is more nuance here, as Spinoza states there are an infinity of attributes; we, however, only know the two attributes that comprise our essence, thought and extension. Therefore, for Spinoza there are two kinds of parallelism: epistemological, concerning the two attributes we know of as humans; and then ontological, the equal powers of all of God's attributes. (Deleuze, 1970/1988, p. 92).

## References

Atmanspacher, H. (2012). "Dual-Aspect Monism a la Pauli and Jung." *Journal of Consciousness Studies* 19, no. 9, 10. http://www.igpp.de/english/tda/pdf/dualaspect.pdf (accessed August 20, 2012).

Atmanspacher, H. & Fach, W. (2013). "A Structural-Phenomenological Typology of Mind-Matter Correlations." *Journal of Analytical Psychology* 58, 219–244.

Atmanspacher, H. & Fuchs, C. (2014). *The Jung-Pauli Conjecture: And its Impact Today.* Exeter: Imprint Publishing.

Barad, K. (2007). *Meeting the Universe Halfway: Quantum Physics and the Entanglement of Matter and Meaning.* Durham: Duke University Press.

Brooke, R. (1991). *Jung and Phenomenology.* London: Routledge.

Bryant, L. (2009). "Deleuze's Transcendental Empiricism: Notes towards a Transcendental Materialism." In *Thinking Between Deleuze and Kant: A Strange Encounter.* Edited by E. Willatt and M. Lee. New York: Continuum. pp. 28–49.

Cambray, J. (2014) "The Influence of German Romantic Science on Jung and Pauli." In *The Jung-Pauli Conjecture: And its Impact Today.* Edited by H. Atmanspacher and C. Fuchs. Exeter: Imprint Publishing. pp. 37–57.

DeLanda, M. (2016). *Assemblage Theory.* Edinburgh: Edinburgh University Press.

DeLanda, M. and Harman, G. (2017). *The Rise of Realism.* Cambridge: Polity Press.

Deleuze, G. (1966/1988). *Bergsonism.* Translated by H. Tomlinson and B. Habberjam. New York: Zone Books.

Deleuze G. (1969/1990) *The Logic of Sense.* Translated by C. Boundas, M. Lester, and C. Stivale. London: Bloomsbury.

Deleuze, G. (1970/1988). *Spinoza: Practical Philosophy.* Translated by R. Hurley. San Francisco: City Lights Books.

Deleuze, G. (1990/1968). *Expressionism in Philosophy: Spinoza.* Translated by M. Joughin. New York: Zone Books.

Gieser, S. (2005). *The Innermost Kernel: Depth Psychology and Quantum Physics. Wolfgang Pauli's dialogue with C.G. Jung.* Berlin: Springer.

Jung, C.G. (1919). "Instinct and the Unconscious." In *The Structure and Dynamics of the Psyche,* 2nd ed. Collected Works of C.G. Jung, Vol. 8, Princeton: Princeton University Press, 1969.

Jung, C. (1921). *Psychological Types,* 2nd ed. Translated by R. Hull. Collected Works of C.G. Jung, Vol. 6. Princeton: Princeton University Press, 1971.

Jung C.G. (1945/1948). "The Phenomenology of the Spirit in Fairy Tales." In *The Archetypes and the Collective Unconscious,* 2nd ed. Collected Works of C.G. Jung, Vol. 9, Part I. Edited by H. Read, M, Fordham, & G. Adler. Translated by R. Hull. Princeton: Princeton University Press, 1969.

Jung, C.G. (1952). "Synchronicity: An Acausal Connecting Principle." In *The Structure and Dynamics of the Psyche*, 2nd ed. Translated by R. Hull. *Collected Works of C.G. Jung*, Vol. 8. Princeton: Princeton University Press, 1969.

Jung C.G. (1955a) "Appendix; Mandalas." In *The Archetypes and the Collective Unconscious*, 2nd ed. *Collected Works of C.G. Jung*, Vol. 9, Part I. Princeton: Princeton University Press, 1969.

Jung, C.G. (1955b). *Mysterium Coniunctionis*, 2nd ed. Translated by R. Hull. *Collected Works of C.G. Jung*, Vol. 14. Princeton: Princeton University Press, 1970.

Leibniz, G (2017). *The Principles of Philosophy known as Monadology*. Edited by J. Bennett. http://www.earlymoderntexts.com/assets/pdfs/leibniz1714b.pdf (accessed June 20, 2018).

Lloyd, G. (1996). *Spinoza and the Ethics*. London: Routledge.

Meier, C.A. (ed.) (2001). *Atom and Archetype: The Pauli/Jung Letters 1932–1958*. London: Routledge.

Nadler, S.M. (2006). *Spinoza's Ethics: An Introduction*. New York: Cambridge University Press.

Ramey, J.A. (2012). *The Hermetic Deleuze: Philosophy and Spiritual Ordeal*. Durham: Duke University Press.

Spinoza, B. (1677). "The Ethics." In *Spinoza: Complete Works*. Translated by S. Shirley. Edited by M. Morgan. Indianapolis: Hackett Pub, 2002.

# 11
# KANT'S INFLUENCE ON JUNG'S VITALISM IN THE *ZOFINGIA LECTURES*

Christian McMillan

## Introduction

This chapter considers the influence of Immanuel Kant's (1724–1804) 'biophilosophy'[1] from the second book of his third *Critique*, *The Critique of Teleological Judgement* (first published in 1790) on C.G. Jung's (1875–1961) 'vitalism'. The rationale for this study concerns conceptual affinities between Jung and Kant which gravitate around Kant's speculations on organic individuation and how these were received by Jung in the late 19th century. Many of Kant's speculations on organic individuation have been broadly classed as holistic and organicistic.[2] The kind of 'vitalism' which Jung appeared to extol in his early *Zofingia Lectures* (1896–1899)[3] and which a handful of Jungian scholars have examined (Nagy, 1991; Addison, 2009) betrays features of Kant's influence from the third *Critique* albeit of a 'second hand' nature given that Jung never engaged with the third *Critique* directly.[4] Rather, it is the filtered effect of Kant's biophilosophy on 19th-century organicism which undoubtedly made its mark on Jung's early reflections concerning what he refers to as a 'pre-existent vital principle' and which he deems as 'necessary to explain the world of organic phenomena' (1896: par. 63). This chapter reflects on the nature of this organicistic vitalism from a critical perspective, one which draws from some of the ideas of French philosopher Gilles Deleuze (1925–1995) and other, more recent contributions presented by scholars in Deleuze studies.

## Kant's biophilosophy and the *Critique of Teleological Judgement*

One of the central pillars of 19th-century organicism (as derived from Kant) was 'the acceptance of living organisation as a postulate: the organism had to be considered the unit of investigation and not a mere aggregate of physical, inorganic, entities' (Esposito, 2011: 18). Moreover, as a 'unit' the organism was often deemed to be a purposive 'whole'. Indeed, Kant considered this to be a veritable 'fact' of 'self-organisation' (*Naturzwecke*) and in the third *Critique* he claimed that '[t]his principle [intrinsic purposiveness], which is also the definition of organised beings, is: *An organised product of nature … one in which everything is a purpose and reciprocally also a means.* In such a product nothing is gratuitous, purposeless, or to be attributed to a blind natural mechanism' (1790/1987, section 66: 376: 255; emphasis original). Hence, the organic 'whole' had a purpose to it and this required new principles to be deployed in order to explain how such purpose or 'final ends' were possible given that this kind of causality did not appear to sit comfortably with the spatio-temporal linear causality that dominated mechanistic theories of cause and effect. As we shall see, Jung refers to the 'fact' of the organic as evidence for the existence of natural purpose and self-organisation in nature. He takes the organism to be a primary unit and one which is not, in the words of Toscano, 'an object-event or a time-position, but rather constitutes an individual the evidence of which demands "indirect" explanation' (2006: 31). Hence the organism is not 'given' in the sense of an object of possible experience; rather it is an evidence or a 'fact' (Jung), and this led Kant to aver that 'were experience not to furnish examples of them [organised bodies] the possibility of such bodies would be dismissed by everyone as fantasies of the Prince of Palagonia' (1993, section 22: 383: 120).[5]

The postulation of a kind of causality proper to 'purpose' was a problem for Kant. In other words the 'organism' as an organised being was a problem; it was an anomaly. There is something about the organism which forces Kant to think in the sense that he is encountering something that is almost paradoxical and which defies all our constitutive explanatory models.[6] The paradoxical status of the organism is only paradoxical relative to a modality of individuation that explains it by recourse to mechanistic principles, principles which Kant sought to grant the highest legitimacy in his first *Critique* (the *Critique of Pure Reason*, 1781). For Kant this legitimacy rested on 'the alliance between Newtonian mechanics and a philosophy of representation' (Toscano, 2006: 24). In the first *Critique*, Kant had presented an epistemological defence of mechanistic cause and effect meaning that any other kind of causality could only be posited as a heuristic device, something Kant referred to in the third *Critique* as a 'regulative' principle as opposed to a 'constitutive' one. As John Zammito put it:

> One might ask how it was even possible, according to Kant's model, to experience such [organic] entities, since experience was necessarily structured in terms of the categories of the understanding, and hence in a model which was already mechanical. … To explain how organisms could be recognised Kant had to deploy his "other kind of judging," that involving "reflection" and "purposiveness," because the determinant form of judgement simply did not suffice. … Purposiveness is never something we

> perceive directly in an experience. It is rather an inference, an imputation, which we make.
>
> *(1992: 219; see Toscano, 2006: 32)*

Hence, it might seem curious that Kant effectively began a process of undermining the alliance between Newtonian mechanics and a philosophy of representation in his third *Critique*. But it is this process which would open the floodgates for 19th-century speculation about ontological modalities of individuation, modalities which Jung took an interest in when he first began to speculate about teleological processes governing the structure and dynamics of the psyche. Just as Kant found it difficult to accommodate a causality of intrinsic purposiveness within the architectonic of his critical philosophy, Jung also admitted to being somewhat 'embarrassed' by its apparent impossibility. In his *Synchronicity: An Acausal Connecting Principle* (1952) he stated baldly: 'Whether we like it or not, we find ourselves in this embarrassing position as soon as we begin seriously to reflect on the teleological processes in biology or to investigate the compensatory function of the unconscious, not to speak of trying to explain the phenomenon of synchronicity' (1952: par. 931). Jung wrote this passage over 150 years after Kant's third *Critique* and over fifty years after his delivery of the *Zofingia Lectures*. This indicates that his interest in teleological processes never diminished. But unlike Kant, Jung does not regard the 'embarrassment' of these apparent anomalous processes to mean that they can only be posited heuristically or in a regulative manner.

It is important to note that as Jung delivered his *Zofingia Lectures* between 1896 and 1899 his references to Kant became cooler.[7] One reason for this is the extent to which Kant was forced to suspend his own insights regarding self-organising individuality in order to hold true to the core tenets of his transcendental philosophy. For Jung, Kant's constricting parameters would have included the *a priori* character of the grounds of scientific knowledge and the subordination of biological evidence to mechanism as the legislating authority within the realm of appearances. In the *Zofingia Lectures* Jung engages directly with Kant and the *a priori*. He is a little inconsistent in how he will deal with this problem, stating in the fourth lecture that 'judgements about purpose are not a priori judgements, for the objectivity of a priori judgements cannot be demonstrated' (1898, par. 175). Furthermore, Jung appears to affirm Kant's view from the third *Critique* that the organism cannot be an object of knowledge when he comments in the second lecture that 'within the categories of space and time, judgement is based on sense perceptions' and that '[o]nly objects in a material form constitute objects of perception' (1897: par. 98). Yet, Jung goes on to affirm what he calls an 'objectivity of purpose' when he resolutely condemns 'radical subjectivists' for not acknowledging 'any teleology external to man' and others who proclaimed that 'we ourselves have projected onto the world, out of our own heads, the idea of purposefulness of nature', i.e. 'the epigones of Kant' (1898: par. 175).[8] Jung, like many before him in the 19th century, was going in 'directions that would have horrified the Königsberg philosopher' (Harrington, 1996: 5) and Bishop ably summaries the reasons why when he writes that '[i]n contradiction to the Third Critique then, which admits only of a critique of teleological *judgement* ('Uretilskraft'), Jung is erecting in this lecture a metaphysic of purpose, a desire which anticipates his later insistence that, against all the odds, life does indeed have meaning' (1995: 37). Bishop draws these conclusions from Jung's comments in the fourth lecture:

> In this sense the category of causality must be interpreted as a totally wondrous a priori reference to causes of a transcendental nature, i.e. to a world of the invisible and the incomprehensible, a continuation of material nature into the incalculable, the immeasurable, and the inscrutable. Surely it is unnecessary for me to add that such an interpretation places the doctrine of the *Ding an sich* in a new light and enables us to get an unexpected glimpse of the superb purposefulness of the animate universe.
> 
> *(1898: par. 184)*

The 'category of causality' as an '*a priori* reference' undercuts the harsh limit that Kant's reflective judgement[9] imposed on the study of life; a judgement that could only provide 'maxims' and inductive generalisations grouped together by the mere subjective heuristic of reason. By undercutting this limit, natural purpose in nature becomes ontologised, and teleology is considered a constitutive or inherent property of organisms themselves, a view which Kant would have deemed 'dogmatic'. As Beiser notes, some of the early *Naturphilosophers* (e.g., Schelling, Hegel, Schlegel, and Novalis) gave constitutive status to the idea of natural purpose: 'First, it refers to a distinctive structure, function, or form of the organic; second, it also denotes a force behind this structure, function, or form ... a form of causal agency, a force whose manifestations are organic structures, functions, or forms' (2006: 17). For Kant, by contrast, the kinds of teleological, purposive processes which constituted the self-organisation of the 'whole' organism were *analogical* and he spoke of our experience of the organism as an 'analogue of life' (1790/1987, section 65: 375: 254). This was bound up with Kant's metaphysical commitment to maintaining the distinction between man and the rest of organic life. Zammito summarises that '[t]he only power capable of self-determination, Kant emphasised, was intelligent will. Intelligent will could never be found in phenomena; it was not part of nature' (2007: 66). This is very important for a number of reasons. The 'life' that Kant refers to is intended as an analogue of human life and more specifically what he regards as the human power of 'desire'. By desire he means the interiority of processes of reason and cognition. In the *Metaphysical Foundations of Natural Science* (1786) Kant argues: 'Life is the faculty of a *substance* to determine itself to act from an *internal principle* ... Now we know no other internal principle in a substance for changing its state except *desiring*, and no other internal activity at all except *thinking*' (1786/2004: 544: 83; emphasis original). He concludes that 'these actions and grounds of determination in no way belong to representations of the outer senses, and so neither to the determinations of matter as matter. Hence all matter, as such, is lifeless' (ibid.).[10] In the *Zofingia Lectures* it is noteworthy that Jung extracts two quotations from a pre-critical work of Kant (*Dreams of a Spirit-Seer*, 1766) which recapitulate the sentiments Kant made twenty years later in the *Metaphysical Foundations*. In 'The border Zones of Exact Science' (November 1896) Jung quotes that 'every substance, even a simply material element, must possess an internal activity as the cause of its external operation' and 'whatever in the world contains a principle of life appears to be immaterial in nature' (pars: 18, 19).[11] Whereas Kant will restrict this 'internal principle' to an anthropomorphic analogy, Jung's dismissal of the 'projection' of 'purpose' in the *Zofingia Lectures* entails the rejection of this kind of analogy. But it does not entail the rejection of the anthropomorphic *form* of the analogy, i.e. the function of the 'internal activity' which Jung equates with an 'immaterial', 'vital principle' (1896–1897: pars. 44, 57, 65, 66, 79, 80, 81, 107) operative in nature at large. Jung goes to say that 'it is a *fact*, verified by a hundred thousand cases, that organic beings never develop out of inorganic matter, but only through contact with life' (ibid.: par. 56; emphasis added).[12] Hence, a matter/life antithesis is projected onto the mereological determination of a special, final causality belonging to self-organisation which goes from the whole to the parts and vice versa (see Toscano, 2006: 33).

## Reflections from a Deleuzian perspective

What Jung has in common with Kant at this early stage in his career is a view of matter as somewhat inert or lifeless and in need of something else such as a force to infuse it with life. In the fourth lecture, 'Thoughts on the Nature and Value of Speculative Inquiry' (delivered in the summer of 1898) Jung refers to 'Life' as being 'the highest activity we know' an activity to which '[t]he entire external environment may act as an obstacle to the degree that it hinders the untrammelled operation of the organism' (par. 224). The 'external environment' is 'material and strives to attain the maximum possible degree of rest'; it is 'obstructive passivity'; the 'obtuseness and inertia of material substance' (ibid.). Kant's negative view of matter emerged before his 'critical' period, but his views on it remained consistent after this.[13] In *Dreams of a Spirit-Seer* Kant grapples with the possibility of immaterial spirits communicating with the material world.[14] He believes that the principle of life is contained within the immaterial and that the upper and lower limits of its communication with the material world are hylozoism and materialism. He wrote that '[h]*ylozoism* invests everything with life, while *materialism*, when carefully considered, deprives everything of life' (1992, section 2: 330: 317). But even in this pre-critical work, Kant is critical of hylozoism and he does not entertain the notion that matter could organise itself or move itself without the impetus of an immaterial principle.

Kant's negative view of matter commits him instead to a kind of hylomorphism and this has been the subject of critical treatment by Deleuze and recent commentators in Deleuze Studies.[15] In *A Thousand Plateaus* (1980) Deleuze and his writing partner Félix Guattari (1925–1992) argue that the 'hylomorphic model' is inseparable from 'a form that organises matter and a matter prepared for the form' (1980/1987: 369). They suggest that this form has a political inflection, and that 'it has often been shown that this [hylomorphic] schema derives less from technology or life than from a society divided into governors and governed, and later, intellectuals and manual laborers' (ibid.). In place of the hylomorphic schema they propose a hylozoic account of matter and although Deleuze and Guattari do not use this term, it has been employed by a number of Deleuzians to underscore what the two authors mean by a 'material vitalism' (ibid.: 411) and a 'matter' that they once referred to as 'matter-movement, this matter-energy, this matter-flow, this matter in variation' which is 'a destratified, deterritorialized matter' (1980/1987: 406). Hylozoism is the claim that matter is self-organising and can generate its own formal principle of organisation. Hence, it is almost the opposite of hylomorphism which, as we have seen, maintains that the formal principle is separate in kind from the matter that it informs.

Kant's reasons for rejecting hylozoism throughout his philosophical career are complicated and I cannot do justice to them here.[16] Needless to say, they concerned a moral commitment to the freedom of the will which Kant imagined would be severely compromised by hylozoism because it would entail the abandonment of the dualism between the noumenal and the phenomenal which he regarded as a precondition of moral action and responsibility (see Beiser, 2006: 24; Zammito, 2007: 66). It also concerned a 'political' commitment against the rise of 'Spinozism' in late 18th-century Germany which formed the bedrock of the 'Pantheism Controversy' from 1786.[17]

Although Jung undermined Kant's commitment to dualism in the *Zofingia Lectures* by attesting to the constitutive status of a vital principle, it is because he tacitly endorsed a view of matter as inert that he affirmed a position which for many in the biological sciences of the late nineteenth century would have been untenable.[18] As a consequence and contrary to my claim at the beginning of this chapter, it becomes somewhat tenuous to label Jung's early vitalism 'organicistic' because the *form* of this vitalism has more in common with the characteristics of the 'analogue of life' that Kant claimed was necessary (as a heuristic device) to help us understand organic self-organisation. Although not an 'analogy' for Jung, the characteristics of Kant's analogy served to radically secure the distinction of organic life from the inorganic, affirming, as Zammito puts it, 'the uniqueness and mystery of organisms as phenomena of empirical nature' (2007: 66). Because there was *no* analogy for Jung, the distinction that Kant had sought to uphold between man and the rest of nature was destabilised. Nonetheless, the *form* of this distinction—the *separation* between an immaterial principle and a matter which it infuses—remains. It is this hylomorphic separation that is the most important hallmark of Jung's early vitalism, although it undergoes radical revision by the time he formally introduces the notion of the psychoid in his essay 'On the Nature of the Psyche' (first published in 1947).[19] When Jung goes beyond Kant in the *Zofingia Lectures* by rejecting the (projected) analogical status of 'intelligent will', he begins to offer a speculative account of the genesis of the origins of life; a 'metaphysic of purpose'. Although Kant intended to block speculations of this kind, dismissing as 'absurd' the possibility that 'another Newton might arise who would explain to us, in terms of natural laws unordered by any intention, how even a mere blade of grass is produced' (1790/1987, section 75: 400: 282–283) this did not stop him from proposing some speculative insights of his own.[20]

In the third *Critique* these speculations centre on what Kant called 'physico-theology' which he defined as 'reason's attempt to infer the supreme cause of nature, and the properties of this cause, from the *purposes* of nature (which we can cognise only empirically)' (1790/1987, section: 85: 436: 324). These speculations are broadly tied up with his 'theism' argument (1790/1987, section 75: 395: 276) which, he claimed, 'does have one advantage over all bases [e.g. mechanism and hylozoism] to explain these [natural] purposes – viz., theism is best able to rescue the purposiveness of nature from idealism; for it attributes an understanding to the original being and introduces an intentional causality for the production of natural purposes' (ibid.). Although Kant will refer to this theistic solution as 'inadequate' (ibid., section 74: 397: 279) he was essentially advocating for a transcendent creator whose intentional will operated like that of a 'divine art' (ibid.). Kant recognised that this would entail a strict separation between 'the products of nature' and 'divine art', meaning that something external was necessary as cause distinct from its products. Kant puzzled over this as follows: 'But if an organised product is to be a natural product, then we cannot make this soul the artificer that constructed it, since that would remove the product from (corporeal) nature' (1790/1987, section 65: 374–5: 254). He reiterates this problem in a later section: 'Once I have determinately stated that certain things are products of divine art, how can I still include them among products of nature, when it was precisely because nature cannot produce such things in terms of its laws that I had to appeal to a cause distinct from it?' (ibid., section 74: 397: 279). Appealing to a 'distinct' cause, like an 'immaterial', 'vital principle' which is external to natural purposes, distinguished Kant's speculative physico-theological organicism from the thought of others in the eighteenth and nineteenth centuries who were struggling to avoid invoking supernatural or occult forces to explain the structure of organisms.[21] Kant's appeal to a 'distinct' cause for natural purposes undermines the possibility of their *self*-organisation. Toscano, borrowing from Kant, argues that 'self-organisation implies a "relational unity of parts" ... an "integrated reciprocal causality" (or self-regulation) and, what is of most interest, their "autoproduction"' (2006: 34). Nevertheless, because Kant thinks that the whole is not the cause of the combination of the parts (this requiring instead some analogical form of final causality), organic bodies:

> [C]annot be self-organising in the complete sense—that is to say, ends-*of*-themselves—hence they must be understood as effects of a supersensible nature (relatively of course). If bodies cannot be regarded as aggregates

caused by the known mechanical laws of nature, then they must, as *self-organising wholes*, be subject to the heteronomous causality of an *idea*. Their individuality thus finds its purely speculative ground in a supplementary, eidetic dimension that can only be thought of theistically, in terms of the hypothetical demiurgic activities of an entity in possession of intellectual intuition.

*(2006: 34–35)*

What Toscano calls the external 'heteronomous causality of an *idea*' is also evident in Jung's account of natural purposes in his *Zofingia Lectures*. Jung refers to the 'soul' as an 'intelligent organisational activity' (1897, para. 118) which reveals in its purposeful acts a 'purposeful idea' (1898, para. 177) responsible for the motivation of an instinctive action. This amounts to an external form of causation; an external act operating the synthesis of the 'whole', meaning that organic wholes may be effects of a supersensible realm as we find in Kant's speculative account.

For Kant, as we have seen, intelligent will could only be ascribed to organic phenomena in terms of an analogy with a human power of desire. Jung's rejection of the analogical status of the intelligent will does not alter its anthropomorphic form, a consequence of Jung having followed Kant's anti-hylozoism from his reading of some of Kant's pre-critical works. The 'purposeful idea' is an idea of the whole which is distinct from matter. Colebrook has argued that '[o]rganicism is an enclosed vitalism: whereas traditional vitalism regards matter as inert and posits an immaterial force that infuses an otherwise lifeless substance, organicism places the form of life in the relations of the whole'. Hence 'life occurs neither at the level of matter itself, nor as some principle in itself, but in organisational wholes' (2010: 154). For Kant, the whole overdetermines the reciprocal production of its parts by analogy with a purely intentional causality according to ideas.

From a Deleuzian perspective the status of the whole in this kind of organicism is problematic along with its separation from matter. The whole is a unity, and it is organisationally closed. The genesis of the whole is blocked because of a matter/life partition, in which matter is presupposed to be inert or lifeless. Because of this the immaterial 'idea' of the whole is *already* individuated and it cannot be decomposed. Distinctions between the organic and the inorganic, the mechanical and the teleological remain at work in this matter/life antithesis as long as matter is considered to be coterminous with mechanism.

## Notes

1 I borrow this term from Deleuzian scholar Alberto Toscano's critical work on Kant's third *Critique*: 'The Paradoxical Object: On Self-Organising Beings in the *Critique of Judgement*' (2006: 19–40).
2 Many early 19th-century natural philosophers such as such as Johann Gottlieb Fichte (1762–1814), Friedrich Schlegel (1772–1829), Friedrich Wilhelm Joseph von

Schelling (1775–1854) and Johann Wolfgang von Goethe (1749-1832), considered themselves to be children of Kant and took inspiration from the idea of an alternative form of teleological causality that they found in his work. Others (sometimes labelled 'teleomechanists') developed an empirical research program derived from Kant's *Critique of Judgement*, (e.g., Gottfried Reinhold Treviranus (1776–1837), Carl Friedrich Kielmeyer (1765–1844), and Johann Friedrich Meckel (1781–1833), and a later generation such as Karl Ernst von Baer (1792–1876), Johannes Müller (1801–1858), Carl Bergmann (1814–1865) and Rudolph Leuckart (1822–1898). For scholarship which has examined Kant's influence see Beiser, 2006: 10; Esposito, 2011: 19, 28–55.

3 Jung became a member of the *Zofingiaverein*, a Swiss Student Fraternity in May 1895, and was elected Chairperson of the Basle section during the winter term of 1897/98. He delivered these lectures between the years 1896–1899 and between the ages of 21 and 23.

4 Bishop contends that '[I]t is both ironic and unfortunate that the one *Critique* which Jung apparently never read in detail was the third! For, if he had, Jung might well have found it more secure to ground his psychology in a variant of Kantian aesthetics rather than in the epistemology of the first *Critique*' (Bishop 2000: 158).

5 This passage appears in Kant's *Opus Postumum*; a work in progress at the time of Kant's death. It is composed of a collection of fascicles written between 1790 and 1803.

6 The phrase 'something in the world forces us to think' comes from Deleuze's *Difference and Repetition* (1968/1994: 139). Here I am thinking of Bennett's characterisation of the 'organism' in Kant's work as a 'wonder' and something 'enchanted'. She writes that 'even in a Kantian world, encounters with nature retain a fascinating but also unsettling power to throw us a tenuous line to another world' (2001: 44), and the 'Kantian world has, then, its own sites of enchantment. These come to the fore in *The Critique of Judgement*, especially in the discussion of teleological judgement, even though they sit uncomfortably with Kant's ongoing project of critique' (2001: 45). Toscano writes that 'paradox, of course, is that one is *forced* to think the organism, insofar as its evidence is such as to show up the lack and limitation of an *a priori* legislation' (2006: 31).

7 Bishop has undertaken a brief analysis of Jung's references to Kant in the *Zofingia Lectures* (see 1995: 28–29): 'It is clear from this analysis that between 1896 and 1899, Jung became very interested in Kant, particularly his pre-critical philosophy, but subsequently moved away from him' (1995: 29).

8 On 'projection' Zammito claims that '[d]riven to admit that it was impossible to see organisms other than as natural purposes, Kant held that this necessity lay in *our* projection, not *their* nature' (1992: 222).

9 In the third *Critique* Kant distinguishes between two forms of judgement, determinative and reflective. Determinative judgements are those which subsume a particular under a universal while reflective judgement finds the universal for the particular.

10 In the third *Critique* Kant wrote: 'And yet we cannot even think of living matter as possible. (The concept of it involves a contradiction, since the essential character of matter is lifelessness, *inertia*)' (1790/1987, section: 73: 394: 276).

11 In the Cambridge edition (1992) of Kant's *Theoretical Philosophy* 1755-1770, both passages are located at section 2: 328: 315.

12 In the second lecture Jung also quotes from Kant's 1766 work: 'It appears that an intellectual being is intimately present with the matter to which it is joined, and that it does not act upon those forces by which the elements relate to each other but rather upon the *inner principle* of their state' (1897: par. 96; emphasis added. Cf. Kant, 1992, section: 2: 328: 315).

13 Kant's 'critical period' is considered to date from 1770 and his *On the Form and Principles of the Sensible and the Intelligible world* of that year. Adkins and Hinlicky

note that for Kant '[t]here is never a question that matter could organise itself or move itself without the impetus of some immaterial principle. While one could argue about the relation between the precritical and critical Kant, he never waivers in his rejection of hylozoism' (2013: 29).
14 Jung makes reference to this in the first lecture (1896: par. 80; cf. Kant, 1766/1992, section 2: 327: 314–315).
15 For example, Adkins and Hinlicky (2013), Toscano (2006), Albert (1999), and Colebrook (2010). It is important to include comment on this scholarship as it attests to the importance of 'matter' in Deleuze's and Deleuze and Guattari's thought. In their accounts of the 'material vitalism' of the two philosophers, Deleuzians find resources to critically investigate the vitalism of other important philosophers, past and present. Kant's bio-philosophy from his *Critique of Judgement* (1790) remains at the forefront of many of these accounts because of his rejection of hylozoism but also for what Toscano has dubbed the 'Kantian legacy' (2006: 59) in some contemporary philosophical and scientific ontologies concerned with the definition of organised beings (e.g. autopoiesis). Likewise Colebrook has critiqued features of what she refers to as an 'active vitalism' (whose character is hylomorphic) which informs 'vitalism in its contemporary mode' (2010: 137), including Humberto Maturana and Francisco Varela's 'autopoietic' model of living systems, Andy Clark's 'extended mind' and the Gaia hypothesis.
16 A good account of the reasons has been presented by Zammito, 1992: 189–213.
17 Zammito claims that Kant's third *Critique* can be regarded as a response to the 'new metaphysical vision which was catching the imagination of Germany in the second half of the 1780's: Spinozist pantheism' (1992: 227). See chapter 11; 'The Pantheism Controversy and the *Third Critique*', 1992: 228–247.
18 This is also evident in Kant's preference for the theory of preformationism in evolutionary theory over epigenesis. Kant was behind the times for reasons pertaining to his metaphysical commitments, i.e. his anti-hylozoism. See Zammito, 'Kant's persistent ambivalence toward epigenesis, 1764–90,' 2007: 51–74.
19 In this essay Jung no longer upholds a radical distinction between form (or idea) and matter. He invokes the idea of a spectrum which can be linked to a continuum.
20 Zammito has referred to this as Kant's 'ethical turn': 'Kant's "ethical turn" must be seen as part of a strategy to defend his crucial metaphysical commitments: to the free will and moral duty of individual human beings, and to the idea of a transcendent-personal Divinity on Christian lines' (1992: 264).
21 Allen distinguishes between 'materialistic holism' (also called 'dialectical materialism') and 'non-materialistic holism' equating the latter with vitalism and figures such as Hans Driesch (1867–1941), whom Jung occasionally referenced. 'Holistic and dialectical materialism' writes Allen, 'share a materialist epistemology, seeking to account for living processes as functioning wholes within the framework of known physical laws. Vitalism, on the other hand, claimed that living organisms defy description in purely physico-chemical terms, because organisms possess some non-material, non-measurable forces or directive agents that account for the complexity' (2005: 267). Jung's holism in the *Zofingia Lectures* broadly fits a non-materialistic holism.

# References

Addison, A. (2009) 'Jung, vitalism and 'the psychoid': an historical reconstruction'. *Journal of Analytical Psychology*, 54, 1, 123–142.
Adkins, B. & Hinlicky, P.R. (2013) *Rethinking Philosophy and Theology with Deleuze: A New Cartography*. London and New York: Bloomsbury Publishing.

Allen, G.E. (2005) 'Mechanism, vitalism and organicism in late nineteenth and twentieth-century biology: the importance of historical context'. Elsevier, 36, 261–283.
Beiser, F. (2006) 'Kant and Naturphilosophie'. In *The Kantian Legacy in Nineteenth-Century Science*, eds. Michael Friedman & Alfred Nordmann, 7–26. Cambridge, MA: The MIT Press.
Bennett, J. (2001) *The Enchantment of Modern Life: Attachments, Crossings, and Ethics*. Princeton and Oxford: Princeton University Press.
Bishop, P. (1995) *The Dionysian Self: C.G. Jung's Reception of Friedrich Nietzsche*. Berlin and New York: Walter de Gruyter.
Bishop, P. (2000) *Synchronicity and Intellectual Intuition in Kant, Swedenborg and Jung*. Lampeter, UK: Edwin Mellen Press.
Brooks, R.M. (2011) 'Un-thought out metaphysics in analytical psychology: a critique of Jung's epistemological basis for psychic reality'. *Journal of Analytical Psychology*, 56, 492–513.
Colebrook, C. (2010) *Deleuze and the Meaning of Life*. London and New York: Continuum Press.
Deleuze, G. (1968/1994) *Difference and Repetition* (P. Patton, Trans.). New York: Columbia University Press.
Deleuze, G. & Guattari, F. (1980/1987) *A Thousand Plateaus: Capitalism and Schizophrenia* (B. Massumi, Trans.). Minneapolis: University of Minnesota Press.
Esposito, M. (2011) 'Between holism and reductionism: organismic inheritance and the Neo-Kantian biological tradition in Britian and the USA, 18901940, Ph. D. thesis, University of Leeds.
Harrington, A. (1996) *Reenchanted Science: Holism in German Culture from Wilhelm II to Hitler*. Princeton: Princeton University Press.
Jung, C.G. (1896/1897/1898) *The Collected Works of C.G. Jung*, eds. Sir Herbert Read, Michael Fordham and Gerhard Adler, executive editor William McGuire, (R.F.C Hull, Trans.) [hereafter *Collected Works*], vol. A, *The Zofingia Lectures*, London: Routledge & Kegan Paul, 1983.
Jung, C.G. (1947/1954) 'On the nature of the psyche'. In *Collected Works*, vol. 8, *The Structure and Dynamics of the Psyche*, 2nd ed., London: Routledge and Kegan Paul, 1969.
Jung, C.G. (1952) 'Synchronicity: an acausal connecting principle'. In *Collected Works*, vol. 8, *The Structure and Dynamics of the Psyche*, 2nd ed., London: Routledge & Kegan Paul, 1969.
Kant, I. (1766/1992) 'Dreams of a Spirit-seer elucidated by dreams of metaphysics'. In *Theoretical Philosophy, 17551770*, (David Walford and Ralf Meerbote, Trans.). New York: Cambridge University Press.
Kant, I. (1786/2004) *Metaphysical Foundations of Natural Science*, (M. Friedan, Trans.). Cambridge: Cambridge University Press.
Kant, I. (1790/1987) *Critique of Judgement*, (Werner S. Pluhar, Trans.). Indiana: Hackett Publishing Company, Inc.
Kant, I. (1993) *Opus Postumum*, (Eckart Förster and Michael Rosen, Trans.). Cambridge and New York: Cambridge University Press.
Nagy, M. (1991) *Philosophical Issues in the Psychology of C.G. Jung*. Albany: State University of New York Press.
Toscano, A. (2006) *The Theatre of Production: Philosophy and Individuation between Kant and Deleuze*. Basingstoke and New York: Palgrave Macmillan.

Zammito, J. H. (1992) *The Genesis of Kant's Critique of Judgement*. Chicago: Chicago University Press.

Zammito, J. H. (2007) 'Kant's Persistent Ambivalence toward Epigenesis, 176490'. In *Understanding Purpose: Kant and the Philosophy of Biology*, ed. Philippe Huneman, 51–74. New York: University of Rochester Press.

# 12
# AN EMERGENT, CRITICAL REALIST UNDERSTANDING OF HOLISM[1]

Ian Hornsby

In many ways, holism is one of the more opaque terms used within the discourses of both philosophy and psychology. It is a term that incorporates both an opposition to atomism, alongside the notion that particular elements cannot be fully comprehended independently from the universal dimensions of the whole. Any word that can be employed so widely, is probably being used to cover too much, as well as, too little ground. As such, a term like holism ends up lacking any useful philosophical and psychoanalytical basis. This chapter sets out to construct a Critical Realist framework, taken from the early writings of Roy Bhaskar, an alternative philosophical approach to that of Poststructuralism's solipsistic 'linguistic turn' and positivism's 'epistemic fallacy'[2], as a philosophical strategy for investigating holism as the concept appears in selected writings of both Deleuze and Guattari, and C.G. Jung.

This chapter will build upon ideas from Deleuze & Guattari and Manuel DeLanda[3] in using the manufacture of bronze, from the forging together of tin and copper, as a metaphor to observe holism as a form of emergence (see Figure 12.1). This form of emergence, as I define later in the chapter, develops from a reality that is stratified into three ontological domains of the *real*, the *actual* and the *empirical* (Bhaskar, 2008a: 56–62). This form of stratification is important for understanding the connection between emergence and holism, as two related but distinct terms. "Emergence may be defined as the relationship between two terms such that one diachronically, or perhaps synchronically, arises out of the other, but is capable of reacting back on the first and is in any event causally and taxonomically irreducible to it, as a society is to nature or mind to matter." (Bhaskar, 2010: 73) Emergence in this sense is the way in which complex systems ascend out of a multiplicity of relatively simple interactions. In other words, emergence can be taken as a theoretical position in which complex forms can develop out of more simple elements with new properties emerging that cannot be reduced to the sum of their parts.

**FIGURE 12.1** 'Gilles and Carl Lose Themselves.' Artwork created by Ian Hornsby *Emergence and Things in Themselves* 2017.

This conceptual understanding of emergence can be seen in Deleuze's association with Guattari in the manner in which their combined writings point to the emergent properties within art as containing the ability to reterritorialize our relations with the world. 'What defines the territory is the emergence of matters of expression (qualities) … Can this becoming, this emergence, be called art?' (Deleuze & Guattari, 1988: 315–316). A similar use of the term emergence can also be seen in Jung's writings on the formation of the transcendent function, which 'makes the transition from one attitude to another' as the engine of individuation, where a third thing emerges from this process, 'a new attitude', through a dialogue between conscious and unconscious (Jung, 1916/1957: pars. 145–146).

The approach adopted in this Chapter, to borrow a phrase from Jacques Derrida (1995), is *An Oblique Offering*, in that it is not *purely* an analytical elucidation of holism, but rather an indirect response that explores the link between holism and emergence. However, before explaining what Critical Realism is and why I have turned to Bhaskar's thinking to help in the under-labouring[4] for this chapter, I would like to suggest why I have brought the two terms of holism and emergence together, without reducing one to the other. Holism, as defined by the racial segregationist, philosopher, and Field Marshal, Jan Christian Smuts, in his book *Holism and Evolution* from 1926, is the study of the relationship between parts and the whole. For Smuts, holism is "a creative tendency" in natural evolution toward "the development of ever more complex and significant wholes" (1926: 105). These wholes he suggests can be observed in both plants and animals, and as such are the driving force of evolution itself, especially as he implements the term in relation to our understanding of how the human mind works, how the human personality develops, and the way in which these parts connect to how human societies operate as a whole. Holism is then for Smuts, in political and militaristic terms, a challenge to what he sees as scientific reductionism, towards a more holistic science that is capable of capturing the rather obscure notion of what he calls the "spiritual and organic" structures which characterise the entire "Holistic universe" (Smuts, 1926: 345).

Although remaining sceptical of Smuts' often contradictory and controversial political views and actions, as well as the overall direction in which he positioned the concept of holism, the term, I suggest, can be rehabilitated by incorporating the general sense of holism, as the study of the relationship between parts and the whole, alongside critical realist ideas of emergence that appear in the writing of Margret Archer, who claims that "emergent properties are relational: they are not contained in the elements themselves, but could not exist apart from them" (1982: 475). This connection between holism and emergence is also supported by Bhaskar in his 2008 book, *Dialectic: The Pulse of Freedom*, where he writes that: "In emergence, generally, new beings (entities, structures, totalities, concepts) are generated out of pre-existing material from which they could have been neither induced nor deduced" (49).

The connection between holism and emergence can also be seen in the writings of both Jung and Deleuze and Guattari, who touch upon similar ideas of emergence in their work. For Jung, individuation, and the development of the individual personality, emerge from the processes of the transcendent function to form a whole made from the sum of its parts. This process takes place via a form of stratification in which less complex aspects of the personality contrast, conflict, and combine with the more complex parts of the self, where "one's true individuality then emerges from behind the veil of the collective personality, which would be quite impossible in the state of reduction since our instinctual nature is essentially collective" (Jung, 1928: par. 110). The emergence of the self as a form of transcendence towards individuation is for Jung a process whereby various aspects and parts of the personality, from various levels of our conscious and unconscious, are brought into conflict in an alchemical process that drives us towards "the urge to individuation [which] gathers together what is scattered and multifarious, and exalts it to the original form of the One, the Primordial Man" (Jung, 1942/1954: par. 401; see Figures 12.2 and 12.3).

Bhaskar, too, addresses this stratified form of emergence, as the relation of higher level mechanisms which produce more than the sum of their parts; such as the process whereby complex aspects of reality (e.g. mind and life) emerge out of more basic and less complex ones (e.g. matter): "the processes of the formation of higher-order entities are reconstructed and explained in terms of the principles governing the elements out of which they are formed, [and this] is compatible with synchronic emergence, on which the higher-order principles cannot be completely explained in terms of the lower-order ones" (Bhaskar, 2015: 98).

For Deleuze and Guattari ideas of emergence can be seen throughout the second volume of their *Capitalism and Schizophrenia: A Thousand Plateaus* (1980). In section 10, *1730: Becoming-Intense, Becoming-Animal, Becoming-Imperceptible*, Deleuze and Guattari return to the question first addressed in *Anti-Oedipus* (1972) of intensive experimentation which emerges from what is in *A Thousand Plateaus*, discussed in terms of "becoming," in which (at least) two systems come together to form an emergent system or assemblage. "These multiplicities with heterogeneous terms, cofunctioning by contagion, enter certain assemblages; it is there that human beings effect their becomings-animal" (1988: 242). In section 12. *1227: Treatise on Nomadology—The War Machine*, Deleuze and Guattari suggest "We will call an *assemblage* every constellation of singularities and traits deducted from the flow—selected, organised, stratified—in such a way as to converge (consistency) artificially and naturally; an assemblage in this sense, is a veritable invention" (1988: 406). And as we can see from reading much of Deleuze and Guattari's writing together, innovations, invention, creation, the new, the event, and art, all emerge from a stratum of smooth and striated spaces, as an immanent unfolding process of rhizomatic becomings moving towards an assemblage of molecular parts that form molar wholes; all of which are biological and creative processes that uncover the all-important 'something new' that emerges above and beyond the stable equilibrium of what existed previously.

Although Bhaskar's use of the term emergence differs somewhat from Deleuze and Guattari's interchangeable and interconnected use of the terms *becoming, emergence, and assemblage*, in that Bhaskar's use of emergence is a much more secure term (2008a: 213), both of their texts come very close in terms of the stratification of parts to wholes in terms of holism. This can be seen in Bhaskar's key early text from 1975, *A Realist Theory of Science*, where he writes "the operation of the higher level cannot be accounted for solely by the laws governing the lower-order level in which we might say it was 'emergent'" (2008a: 113).

Critical realism as a strategy puts forward the idea that the world exists independently of our thoughts about it, and that the vast majority of reality is mind-independent. Therefore, a major question for critical realists to ask is: "what must the world be like for our science to be possible and for our thoughts about the world to be both practical and meaningful?"[5] In philosophical terms, this question is a form of pragmatism, the approach to thinking about the world that evaluates the success of a set of beliefs in terms of their practical application.

*Plate 2*

**FIGURE 12.2** 'Carl is Served.' Artwork created by Ian Hornsby *Emergence and Things in Themselves* 2017.

Critical realists attempt to apply this pragmatic approach towards questions such as: What must the natural world be like for our scientific experiment to be meaningful? (Bhaskar, 2008a). What must the social world be like for our analysis of social activities and culture to be helpful? (Bhaskar, 2015). What must social structures be like, for our practices to aid human agency and emancipation? (Bhaskar, 2008b).

In addressing these questions this chapter presents critical realism as a form of what I'm calling *pragmatic ontological materialism*, as the best approach to summing up Bhaskar's position in his writings from 1975 to 2008, and as a way of moving beyond the stagnation of much contemporary thinking in terms of poststructuralism and positivism. This process is *pragmatic*, I suggest, in the sense that it's about judging a set of beliefs through practical application. It is a form of *ontology* in that it is a theory concerned with questions about the nature of being and asks what kind of beings populate our world and what kind of entities we are committed to claiming exist in our world. Ontological ideas are concerned with the most basic presuppositions of any philosophy, the things that underpin our ideas and that we take for granted, ideas that we are not going to have to explain over and over again before we can move forward with explaining so many other important things about our world. Everything we say and think is based upon presuppositions, every philosophical idea, every scientific law, every sociological attempt to understand the complex relationships between individuals, every psychoanalytical interpretation of the complex pathologies of each individual, and every practice, all of these are based upon several undefined assumptions that we must take for granted. If you don't have presuppositions you are condemned to wait like *Vladimir and Estragon* and say nothing, repeatedly. This process of basing our larger ideas upon assumptions is better known as *metaphysics* and it is time we reclaimed metaphysics from its place of condemnation in contemporary thinking where it is used as a term of derision. Metaphysics, as an insult, is the one thing that seems to unite continental and analytic philosophers; "Oh, that's just pure metaphysics", they say, as if this 'presupposition' itself were a way of dismissing 'things' out of hand.

The third word in my phrase is a return to the dismissed 'thing,' our material existence, realism or *materialism*[6], the idea that the world has an existence independent from the contents of our minds, that there is a mind-independent reality outside of our consciousness of it. But I want to clarify a couple of things here before moving on. As a realist, if all the human minds in the world vanished overnight, then although cities, communities, works of art, and the buildings that house institutions such as universities and banks would still exist; they would, however, cease to function in the way they do in a world that includes human minds. In this sense, they would not be real in any meaningful sense of the term, because all meaning, as we understand the term as humans, is human. Rather they would be simply physical objects, existing independently of meaning and the contents of the human mind. For materialists, although the world exists independently of our minds, meaning does not, and therefore, communities, institutions, art, and science, do not exist without minds and bodies to create, activate, and interpret them.

Although this does not appear as a huge claim when put in this way, calling yourself a realist today is like calling yourself a metaphysician; it places you outside of the predominant thinking of our era. Therefore, this pragmatic ontological materialist argument as an extension of critical realism suggests that it is ambition enough to be part of a community of thinkers who are underlabouring with a commitment to creating coherent methodologies, via an immanent critique of the presuppositions used, and committed to constructing a practical set of ideas. This process is not about building grand systems, uncovering first principles, or building the foundations upon which to erect a whole set of laws and axioms for our knowledge of the world as it is *in-itself*. Or, and this is perhaps the worst of all, presenting oneself as the '*philosopher genius*' who comes up with these ideas, all by *him*self, and gifts these ideas to the world as if they came out of *his* head fully formed without the rest of the community being in any meaningful way a part of this process.

Obviously, some thinkers present things in a wonderfully new way that enables the rest of us to stand back and say, "I thought exactly that, but could not have put it into such sublime language, or beautiful prose." However, these individuals are not geniuses, rather they are the end point of a process that emerges from the myriad of thoughts being spoken and debated within any community. These ideas are the dialectic thoughts drawn from the social, and intellectual levels of an active society. They are shared ideas that emerge from the *scenius*, to use Brian Eno's term[7], which suggests that scenius is like genius only emerging holistically from cultural scenes as a whole that is greater than the sum of its parts, and not merely in the genes of certain individuals. In this way, the present patriarchal white supremacist and bourgeois world of academia, and philosophy especially, is retarding us from a truly useful and inclusive form of thinking that is pragmatic ontological materialist thinking, with its goals of being meaningful, useful and emancipatory.

Therefore, doing metaphysics with quality today should be concerned with articulating the conditions for the possibility of *practice*; looking at the theory behind *practice*, presupposed by *practice*, and implied within *practice*. This form of ontological realism reduces linguistic confusions while attempting to forge new forms of emancipation that would give us the conditions for the possibility of *practice*.

So, what are the forces holding this process back? Well, one of the most pernicious culprits is *positivism*, the idea that there is no knowledge other than *a posteriori* knowledge and that all *a priori* (presuppositions) are nonsense and merely pure metaphysics. Positivism's claim is that all knowledge must be based on logical deduction and proven through empirical investigation (i.e. sensory experience) which then produce universal laws. This may seem like the very gold standard of science and proof today, but not only is it based upon certain assumptions and presuppositions, but it also creates what critical realists like Bhaskar, term, an *epistemic fallacy*. This is the fallacious idea that statements about being should be eradicated in favour of statements about knowledge (Bhaskar, 2008a: 16). But this would mean that we are addressing the map and not the territory.

The ontological challenge to positivism is that all of its laws and lawlike predictions are actually produced in closed systems like laboratories or in the rooms of economics professors and that these are unreal environments, fixed in time, rather than being in the open systems of change and multiplicity (Bhaskar, 2008a: 117–118). Therefore, positivism and its laws work fine in false situations i.e. they work fine as fixed ideas about how free market systems work as models, how physics works as laws, and how philosophies work as maps, so long as they are kept in the hermetically sealed world of the laboratory. But if these laws, models, and maps are used in the world, they implode. And today these laws, models, and maps have become more real than the open systems that they are meant to interact with and represent. The map, the law, the model, have become our real; and this is not just the hyperreal in Baudrillard's use of the term (Baudrillard, 1994: 6)[8] but is in actuality, when you think about it, completely illogical (Bhaskar, 2008a: 127–142).

Critical realism avoids these problems by suggesting that research is not about maps, models, and laws but about exploring the powers, structures, and mechanisms, which under certain conditions provide temporary pragmatic methods and results. In this way, we ask what the world must be like for our understanding of it to be possible and meaningful. To do this Bhaskar identifies the stratification of three overlapping levels or ontological domains: There is *the real*, which is the level of 'generative mechanisms': causes, powers, and structures that produce the events we experience. It is very rare for us to know *the real*, to understand the generative mechanisms that structure our world. But we begin by assuming that they are there because the world exists independently of our minds. The next level is *the actual*, the events, things, products; the very basis of our experience and the symptoms through which we analyse the real. And the final level is *the empirical*, our experience, observations and measurements of these events. Through sensory experience, we explore the symptoms of the actual world to make predictions about the *real* (Bhaskar, 2008a: 56–62).

These ideas are perhaps best illustrated in the ideas of assemblages that emerge from the event of making 'bronze'; a wonderful chemical example of holism in that it is an alloy made from the combination of tin and copper[9]. Tin has a tensile strength of 22 megapascals (MPa), Copper 24 MPa, which should if combined together add up to 46 megapascals of tensile strength, whereas bronze has a tensile strength of 59MPa, much more than the sum of its parts[10]. Those extra 13 MPa emerge from the new properties in the structure of tin and copper combined. As I illustrate in the comic book this process also contains another holistic assemblage with emergent qualities, i.e. the combination of oxygen and hydrogen atoms to form the water molecule $H_2O$, which has very different properties from each element taken separately[11].

Assemblages are not only holistic in terms of chemical processes, they can also be holistic in regard to social activities, in the way that assemblages have the ability to move from one level of existence to another, that is, from inorganic to

**FIGURE 12.3** 'Mic Drop.' Artwork created by Ian Hornsby *Emergence and Things in Themselves* 2017.

biological, from biological to the social, and from the social to the intellectual. And it must be remembered that as these assemblages go upwards they gain emergent properties which means you can't move downward without losing certain properties. Therefore, entropy happens when you move down the levels and holism when you move up.

Emergent properties also have the ability to block reductionism: molecules cannot be reduced to atoms, cells cannot be reduced to molecules, organs cannot be reduced to cells, organisms cannot be reduced to organs; and intelligence cannot be reduced to a single organism, namely, the male genius; because at every level new properties emerge that create a whole greater than the sum of its individual parts.

However, it is important to keep in mind that Bronze is simply an alloy and is only greater than the sum of its parts when understood in materialist terms as being part of our understanding of the world. Bronze is only ever as 'good' as the intentions of its user; outside of this, it's simply an object.

## Notes

1 This chapter includes three black and white plates taken from the comic book I created for the *Holism: Possibilities and Problems* conference held at the University of Essex in the autumn of 2017. The comic was designed to elucidate particular ideas relating to the texts of Critical Realist philosopher Roy Bhaskar, on the theme of emergence as it relates to our holistic comprehension of "what the world must be like for our understanding of it to make sense" (2008a: 23). The form of the comic book was important because of the inherent aspects of holism in the construction and comprehension of works of sequential art. By bringing together its separate elements, such as images, word bubbles, panels and boarders, the comic book emerges as a whole that is greater than the sum of its parts.
2 Bhaskar writes: "Empirical realism is underpinned by a metaphysical dogma, which I call the epistemic fallacy, that statements about being can be transposed into statements about our knowledge of being. As ontology cannot, it is argued, be reduced to epistemology..." (1975/2008a: 16).
3 Deleuze and Guattari (1980/1988) address the issues of creating bronze in 'A Thousand Plateaus' in §12 *1227: Treatise on Nomadology–The War Machine*: 399-404 and Manuel DeLanda addresses the "assemblage formed by copper and tin when they interact to form an alloy, bronze, with its own emergent properties and capacities' (2010: 72).
4 Underlabouring is an idea Bhaskar takes from the writing of British empiricist philosopher John Locke in which he indicates that it is ambition enough for each thinker to clear a little the ground in a process that can slowly uncover knowledge about the world. "Under-labourer – for how else is one to construe his activity, save as an attempt to remove 'some of the rubbish that lies in the way to (social) knowledge'? 'Epistle to the Reader', *Essays Concerning Human Understanding* (New York 1959): 14. (See Bhaskar, 1979/2015: 151).
5 Bhaskar writes: "The Answer to the transcendental question 'what must the world be like for science to be possible?' deserves the name ontology" (1975/2008a: 23). I have added to this line to incorporate ideas presented the following five titles Bhaskar wrote between 1978 and 2008 including texts such as *The Possibility of Naturalism* (1979) *Reclaiming Reality* (1989) *Plato Etc.* (1994) and *Dialectics: The Pulse of Freedom* (2008).
6 I realise that I am using the two terms, materialism and realism, as though they were interchangeable here, even though they are very different terms. However, my point is that all materialists must also be realists and therefore the two terms in this current use are very closely related.
7 "Scenius is like genius, only embedded in a scene rather than in genes. Brian Eno suggested the word to convey the extreme creativity that groups, places or "scenes" can occasionally generate. His actual definition is: "Scenius stands for the intelligence and the intuition of a whole cultural scene. It is the communal form of the concept

of the genius." (website accessed 29/03/18 https://www.wired.com/2008/06/sceni us-or-comm/)
8 See Baudrillard, 'Simulacra and Simulation' (1994).
9 Which can be seen in pages 5 to 8 of my comic book http://ihornsby.co.uk/eme rgence-comic-paper
10 Data taken from the *Journal of Materials* Volume 2013 (2013), Article ID 352578, 6 pages http://dx.doi.org/10.1155/2013/352578 Research Article *On the Prediction of Strength from Hardness for Copper Alloys* S. Chenna Krishna, Narendra Kumar Gangwar, Abhay K. Jha, and Bhanu Pant.
11 Although I acknowledge the points made by John Protevi in his informative article *Deleuze, Guattari and Emergence* in *Paragraph: A Journal of Modern Critical Theory*, 29.2 (July 2006): 19–39; "…that quantum mechanics has shown ways to explain water's properties on the basis of the properties of hydrogen and oxygen. (Schröder, 2000; Sawyer, 2001: 560)." I still suggest that on a molecular level the combination of oxygen and hydrogen produce a very different material from the elements taken separately.

## References

Archer, M. 1982 'Morphogenesis versus Structuration: On Combining Structure and Action', *British Journal of Sociology* 33(4): 455–483.
Baudrillard, J. 1994 *Simulacra and Simulation* Translated by Shelia Glaser, Michigan: University of Michigan Press.
Bhaskar, R. [1975] 2008a *A Realist Theory of Science* (Third Edition), London: Verso.
Bhaskar, R. [1979] 2015 *The Possibility of Naturalism: A Philosophical Critique of the Contemporary* Human Sciences (Fourth Edition), London: Routledge.
Bhaskar, R. [1994] 2010 *Plato Etc. The Problems of Philosophy and their Resolution* (Second Edition), London: Routledge.
Bhaskar, R. 2008b *Dialectics: The Pulse of Freedom*, London: Routledge.
DeLanda, M. 2010 *Deleuze: History and Science*, New York: Atropos Press.
Deleuze, G. & Guattari, F. [1972] 1984 *Anti-Oedipus: Capitalism and Schizophrenia Volume 1* Translated by Robert Hurley, Mark Seem, and Helen R. Lane, London: Athlone Press.
Deleuze, G. & Guattari, F. [1980] 1988 *A Thousand Plateaus: Capitalism and Schizophrenia Volume 2* Translated by Brian Massumi, London: Athlone Press.
Derrida, J. [1993] 1995 *On The Name* Translated by David Wood, John P. Leavey, JR., and Ian McLeod, Stanford: Stanford University Press.
Jung, C.G. [1916/1957] 1969 'The Transcendent Function', in *Collected Works* vol. 8, *The Structure and Dynamics of the Psyche*, 2nd ed, London: Routledge and Kegan Paul.
Jung, C.G. [1928] 1969 'On Psychic Energy', in *Collected Works* vol. 8, *The Structure and Dynamics of the Psyche*, 2nd edn, London: Routledge and Kegan Paul.
Jung, C.G. [1942/1954] 1969 'Transformation Symbolism in the Mass', in *Collected Works*, vol. 11, *Psychology of Religion: West and East*, 2nd edn, London: Routledge and Kegan Paul.
Smuts, J. C. [1926] *Holism and Evolution*, New York: MacMillan.
Sawyer, R. Keith (2001). 'Emergence in Sociology: Contemporary Philosophy of Mind and Some Implications for Sociological Theory,' *American Journal of Sociology* 107(3), 551–585.
Schröder, Jürgen (2000). 'Emergence: Non-Deducibility or Downwards Causation?' *The Philosophical Quarterly* 48(193), 433–452.

# 13

# SYNCHRONICITY: BETWEEN WHOLES AND ALTERITY

*Rico Sneller*

## Introduction

In this chapter I would like to explore the viability of thinking wholes without excluding alterity. It seems that 20th-century philosophy, from Heidegger and Levinas onwards, in a critique of the Western tradition exhaustively unmasked any attempt to totalise while thinking. However, this critique may have unnecessarily rejected *experience*. Yet, what cannot be thought or articulated can perhaps still be experienced.

It is my hypothesis that the notions of 'synchronicity' and 'image thinking' could bring a solution to the apparently mutual exclusion of 'whole' and 'alterity'. I will argue that a re-conception of (1) nature, (2) consciousness and (3) language is requisite here. Nature needs to be reinterpreted as *psychoid*, such as to mitigate the strict boundaries between it and consciousness. Consciousness should be seen as endowed with a 'slider' that oscillates between alternate states of mind. And language should similarly be seen as a multifaceted reality rather than as a useful yet one-dimensional instrument. Synchronicity experiences, so I would argue, are not only those *eliciting* the said re-conception of nature, consciousness and language; they are also those that are likely to *produce* themselves once this re-conception has taken place. In order to articulate them, we may have to resort to images rather than to concepts.

Thinkers on whom I will be drawing in this chapter, whether implicitly or explicitly, are the Japanese philosopher Yasuo Yuasa (1925–2005), the philosopher-spiritualist Carl du Prel (1833–1899), the philosopher of life and thinker of ecstasy Ludwig Klages (1872–1956), the panpsychical philosopher Gustav Fechner (1801–1887) and the psychiatrist C.G. Jung (1875–1961).

## Main question

The main question I would like to discuss here is, do 'wholes' exclude alterity, otherness, and transcendence? Would not being part of any whole be suffocating for its constituents? And, if wholes are conceived of as being *cosmic* in nature, would not such a cosmic whole simply be an extrapolation of a totalitarian state, inasmuch as the 'dictator' has been simply substituted here by an 'ultimately governing or determining principle'?

That this question cannot be neglected appears from the philosophies of, for example, Heidegger (who criticised the entire metaphysical tradition of Western thinking as a forgetfulness of Being), or Levinas (who similarly qualified Western thinking as totalising and as being oblivious of the other). My point, however, is that these critiques, different though their respective framings be, primarily apply to *thinking*. To *think* a whole comes down to a subsumption of each particular being under a common, abstract denominator, which is *thought* or *conceived* (whether it is called Being, Spirit, omnipotent God, or Laws of nature). I would argue that the *experience* of wholes is not necessarily totalitarian, to the extent that experience excludes exhaustion and thrives on alterity.

## Synchronicity and image-thinking

In order to articulate holistic experience (as opposed to holistic thinking), it will be helpful to resort to two notions, 1) synchronicity experiences and 2) image 'thinking'. If at all, these notions could possibly make 'wholes' and 'alterity' compatible. Without alterity, wholes will be at risk of representing a purely totalitarian structure that undercuts the very whole it attempts to render. However, neither synchronicity experiences nor image thinking seem to be obvious notions. Instead of synchronicity, causality largely dominates thinking; most particularly in what is called 'science' today, but implicitly also in our daily lives. And instead of image thinking, conceptual thinking prevails. Therefore, the notions of synchronicity and image thinking, indispensable tools in making wholes and alterity compatible, can only catch on if at least three conditions are met. First, a re-conception of 'nature' becomes necessary. Second, 'consciousness' needs to be deprived of its apparent univocity. Third, the phenomenon of 'language' should be reinterpreted.

### *1. Nature*

What is 'nature'? Before attempting to answer this question using some philosophical definition $X = Y$, we should be clear that the very form of the question misleadingly appeals to a stable, unequivocal entity. 'Nature' as a concept confusingly implies an unambiguous, univocal referent, a 'thing' or an 'object' *reflecting* our 'concept'. Evidently, a refined idea of language itself and a more subtle interpretation of linguistic referentiality may mitigate language's hypostasising tendencies. But I fear that the so-called 'speech act theory'—which aims at widening our understanding of how language works—is not powerful enough in rescinding those tendencies.

This linguistic fallacy conceals another one, which I propose to call 'ontic'. The latter consists of attributing an object-character to phenomena. Turned into an *object*, phenomena erroneously imply accomplishment, delimitation, definition, or at least definability. Consequently, they are exempt from change, albeit for thinking. Objects may not even exist outside thinking, and yet, object-character is imposed upon the phenomenal world.

I would go one step further. To the extent that self-transcendence—which I take to be the opposite of objectivity—seems to be a viable if minimalistic description of *consciousness*, I would even attribute consciousness to phenomena, or to nature at large. Rather than crossing the boundaries of what can be known, such an attribution respects nature as irreducibly self-transcending. For, we do not really know what consciousness is, nor can we define it.

The idea of ascribing consciousness to nature, even beyond the minimalistic sense intended above, has a long-standing philosophical tradition, from Plotinus, Spinoza, and Hegel, to Fechner and Klages. Materialism consists of the suppression of this idea. However, as long as a satisfactory and exhaustive conception of 'matter' is lacking, rejecting consciousness in nature is as pointless as it is premature.

## 2. Consciousness

The second notion to be reconsidered is 'consciousness'. A univocal conception of consciousness, i.e. one in which consciousness *coincides* with its immediate awareness, can only account for unilinear causality. This 'flat' conception of consciousness is shared both by classical empiricism and Enlightenment rationalism. To the extent that empiricism and rationalism reduced consciousness to immediate self-awareness, they elicited German Idealism, and ultimately even the *explicit* notion of an Unconscious—as defended by the Schopenhauerian tradition, from Eduard von Hartmann and Carl du Prel to Freud and beyond.

Doing justice to consciousness, so I would argue, entails as a minimum requirement that it not be reduced to non-conscious elements (i.e., 'brain activity'), albeit that the latter may well create the former's constituents. Instead, consciousness is best approached from within, since, as opposed to anything else, it *consists* of self-access (even if this self-access entails an irreducible detour over the phenomenal world—as, for example, Derrida affirms).

These succinct preliminary remarks cannot exhaust the extremely complex issue of consciousness. It seems to me, though, that any account of consciousness cannot dispense with notions of 'self' (even if the self is believed to be non-existent, as in the Buddhist tradition) and 'mirror'. Above, I suggested that consciousness should be seen as self-transcendence. Now, I would add that 'self' or 'selfhood' is that which is *produced* in the act of self-transcendence (*albeit* as an illusion). 'Mirroring', then, could be a description of the nature of this act. I am partly drawing here on Ludwig Klages, who in his main book *Der Geist als Widersacher der Seele* (1929–1932) qualifies consciousness in a similar vein (*Bewusstsein als Spiegelung*, 'consciousness as mirroring').[1] The more current word 'reflection' is synonymous to 'mirroring'; yet, it has a stronger intellectualist connotation, which makes it perhaps less adequate for a fuller account of consciousness.

In what way is a re-conception of consciousness necessary for synchronicity experience and image thinking? How does it enhance susceptibility to the latter, and thereby make totality or wholeness compatible with alterity?

Provided that consciousness is not self-coincident but always self-transcending it seems possible (though *not* inevitable) to assume that this self-transcendence is multifocal and versatile. As a rule, and also according to Husserlian phenomenology, the self-transcendence of consciousness is extensive, that is, intentionally directed at present, past or future. One could equally say that this extensive intentionality creates *time* and *space*, as it temporalises and spatialises. However, nothing forbids that the self-transcendence of consciousness be intensive as well—that is, that it penetrate its own temporalisation and spatialisation.

Such a theoretical possibility, which stated thus is still too abstract to make sense, may well be confirmed by experience. In an attempt to account for *altered* states of mind, the almost forgotten 19th-century German philosopher Carl du Prel conceives of consciousness as endowed with a 'slider'. This slider (*Empfindungsschwelle*, 'threshold of experience') supposedly oscillates between distinct and yet *simultaneous* states of mind. Possible examples are phenomena of telepathy, ecstasy, intuition, clairvoyance, dreaming, insanity/psychosis, eroticism, and the like.

Most often, an emphasis is put on an 'average' mind-set, which is in itself *already* hard to define, and which moreover may be liable to normalisation procedures. However, other, exceptional mind-sets occur which are perhaps not at our free disposal but which are just as significant to those that have them, if not more.

I want to argue that altered states of mind, in virtue of their *intensive* self-transcendence, are neither governed by linear temporalisation nor by concordant spatialisation. This could be verified by numerous examples, some of which have been significantly analysed in the works of William James (*Varieties of Religious Experience*), Carl du Prel (*Philosophie der Mystik*), Freud, Jung (case studies), and others.[2]

## 3. Language

A third notion in need of being revised is 'language'. Language should perhaps rather be seen as a multifaceted *reality* than as a useful yet one-dimensional *instrument*. The latter conception usually prevails in accounts based on Wittgenstein's *Tractatus logico-philosophicus*.

First, it should be noted that *prior* to its being used as a tool language establishes communication between a 'subject' and an 'object'. Language may even be said to precede the hierarchies and patterns it establishes. Stating this approximates having a 'mystical' conception of language and reality. We find such a conception not only in medieval traditions (Kabbalah, Sufism), but also in J.G. Hamann, Walter Benjamin, and Heidegger. Benjamin, for example, argues that the essence of language is communication, and that communication takes place both in a soniferous and a non-soniferous way.[3] Language, in Benjamin, is another word for the divine spirit that communicates itself in creation and in which humans can in principle have a share. Corroborating Benjamin's view may not be an easy task; rather than doing an 'experiment' to 'test' it, what is required here is submitting oneself to *experiencing* language. Poets or philosophers could possibly testify to such an experience, though they are not likely to convince those whose scientific credentials rely on an initial blocking of linguistic experience.

Secondly, drawing upon the previous insight, one could say that words and sounds, prior to being *chosen* or *selected* by human subjects, always already *respond* to antecedent experiences of phenomena, always already *convey* experiences of previous generations, and also *reverberate* meanings that cannot be kept in control. Words, names, nouns, verbs, and so on are no self-identical units that can be moulded at will. Our transmission or 'tra-dition' of them both enhances their 'traditional' resonance and renews it. Language inevitably moves between past determinations and continuous renewal. Paradoxically, in its incipience it is response.

Finally, it should be emphasized that language, especially 'scientific' language, can become *occluded* by the introduction and imposition of concepts that tacitly *presuppose* a worldview impoverished by 'empirical science's' power claims; what is called 'literature' or 'poetry' may testify to an awareness that our average language is *obnubilated*. Examples of concepts that rely on an impoverished worldview are 'evidence', 'experiment', 'natural law', 'test', 'scientific', 'argument', 'principle', 'sense data', 'sample', 'content', 'certainty', 'observation', and 'theory'. Without suggesting that the origin of a word is ever sacrosanct, it can be safely assumed that, in the course of their history, the aforementioned concepts underwent a considerable connotative reduction.[4]

## Synchronicity and image thinking

In this chapter I want to make a case for compatibility of wholes and alterity when mediated by synchronicity experiences and image thinking. The latter can become comprehensible once the notions of 'nature', 'consciousness', and 'language' are enlarged.

It is my contention that synchronicity experiences not only *elicit* a re-conception of nature, consciousness and language (in order to make sense of them), but also are likely to *produce* themselves in *virtue* of this re-conception. For substantiation of this hypothesis one may seek in the confirmed experience of those who are already drawing on an enlarged notion of nature/Being, consciousness, and language: artists, literary authors, poets, and philosophers. Regarding artists, this does not seem to be a bold claim. Especially in poetry, the meaningful coincidence of rhythm, rhyme, sound, and/or scripture, seems to be the very embodiment of synchronicity. In literary language, Being and language conflate.

A philosopher whose work is rife with synchronicity experiences is Jacques Derrida. Many of his textual analyses are in themselves endeavours in digging up the most remarkable synchronicities. As appears from the more 'autobiographical' introductions to his later texts, his personal vicissitudes are not foreign to synchronicity experiences, either.[5] Obviously, this is not to say that similar conceptions of 'consciousness' or 'nature' are defended whenever openness to synchronicities can be detected. Nor does this entail that the occurrence of synchronicity experiences is accompanied by an *explicit* reflection on them.

In order to express synchronicity experiences, *conceptual* language may be unfit. Such language rests on the same presuppositions that suggest the arbitrariness of those experiences. In the Aristotelian tradition of Western philosophy, concepts are seen as abstractions from particulars, allowing one to expand one's intellectual grasp of them. The coincidence of the particular with the eternal Form it embodies is but *a* coincidence.

Instead, we may rather have to resort to 'images', that is, constellations of singulars that are experienced as mutually coherent and corresponding. Thereby, they are intrinsically significant. Images meaningfully connect particulars and invite our intellect to embrace rather than to conceive them. It is my claim that original philosophical or artistic insights, ideas, or views are such 'images', that is, primordial, 'synchronistic' patterns immediately 'perceived' and not immediately explainable in conceptual language. Deleuze and Guattari also defend this view, even though they define philosophy as the science of concepts. However, their conception of 'concepts' greatly differs from the prevailing 'intellectualist' one.[6]

## Conclusion

Rather than 'thinking' wholes we had better 'imagine' or 'intuit', if not *experience*, them. The synchronicity experiences introducing them, however 'coincidental' to the logic of what is called 'science' today, invite us to see them as images rather than as a temporal sequence (in the form of a *sub*sequence, let alone of a *con*sequence). Such images remain incomprehensible to an intellect that proceeds by making abstraction from particulars, and is even identified with this capability. Obviously, it would be inane to deny science the right of making abstraction, even more so as many beneficial technological improvements rely on them. However, science should be denied the right to usurp thinking and to promote a worldview. Scientific worldviews tend to be suffocating, if not in their explicit aim (it hardly ever is), at least in their implicit procedure of generalising. Paradoxically, empirical science has no access to experience. It can only conceive of it in the form of manipulable experience, that is, in the form of testing. What counts as 'evidence' is only controllable experience. Whereas this seems 'evident' to many scientists, what is overlooked is the power drive behind it.

It remains highly doubtful if Neo-Kantian attempts to reconceive of scientific laws as 'hypotheses' or as infinite 'approximations', however sympathetic, truly solve the issue. They also tacitly assume the priority of the general over the particular.[7]

It is equally uncertain if Husserlian phenomenology can meet the demands of a satisfactory approach to Being. Its complete refusal to be metaphysical and totalising may seem sympathetic, but it throws out the baby with the bathwater. To the extent that it neither puts into question the *primacy* of the subject of intentionality nor considers its *abysmal* nature, it cannot rethink wholeness, not even in the moderate form, proposed in this chapter, of an experienced whole that thrives on synchronicity experiences.

Experienced wholes need not be suffocating; they leave room for *incessant extension* and *always increasing* circles of perception and awareness. We can perhaps compare this to a stone thrown into the water, or to a pastor circulating his flock through the fields searching for grass. Or, to give a psychological example, it could also be compared to the Platonic notion of Eros, especially as taken up by Freud. Eros, Freud argues, comes down to a desire to adhere to, and unite with, an always-bigger whole. The least we can say is that such a whole is not identical to an intelligised or a comprehended whole. It can only be an experienced whole, that invites the lover to see, hear, smell, or even touch, their beloved everywhere.

The following passage from the *Song of Songs* can be read as a testimony (not a 'test') to this Erotic experience. More than the English translation can show, the verses abound with references to 'herding' (*ra'a*), or 'herd' (*ro'ê*). Perhaps the experience of 'herding' or 'grazing one's flock' can be an adequate substitute for the reductionist power claims of generalising science.

> Tell me, you whom I love,
> where you graze your flock
> and where you rest your sheep at midday.
> Why should I be like a veiled woman ('*oteya*)[8]
> beside the flocks of your friends?
>
> – If you do not know, most beautiful of women,
> follow (*tse'i*) the tracks of the sheep (*tso'n*)
> and graze your young goats
> by the tents of the shepherds.
>
> (*Song of Songs I, 7–8; NIV*)

## Notes

1 Ludwig Klages, *Der Geist als Widersacher der Seele*, 3. Buch 2. Abschnitt ‚Vom spiegelnden Schauen', Bonn, Bouvier Verlag, 1981.

2 Also cf. recent studies as Edward F. Kelly et al. (eds.), *Irreducible Mind. Toward a Psychology for the 21$^{st}$ Century*, New York: Rowman & Littlefield Publishers, 2010; Imants Barušs & Julia Mossbridge, *Transcendent Mind. Rethinking the Science of Consciousness*, Washington: American Psychological Association, 2017; Etzel Cardeña, Steven Jay Lynn, and Stanley Krippner (eds.), *Varieties of Anomalous Experience: Examining the Scientific Evidence* (2$^{nd}$ ed.), Washington, DC: American Psychological Association 2014 (2004).
3 Cf. Walter Benjamin, 'Über Sprache überhaupt und über die Sprache des Menschen', in: *Gesammelte Schriften*, vol. II-1, Suhrkamp: Frankfurt a.M. 1991.
4 Among many philosophical texts which might support my claim, see e.g. H.-G. Gadamer, *Wahrheit und Methode. Grundzüge einer philosophischen Hermeneutik*, J.C.B. Mohr (Siebeck): Tübingen, 1990 (1960), III.3 'Sprache als Horizont einer hermeneutischen Ontologie'.
5 To limit myself to only one example, see the introduction to 'Comment ne pas parler. Dénégations', in: *Psyché. Inventions de l'autre*, Paris: Galilée, 1987, 547f. n.1. Also see Hein van Dongen, Hans Gerding and Rico Sneller, *Wild Beasts of the Philosophical Desert. Philosophers on Telepathy and Other Exceptional Experiences*, Newcastle upon Tyne: Cambridge Publishing, 2014, Ch. 8 'Derrida and Telepathy'.
6 Cf. Deleuze/Guattari, *Qu'est-ce que la philosophie?*, Paris: Minuit 1991. Also cf. Yuasa Yasuo, *Overcoming Modernity: Synchronicity and Image-Thinking*, Albany: SUNY 2009.
7 Cf. e.g. Hermann Cohen's 1902, *Logik der reinen Erkenntnis*, Berlin: B. Cassirer; Paul Natorp, 1903 *Platons Ideenlehre: Eine Einführung in den Idealismus*, Leipzig: Dürr'sche Buchhandlung.
8 Hebr. *'oteya*; Buber/Rosenzweig translate *eine Schmachtende*, 'a yearning, languishing one'.

# 14

## WHY DON'T HOLISMS DESCRIBE THE WHOLE? THE PSYCHE AS A CASE STUDY

*J. Linn Mackey*

Three perspectives will be presented which indicate that holisms never describe the whole. These perspectives are those of John Macmurray, Georg Henrik von Wright, and dual-aspect monism proposed by Carl Jung and Wolfgang Pauli. The human psyche as approached by complexity theory and by Carl Jung will be used as a specific case study. It will be helpful to have a definition of holism. A useful definition of holism is "the theory that whole entities as fundamental components of reality have an existence other than as the mere sum of their parts."[1]

### John Macmurray

John Macmurray (1891–1976) was a Scottish philosopher and professor at the University of London and later at Edinburgh University. Macmurray's *Interpreting the Universe*[2] can be read as a discourse on holism and the whole. Although the word holism does not appear in *Interpreting the Universe*, it is implicit in Macmurray's discussion of organisms and elsewhere in the book. "We must represent the unity of what is alive as a unity of differences, not as a unity of identities. It follows that the organic whole cannot be represented as the sum of its parts. You cannot sum differences,"[3] and "no element in an organic whole can be really individual. Only the whole can possess true individuality."[4]

Macmurray carefully builds a case from a base of immediate experience that three unique "sciences" exist. He calls them *unity patterns* and they apply to different areas of human experience. By unity pattern he means "a formal conception of the way in which the different symbols can be united to constitute a whole."[5] They are mathematical and mechanistic, the biological and organisms, and the psychological and personhood.[6] The unity pattern of one area of experience can have some limited applicability to another area of experience. Thus, organisms are composed of matter and the mathematical mechanistic unity pattern is applicable to the material aspects of organisms. However, Macmurray says this unity pattern is not applicable to new kinds of characteristics of organisms that are properties of their holism like growth, development, and differentiation. These things point not to the present but to a future only revealed when achieved, thus to teleology. This is an aspect not present in the mathematical mechanical unity pattern according to him. "It is these characteristics of things which must be represented in the unity pattern which reflection uses for the understanding of life, and they are such that none of them can be represented by the mechanical unity pattern of mathematical thought."[7] Likewise persons are material and also organisms so that the mathematical and mechanistic and biological and organism unity patterns will be applicable to those aspects of persons. However, characteristics of persons cannot be addressed by these unity patterns. Macmurray's discussion of the uniqueness of persons and why a third unity pattern is needed is detailed and complex. A major issue is that with the previous areas we stand outside what we are experiencing. This is not true of persons. We ourselves are implicated. "We know persons, in fact, only by entering into personal relationship with them as equals."[8] Thus a third unity pattern is needed.

Macmurray argues in *Interpreting the Universe* that mathematical and mechanistic science is only capable of seeing the whole as the sum of the parts.[9] In his view this unity pattern is incapable of accounting for organisms or any holism. The biological and psychological unity patterns embody holisms. *Interpreting the Universe* was published in 1933 before the developments of fractals,[10] nonlinear dynamics, and chaos and complexity theories.[11] These mathematical developments embody self-organization and emergence and thus yield holisms. As Waldrop says they show "a disconcerting fact: *the whole can be greater than the sum of its parts* (my emphasis)."[12] So Macmurray has been proven wrong when he stated that mathematical science is only capable of seeing the whole as the sum of its parts. The new mathematics is capable of modeling holisms and is applicable to biology and organisms. Fractals and nonlinear dynamics reveal a new kind of holism, the pattern of the whole is present in the parts. "Whereas in linear systems we detect the whole additively as the sum of the parts, in chaotic systems we detect the whole nonreductively within the parts themselves."[13] To summarize Macmurray on holism and the whole, three distinct unity patterns are needed to account for immediate experience. In the case of a person all of these are necessary for the whole.

## Holism, teleology, and emergence

Holism, teleology and emergence are related. Macmurray writes,

> to understand a process of development, it is necessary to know its final state, or at least its state of complete development. ... The conception of teleology is merely a way of describing natural processes of growth.[14]

This means that Macmurray's second unity pattern, biological thought and organisms, requires a final state that is unknowable until achieved. It *emerges*. Emergence is a term that has come into common use since Macmurray wrote. It is used to describe states unpredictable before they are achieved. It points to the unpredictability we find in teleology. And why are teleology and emergence unpredictable before they are achieved? It is because they describe whole entities as components of reality that have existence beyond the sum of their parts. They are holisms.

## Georg Henrik von Wright

Georg Henrik von Wright (1916–2003) was a Finnish-born philosopher who succeeded Ludwig Wittgenstein as professor at the University of Cambridge. In *Explanation and Understanding*[15] he reached conclusions similar to John Macmurray's. Rather than the three sciences or unity patterns proposed by Macmurray, von Wright proposes only two. He does not propose a separate biological and organism science like Macmurray. His two sciences roughly correspond to Macmurray's mathematical mechanistic and psychological and personhood unity patterns. Von Wright did not reference Macmurray's earlier work; he apparently was unaware of it.

Von Wright considers two main traditions in the history of ideas that he calls Aristotelian and Galilean.

> Two main traditions can be distinguished in the history of ideas, differing as to the conditions an explanation has to satisfy in order to be scientifically respectable … The contrast between the two traditions is usually characterized as causal *versus* teleological explanation. The first type of explanation is also called mechanistic, the second finalistic.[16]

The Galilean tradition came to its full flowering with the scientific revolution of the 16th and 17th century. It comes down to today as positivism whose tenets are methodological monism or the unity of method across the subject matter studied, the view that the exact natural sciences, like physics, set a methodological standard for all other sciences. Scientific explanation is causal, and rejects final cause as an explanation, i.e. any attempts to account for facts in terms of intentions, goals, and purposes.[17]

The second tradition goes back to Aristotle's idea of a final cause. This tradition underwent what von Wright calls a "great awakening or revolution in the 19th century in the systematic study of humans, their history, languages, mores and social institutions."[18] Von Wright identifies this second revolution in the human sciences as hermeneutics. Two features of the contemporary version of the second tradition are, first, emphasis on language-oriented notions such as meaning, interpretation and understanding and second, an opposition to positivism's idea of the unity of scientific method.[19]

Von Wright's conclusion is that there is irreconcilable opposition between the two traditions.

> There is also basic opposition, removed from the possibility both of reconciliation and refutation even, in a sense removed from truth. It is built into the choice of primitives, of basic concepts for the whole argumentation. This choice, one could say, is 'existential.' It is a choice of a point of view which cannot be further grounded.[20]

Von Wright's conclusion would mean that, although each tradition could address the same phenomenon, their accounts would differ leaving open the possibility that even if each account was a holism it inadequately or incompletely described the whole.

## Dual-aspect monism

The third perspective is dual-aspect monism. We see this perspective in the collaborative efforts of Carl Jung and Wolfgang Pauli. Carl Jung (1875–1961) was a Swiss psychologist who early on collaborated with Sigmund Freud but broke with him and founded his own approach that he called analytic psychology. Wolfgang Pauli (1900–1958) was a Nobel Prize winner and one of the most influential 20th-century physicists. He and Jung had a 26-year interaction and collaboration.[21] One of the fruits of this collaboration was a perspective that Harald Atmanspacher calls dual-aspect monism. This draws on a close analogy to quantum physics that Pauli played a key role in founding. To describe entities like electrons, quantum physics must use the complementary descriptions of waves and particles to fully describe the whole.[22] "Two descriptions are complementary if they mutually exclude each other, yet are both necessary to describe a situation exhaustively."[23] To describe the whole of reality in dual-aspect monism requires the incompatible but complementary aspects of matter and psyche. This is similar to Macmurray's perspective of the need for two incompatible unity patterns to describe the material and personhood aspects of humans. In dual-aspect monism the matter aspect would be elucidated by von Wright's Galilean science while the psyche aspect would be elucidated by von Wright's Aristotelian science or Macmurray's psychological and personhood unity pattern.

## Comparisons

The three perspectives that have been considered will be compared. All three perspectives imply that holisms do not describe the whole. Dual-aspect monism is a metaphysical conjecture. It considers only matter and psyche. It does not address Macmurray's domain of biology and organism. Matter would seem to be limited to Macmurray's domain of mathematical and mechanism.

This perspective would not address the domain of the biological and organism with its teleological aspects that the other two perspectives consider.

Macmurray's perspective is philosophically grounded and carefully nuanced. He proposes three different areas of experience each with its respective unity pattern. For him the whole would incorporate at least all three of the unity patterns. Von Wright takes a historical approach and traces the development of two approaches or traditions, the Aristotelian and Galilean. Both Macmurray's philosophical approach and von Wright's historical approach are useful, reach similar conclusions, and can be viewed as complementary. Although von Wright does not set out as explicitly the three areas that Macmurray calls mathematical and mechanism, biological and organism, and psychological and personhood, they do clearly emerge in his discussion of teleology.[24]

Since dual-aspect monism seems to lack the realm of biology and organism the issue of teleology is not directly addressed. However, as the remainder of this paper makes clear, Jung clearly attributed teleology to the psyche that would be a part of Macmurray's domain of psychology and personhood.

## Two approaches to the psyche

These general perspectives on holism and the whole can clarify issues regarding approaches to the human psyche. Consider two approaches to the human psyche, Jung's approach and complexity theory. It has been suggested that these approaches can be conflated.[25] Complexity theory and Jung's view of the psyche are system approaches that share some commonalities. Jung viewed the psyche as a whole made up of relatively independent but interacting parts such as persona, ego, anima, animus, and shadow. Both views of the psyche are dynamic systems of interacting subprocesses. Jung viewed the psyche in its development as a dynamic system. He likened it to the alchemical process, moving from base metal to gold. Another commonality is that both complexity theory and Jung's view of the psyche exhibit self-organization and emergent behavior. Jung called this individuation, which is clearly teleological. As discussed above in the section "Holism, Teleology and Emergence," this means both complexity theory and Jung viewed the psyche holistically. Jung called the self-organizing aspect of the psyche the Self.

Complexity theory is a recent attempt to model complex adaptive systems.[26] West defines a complex adaptive system (CAS) this way: "Closely related to the concepts of emergence and self-organization is another critical characteristic of many complex systems, namely their ability to adapt and evolve in response to changing external conditions. The quintessential example of such a complex adaptive system is of course, life itself in all its extraordinary manifestations from cells to cities."[27] West's recent book, *The Universal Laws of Life and Death: Scale in Organisms, Cities and Companies* demonstrates, contra Macmurray, the success of mathematical approaches to the teleological realm of biology and organisms.

It is not surprising, then, to find Jungian writers exploring how complexity theory connects to Jung's psychology. Butz, a psychologist, reviews these efforts and writes:

> One can identify many parallels between the theories of development described by Freud, Jung, and Erikson and the ideas under the terms chaos and more recently complexity. ... These three theories may be given greater clarity of reformation by applying some of the new scientific notions to each.[28]

Joseph Cambray writes: "It can be argued that Jung's theories, practices, and clinical methods bear direct relationship to what currently is referred to as complexity theory."[29]

So is the psyche a complex adaptive system (CAS) and can complexity theory be usefully applied to it? My answer is, yes, the psyche is to some degree a CAS and complexity theory may be applicable to aspects of the psyche, but it is more. Complexity theory does not encompass the whole of the psyche.

Jung viewed the conscious focus of a person in the first half of life as adapting to the external world. In that sense the person could be viewed as a CAS. Certainly a person continues to respond to changing external conditions. Jung called this dynamic individuation and he identified a tendency in the second half of life for consciousness to focus on the inner aspects and processes of the psyche, the prompting of unconscious processes and materials. He proposed a teleological dynamic towards meaning and wholeness within the psyche.

The psyche lies beyond the reach of Macmurray's first two unity patterns and requires the psychological and personhood unity pattern. It is clearly within von Wright's Aristotelian or hermeneutical tradition and eludes the Galilean tradition. Dual-aspect monism postulates that matter and psyche are incompatible but complementary descriptions of the whole. All perspectives considered agree holisms do not describe the whole.

## Notes

1. *Random House Dictionary of the English Language,* The Unabridged Edition, Random House, New York, 1969, p. 677.
2. John Macmurray, *Interpreting the Universe,* Amherst, New York, Humanity Books, 1933.
3. Ibid., p.62.
4. Ibid. p. 79.
5. Ibid. p. 32.
6. Macmurray used personality rather than personhood but later dropped the use of personality in his writing.
7. Ibid. p. 61.
8. Ibid. p. 71.
9. Ibid. p. 51.
10. B. B. Mandelbrot, *The Fractal Geometry of Nature,* New York, W. H. Freeman, 1977.
11. M. Waldrop, *Complexity,* New York, Simon and Schuster, 1992.

12 Ibid., p. 64.
13 Terry Marks-Tarlow, *Psyche's Veil*, London and New York, Routledge, 2008, 272.
14 Macmurray, *Interpreting the Universe*, p. 63.
15 G. H. von Wright, *Explanation and Understanding*, Ithaca and London, Cornell University Press, 1971.
16 Ibid. p. 2.
17 Ibid. p. 4.
18 Ibid. p. 3.
19 Ibid. p. 30.
20 Ibid. p. 32.
21 C. A. Meier, *Atom and Archetype*, Princeton, NJ, Princeton University Press, 2001.
22 H. Atmanspacher, *The Pauli-Jung Conjecture and its Impact Today*, Andrews, UK, Imprint Academics, 2014, 23.
23 H. Atmanspacher, "Dual-Aspect Monism a la Pauli and Jung", *Journal of Consciousness Studies,* 2012, vol. 9, pp. 96–120, 25.
24 G. H. von Wright, *Explanation and Understanding*, p. 16.
25 J. Cambray, *Synchronicity: Nature and Psyche in an Interconnected Universe,* College Station, TX, Texas A&M University Press, 2009, p. 2.
26 M. Waldrop, *Complexity,* 1992.
27 G. West, *The Universal Laws of Life and Death: Scale In Organisms Cities and Companies,* London, Weidenfeld and Nicolson, 2017, p. 23.
28 M. Bütz, *Chaos and Complexity,* Washington, DC, Taylor & Francis, 1997, p. 53.
29 J. Cambray, *Synchronicity: Nature and Psyche in an Interconnected Universe,* College Station, TX, Texas, p. 2.

# PART IV
# Practice and the arts

# 15

# A SYNCHRONISTIC EXPERIENCE IN SERBIA

*Richard Berengarten*

## Introduction

In May 1985, I visited Serbia from my home in Cambridge, England, to run a series of poetry writing workshops for pupils in Serbian schools, mostly in their early teens. With my daughter Lara, who was then 17 years old, I travelled to Belgrade and some smaller towns and villages in the central and western region of the republic, known as Šumadija (*šuma*, 'wood', 'forest'). The project, which included a group of local teachers of English, was set up and led by my friend and colleague Branka Panić, director of a language teaching centre in Belgrade, in collaboration with a Serbian publisher of children's books and magazines. As I didn't know Serbian at that time, when conducting these workshops, I spoke in English and the teachers translated for me. The boys and girls wrote their poems in Serbian. Our group travelled from town to town in a minibus.

One of these poetry workshops took place on a sunny morning on 25 May in a school in the city of Kragujevac (*kraguj*, 'vulture'). Many pupils were involved in several sessions, and the events filled the school hall. There was a bright, enthusiastic, expansive atmosphere and a sense of novelty and pleasure about these workshops. Afterwards, with Branka and Lara, I visited the city's memorial museum in Šumarice ('woodland', 'spinneys'), a hilly park of 350 hectares just outside the town (Berengarten, 2011: 123–125).

Nothing could have contrasted more strongly with the mood of these poetry workshops than the history of Šumarice. Here, on 21 October 1941, 2,272 people were massacred. Most of these victims were male Serbs, including boys pulled directly out of classes from one of the main schools. Victims included forty local Jews, an unregistered number of Roma, as well as prisoners from local jails, and some Serbian women and girls (Brkić, undated; Berengarten, 2011: 125–128).

Following their whirlwind invasion in April 1941, the Nazis had fully occupied Serbia by the beginning of May. The massacre was a punitive reprisal for a night-time ambush by a Serbian resistance group, near the village of Ljuljaci, on the narrow hilly road between Kragujevac and Gornji Milanovac, at a spot lined by woodland on both sides, on 16 October. Nine German soldiers were shot and twenty-seven wounded, of whom one died later. A ruthless edict had been published by the occupiers, stating that in the event of a single German being killed, one hundred members of the Serbian population would be executed. For a single wounded German soldier, the toll would be fifty executed (see Berengarten, 2011: 4, 127).

Three days after the ambush, the reprisals were swift and merciless. On 19, 20 and 21 October 1941, 2,797 people were massacred at Šumarice, in Kragujevac itself, and in the four nearby villages of Maršić, Mečkovac (*aka* Ilićevo), Grošnica and Beloševac. Those killed included at least 27 women, 217 children of high school age, and 25 children aged between twelve and fifteen. The largest killing site was at Šumarice (Brkić, undated; Brkić, 2007; Berengarten, 2011: 4, 5, 125–135).

Our visit to Kragujevac coincided with a national holiday linked to the birthday of the former Yugoslav president, Josip Broz Tito. Five years after his death, May 25 was still being observed as *Dan mladosti* ('Youth Day'). But because our entire focus had been on the poetry writing workshops, Lara and I had been given no advance knowledge by my Serbian colleagues either of this event or of the wartime massacre, so we had no idea at all of what to expect. Our friends had told us after the workshops that we really ought to visit the museum, but excused themselves from coming with us. They had already been there; a repeat visit would be "too upsetting"; they had other things they wanted to do. But Branka Panić kindly agreed to accompany us. I had never visited the site of a massacre, and nor had Lara. I was curious to visit Šumarice, even though I knew nothing about it and the visit hadn't been envisaged in any way, let alone prepared.

As we arrived, the memorial park presented a curious and completely unexpected scene. The place was thronging with people on special outings. Groups were arriving from many other Serbian towns and villages. Children and teenagers poured out of various hired buses, and pensioners out of others. Many families were coming in by car. Hundreds of people milled around us, and in the queue outside the museum there was a good deal of noisy chatter and friendly jostling. The weather was balmy, and the area around the museum brimmed with youthful energy. In extreme contrast, the memorial park itself, an area of 350 hectares, a space expressly dedicated to the commemoration of the massacre, retained its own underlying, passive, greeny calm. It would be hard to visit this place at any time and not be reminded of the events that had taken place there in 1941.

On both sides of the straight road leading from the town to the museum, large banners had been strung up, on which fluttered phrases inscribed in Cyrillic script. Branka explained to us that these were blow-ups of short messages that had originally been scribbled on scraps of paper by some of the men and boys who had been selected by the Germans for execution. They had been interned overnight in a disused barracks before being marched out to be shot the next morning. They had known or at least expected the fate that was awaiting them. These short messages, written out of communal and individual terror, overwhelming panic, utter helplessness, and extraordinary bravery, were remarkable documents. Much later, when I tried to render some of them into English, I discovered that they had a heartrending, tragic poignancy and dignity that utterly defied adequate translation ('Don't send bread tomorrow', Berengarten, 2011: 6–7).

Eventually, Lara, Branka and I found ourselves in a queue of people waiting to get into the museum. The building was quite small and, once a hundred or so people had entered, the keepers closed the glass doors to prevent overcrowding inside. The previous group needed to be allowed to percolate through the building to the exit on the floor below, before we could be admitted. We stood outside, in a crowd of strangers, waiting our turn.

I have a crystal-clear memory of what happened next, in all its detail. Lara and I were standing close to the glass doors of the museum, slightly bemused by the chatter and bustle around us. I had my arms folded in front of me, so that my right hand cradled my left elbow and my left hand was slightly raised. Lara stood to my right, holding our camera. My eyes were focused on the statement printed in large letters on the partition wall inside the museum, facing through its glass doors so that it could be read from outside: *Machen si mir dieses Land Deutsch* ('Make this land German for me'). Beneath it was attached the name *Adolf Hitler*. At that moment, out of the corner of my eye, I noticed a small movement on my left hand.

Looking down, a small blue butterfly was perched on my left forefinger, its wingspan hardly more than the size of my thumbnail. I gazed at it in disbelief for a second and nudged Lara with my right elbow. "Look," I said. "Quick, take a photo."

Lara pulled out our camera and took the first of two photos. In my astonishment, a vast number of impressions and ideas flashed (flooded) across my mind at once, as the horizons and boundaries of 'normal' perception, thought, and observation suddenly opened wide. Then the tiny butterfly lifted off my finger but, rather than flying away, fluttered before my face and just above it. It seemed to be performing a little aerial dance. Then, it settled back down on my finger again, the same finger as before. "It must *like* me," I thought. I asked Lara to pass me the camera, slowly stretched my left arm out in front of me and, using only my right hand, managed to focus the apparatus so that I could take a slightly better close-up shot. I had to manipulate the camera carefully because I'm left-handed, and my right hand isn't as flexible as my left.

In terms of clock-time, although all this must have happened in a few seconds, I remember it as a moment in and through which the here-and-now expanded into a kind of timelessness, and time and space either stopped, or stopped being relevant. Time itself seemed to expand (disperse) and collapse (implode) simultaneously, and while 'things' were transformed because of this – somehow (and paradoxically) they also remained entirely 'normal': that is, exactly as they had been previously. I have captured, or at least suggested, some of these complexities of response in 'The telling, first attempt' (Berengarten, 2011: 10–11); though the word *attempt* in the title clearly indicates my sense at that time that language itself—even language, the richest, finest, clearest of our communicative gifts—wasn't adequate to expressing the fulness and subtlety (essence?) of such an experience, which leaks away, as it were, through minute cracks in language's jar.

I don't remember much, if anything, of what happened immediately after that. I know that I retained some immediate visual and spatial impressions of the museum's interior, because I remembered them later on, when they became relevant to me as triggers for research. But the incident itself, of the butterfly perching on my finger—and then returning, and then flying away again—together with everything that had led up to it, has been engraved into my memory ever since, with a cut-glass clarity, scattering multiple refractions.

Our tour of Serbia continued and we moved on to other towns. As soon as Lara and I returned home to Cambridge, I had both our photos developed. Although these were of nowhere-near-professional standard, especially by comparison with the extraordinarily fine detail of modern digital photography, the first shot that Lara had snapped and the second that I had taken both yielded quite clear images of the little blue creature astride my finger, almost as if it had been posing there, sunning itself, waiting—even somehow wanting (?)—to be photographed. Our camera had contained a colour film, so the butterfly's delicate blueness came out clearly: wings edged in lacy whiteness, and a black contoured band, a kind of wavering border, between wingtips and the inner dominant blue.

Around that time, I wrote two poems to record the experience. They arrived spontaneously and effortlessly: first, 'The blue butterfly' (see the Appendix below; Berengarten, 2011: 7; Wilson, 2009, for a critical commentary; and for an interview, Berengarten and Rys, 2017: 111), followed by 'Nada: hope or nothing' (Berengarten, 2011: 8 and 9). The second poem contains two lines ("A blue butterfly takes my hand and writes / in invisible ink across its page of air…") which express my acute sense at that time that, rather than *my* writing them, both of these poems were being written *through and out of me*. That is to say, rather than my own will, intention (ego) being in control, the butterfly had somehow entered my imagination (psyche), and was guiding and guarding my hand in, through and along the entire compositional pathway.

It was hardly surprising that after the arrival (delivery) of these two poems, I realised that there was considerably more to be said – and done. As it turned out, these two poems eventually became the core of a book, entitled *The Blue Butterfly* (Berengarten, 2011; first edtn. Burns, 2006; Serbian edtn. Burns, 2007).

Thanks to the resources of Cambridge University Library, one of the great libraries of England, was able to do some preliminary research into the Second World War in Yugoslavia. I began to delve into this subject from as many angles as possible, including records of German war documents. During this period,

I also received and accepted several further invitations to various parts of the then-Federation of Yugoslavia, including Croatia and Slovenia, as well as Serbia. These visits were short, usually lasting no more than one or two weeks: I went either to train English teachers on residential courses sponsored and planned by the British Council, or to attend literary events organised by the Serbian Writers' Association. As a result, by 1986 I had a good number of friends among both teaching and literary communities in Belgrade and in Split.

In my early twenties, I had lived in Italy and then in Greece, and knew both countries well. Now, in my mid-forties, I was discovering that the more I learned about Yugoslavia – which, at that time, I first thought of as the 'space between' Italy and Greece – the more curious I became, the more attracted, and the more I wanted to discover about it as an entity in its own right.

Then a new idea emerged. Branka Panić's language centre in Belgrade needed a qualified native-speaker to teach English, and a job was to be advertised in the UK through the British Council. By this time, I had already given poetry readings and run several poetry workshops at this centre, and had several friends there. If I went to live in Belgrade, I would have the chance to experience Yugoslav and more specifically Serbian culture first-hand, learn some Serbo-Croat, and work on *The Blue Butterfly*. I decided to apply for the post, and was interviewed by a laconic mandarin at the British Council's head office in Davies Street, London. "I see no reason," he drawled, "why we can't accept you". A new phase in my life was underway.

In 1987, Yugoslavia didn't figure especially prominently in the consciousness of most of my English literary acquaintances. I found myself being asked sceptical questions: "Yugoslavia? Why on earth are you going to live in *Yugoslavia?*" But I didn't feel like arguing, and in any case, had always been attracted by edges, borders, and zones of intersection and crossover, rather than self-appointed, self-important, big-time 'centres'. So, I took the easy way out and answered, "I'm going to chase butterflies," thinking of Georges Brassens's song, 'La chasse aux papillons'.

I lived in Yugoslavia from 1987 to 1990. I was 44 when I arrived and 47 when I left. During that time, I wrote many poems that would eventually find their way into *The Blue Butterfly*. Following my return to Cambridge, I worked sporadically on the book, doing more research, following up various themes, and writing more poems as and when they appeared. I wasn't in a hurry. I knew that this book, with its inception in the synchronistic event of 1985, needed to gestate, emerge, and ripen, in its own way and its own time. I thought of this book as a single composite poem, an organic whole, rather than as a collection of disparate shorter pieces. As things turned out, it took me twenty years to complete. (Another way of putting this is that my butterfly turned out to be a particularly heavy specimen, and that it took me 20 years to free myself from the almost weightless weight of its momentary touch on my finger.) The first English edition was published in 2006. Since then the book has been translated into Serbian (Burns, 2007), and this translation was utilised as the oratorio for the open-air choral and dramatic commemoration at Šumarice in the same year.[1]

After writing 'The blue butterfly' and 'Nada: hope or nothing' in 1985, very soon after my return to Cambridge from Serbia, I began to realise that something larger was gestating in me (gesturing to me), of which these two small poems were only indications (forerunners, harbingers). What this something was or where it came from, I didn't at first understand at all. Even so, I did trust its source and its impetus, and did so instinctively. I also fully recognised what it was *doing*—which was *calling me (calling on me, calling me out)*: to write. And while I could scarcely help recognise that these two small poems possessed their own intrinsic qualities of authenticity and depth, it dawned on me that they were also glimpses of a vastly larger and more extensive inner seam, which, so long as I was attentive and patient, I might possibly be capable of exploring and mining. This seam, I recognised at the time, and expressed later, ran deep into and through my own personal psyche, both as a Jew and as a poet. And from responses to these poems in Serbia, later on I also realised how deeply this seam runs through the intersubjective identity and history of the Serbian people. This set of discoveries surfaced very slowly and gradually: it assembled itself piecemeal, during and along with the composition of the book itself, evidently incorporating (embodying) my full volition, while somehow, appearing of its own accord, and only revealing the whole of itself in its own good time.

Evidently, my job was to listen, watch, scry, follow, delve, and keep listening and watching for the deeper sources of these two initial poems. Eventually, my butterfly-experience and the poems that flowed out of it would touch and activate (resonate) an archetypal chord not only in myself but in others.

In the Greek tradition, the paradigmatic call to the poet to sing is delivered, mysteriously, by one of the Muses, daughters of Mnemosyne, goddess of Memory, and of Zeus, king of the Gods. The nine daughters of Memory are the nurses, guides, and guardians of poetic inspiration. In the opening of his epic masterpiece, *Paradise Lost*, John Milton calls on his Muse, Urania: "Sing heavenly muse" (Milton, 1958, Book 1: l. 6). Urania, highest of the Muses and patroness of astronomy, is named after the heavenly god Uranus or Ouranos. Even in Modern Greek, the word ουρανός means 'sky, heaven'.

Who, then, was calling me, on me, calling me out? Certainly, not Urania.

I had felt, even during or immediately after the event, that the butterfly landing on my hand was a message that involved *the soul*. I knew, too, that in ancient Greek the single word ψυχή (ancestor of our word *psyche*) meant *both* 'butterfly' *and* 'soul'. What is more, in my mind, as I stood outside the museum gate at Šumarice, it wasn't so much that the butterfly *symbolised* the soul in any conventional modern sense, but that *butterfly and soul were one*. And this integral cognitive and linguistic connection between *butterfly* and *soul*, through the word ψυχή, occurred to me *at that time*. Whether this recognition happened simultaneously with the butterfly landing on my finger or in the nano-seconds after it, I can't be sure; but, certainly, this meaning (meaningfulness) was key to both the core-event and the entire experience. And as for this *particular* butterfly, I was now coming to think of it as 'my' butterfly, sensing that I had a special bond with it. And I began to have extensive discussions with myself about the creature; and in some of these I found myself addressing the creature as *part of myself*.

Clearly, then, my Muse was ψυχή, the butterfly-soul. And this entity or being had *already* chosen me, simply by sitting on the forefinger of my writing hand. And equally clearly, this Muse of mine scarcely belonged to the Empyrean (aetherial) heights, but rather to the lower air, and to the gates between life and death. What is more, I recognised that these gates had been opened up to me—in me, and through me—gradually and progressively, ever since 1957, when as an Anglo-Jewish boy of thirteen growing up in London, I had first learned about the Nazi Holocaust.

Nor did I need anyone to explain to me that, in Greek mythology, the gates between life and death are those between this world and the Underworld, ruled over by Hades and his queen, Persephone, daughter of Demeter. I knew, too, that the myth of Persephone enacts (re-enacts, embodies, encapsulates) the natural annual cycle and the theme (motif, imagem, symbol—and also archetype) of *rebirth*, even though it did not occur to me *consciously* at that time to connect this intellectual (bookish, theoretical) knowledge with the fulness of the emotional (heuristic, transformational) experience that I was undergoing in the wake of this synchronistic event.

Thinking of this (and thinking it through) now in retrospect, as I write this account in 2018, 33 years later, it is clear to me that the meaning of the proximity of the massacre and the butterfly soul or soul butterfly in the synchronistic event, involves *rebirth*. And at the time, to me at least, an immediate, direct coincidence (connection, link, mesh, merging, bind, bond) was established between the butterfly and the massacre. This involved a *metamorphosis*—perhaps even a *metempsychosis*.

But if I were to interpret the creature as a perfectly articulated materialisation (embodiment, incarnation, appearance, epiphany) of the soul, the question was, *whose*? At some point in this inner debate with myself, now indiscernible and unrecapturable, I developed the sense that the butterfly's message to me wasn't only personally directed at me—to me, for me—but that it was entirely clear and very simple. After all, the creature had come, whether by chance, accident, or 'of its own accord', to sit on the forefinger of my writing hand, no-one else's. Wasn't there, then, at least according to the mode of thinking that I was applying then—and am also and still applying here—that is, the ancient, neolithic, symbolic, mythical, mythopoeic mode of poetry, rooted in correspondences and their accretions—wasn't there at the very least a kind of *elective affinity* between my writing hand and this soul butterfly or butterfly soul?

As for the inner meaning of my butterfly's message, my sense developed that I was being directed (asked, tasked), *called (called on, called out)*, told (and even *tolled*—almost as if I were some kind of bell)—to write about (and to *write out*) the massacre. This calling to me at least was as clear as any call (or call-out or call-up) possibly could be, delivered in the soul's own code-language (see Hillman 1977 and 1979) – a code that had no need of human words. Its meaning and meaningfulness were self-evident, in the blue butterfly's arrival on my writing hand.

## Appendix

The blue butterfly

On my Jew's hand, born out of ghettos and shtetls,
raised from unmarked graves of my obliterated people
in Germany, Latvia, Lithuania, Poland, Russia,

on my hand mothered by a refugee's daughter,
first opened in blitzed London, grown big
through post-war years safe in suburban England,

on my pink, educated, ironical left hand
of a parvenu not quite British pseudo gentleman
which first learned to scrawl its untutored messages

among Latin-reading rugby-playing militarists
in an élite boarding school on Sussex's green downs
and against the cloister walls of puritan Cambridge,

on my hand weakened by anomie, on my
writing hand, now of a sudden willingly
stretched before me in Serbian spring sunlight,

on my unique living hand, trembling and troubled
by this May visitation, like a virginal
leaf new sprung on the oldest oak in Europe,

on my proud firm hand, miraculously blessed
by the two thousand eight hundred martyred
men, women and children fallen at Kragujevac,

a blue butterfly simply fell out of the sky
and settled on the forefinger
of my international bloody human hand.

## Afterword: The Butterfly, the Soul and Rebirth

Any child who has watched any one of the mysterious transitions in the lifecycle of a butterfly—from egg to caterpillar, from caterpillar to chrysalis, and from chrysalis to flying adult (imago)—is likely to be enthralled by the experience. And it's a small leap from this natural observation to an adult's understanding of how in ancient Greece this creature should have become identified with ψυχή, the soul, and to have evolved as a symbol for both emergence and transformation. For, since the transformations in a butterfly's life are visible embodiments of natural metamorphoses, by extension and analogy they are evidently interpretable in terms of both rebirth and metempsychosis.

C. G. Jung introduces the key theme of rebirth into his famous discussion of his patient's dream of a scarab, which was followed by a similar insect flying in through the window of his consulting room during an analytical session with the same patient. This episode has almost come to be read as a paradigm for his theory of synchronicity itself:

> It was an extraordinarily difficult case to treat, and up to the time of the dream little or no progress had been made. [...] Evidently something quite irrational was needed which was beyond my powers to produce. The dream alone was enough to disturb ever so slightly the rationalistic attitude of my patient. But when the "scarab" came flying in through the window *in actual fact*, her natural being could burst through the armour of her animus possession and the *process of transformation* could at last begin to move. Any essential change of attitude signifies *a psychic renewal* which is usually accompanied by *symbols of rebirth* in the patient's dreams and fantasies. The scarab is a classic example of a *rebirth symbol*.
> (Jung, 2014 [1960], CW 8 §845; emphases added)

In commenting on the transpersonal or archetypal nature of this episode, Roderick Main writes:

> Whether or not the patient in the incident [...] had prior exposure to images of scarabs, and whether or not she could have acquired from her personal experience a disposition to produce symbols of rebirth, the synchronicity suggests that some *factor larger than her personal psyche has been involved in the organisation of the events* – a factor that *encompasses the external world of nature* in addition to her psychic world.
> (Main, 2014: 133; emphasis added)

And he adds:

> Further, as Jung's example of the scarab beetle indicated, the content of synchronistic events is often *mythic*. This is not surprising if we bear in

mind that, for Jung, *synchronistic events are based on the activation of archetypes and myths are the narrative elaboration of archetypal motifs.*

(Ibid. 163; emphasis added)

Jung's and Main's perspectives richly *in*form my 'understanding' of the incident of the blue butterfly landing on my hand. Experientially, this event involved both *the process of transformation* and *psychic renewal*; it included a *factor larger than the personal psyche in the organisation of the events*; and this factor not only *encompassed the external world of nature*, but did so in ways that *activated archetype and myth*. And even though the word 'understanding', with all its connotations of logically presented, rationally argued, causally derived, and consciously motivated and directed interpretation, is hardly the right one here – since the core of whatever I do understand remains richly incomprehensible, radically inexplicable, ineluctably acausal, and ineffably mysterious – in short, entirely *beyond* me – I can still think of no better word. This event changed my life, and it still resonates in and through me. I return to it again and again, and it won't let me go. *But that's all right.* The blue butterfly binds me into joy. For whatever may come after it, to have been visited even just once by the muse in a form that the Greeks designated as that of the soul itself, can scarcely be construed as anything less than a blessing.

*Cambridge, June 2019*

## Notes

1 *Veliki školski čas* [the' Great School Lesson'], an event commemorating the massacre, held at Šumarice each October since 1957 (Berengarten, 2011: 136–137).
2 References to the author appear under the names Berengarten and Burns.

## References[2]

Berengarten, Richard. (2011). *The Blue Butterfly*. Exeter: Shearsman Books.
Berengarten, Richard and Rys, Sean. (2017). 'I Must Try This Telling'. In *A Portrait in Inter-Views*, eds. Nikolaou, Paschalis and Dillon, John. Z: 110–146. Bristol: Shearsman Books.
Brkić, Staniša. (undated). *Kragujevačka tragedija / Kragujevac Tragedy*. Bilingual booklet. Kragujevac: Kragujevac October Memorial Park.
Brkić, Staniša. (2007). *Ime i broj: Kragujevačka tragedija 1941* ['Name and Number: the Kragujevac Tragedy 1941']. Kragujevac: Kragujevac October Memorial Park.
Burns, Richard. (2006). *The Blue Butterfly*. Cambridge: Salt Publishing.
Burns, Richard. (2007). *Plavi leptir*. Serbian tr. of *The Blue Butterfly*, Vera V. Radojević. Kragujevac and Belgrade: Spomen Park, Kragujevački oktobar with Plava tačka [Kragujevac October Memorial Park with Blue Spot].
Hillman, James. (1977). *Re-Visioning Psychology*. New York, NY: Harper.
Hillman, James. (1979). *The Dream and the Underworld*. New York, NY: Harper.
Jung, C. G. (2014) [1960]. *The Structure and Dynamics of the Psyche*. CW 8. Hull, R. F. C. (trans.). London: Routledge.

Main, Roderick. (2014) [2004]. *The Rupture of Time: Synchronicity and Jung's Critique of Modern Western Culture*. London and New York: Routledge.
Milton, John. (1958). 'Paradise Lost'. In *The Poetic Works of John Milton*, ed. Helen Darbishire. London, New York, Toronto: Oxford University Press.
Wilson, Stephen. (2009). 'Hath Not a Jew Hands'. *International Literary Quarterly* 8. Online at: http://interlitq.org/issue8/stephen_wilson/job.phphttp://interlitq.org/issue8/stephen_wilson/job.php. Accessed, February 14, 2018. Also published in Jope, Norman, et al. (2017). *Richard Berengarten: A Critical Companion*: 357–369. Bristol: Shearsman Books.

# 16
# THE CONCEPT OF *KAMI* IN SHINTŌ AND HOLISM: PSYCHOTHERAPY AND JAPANESE LITERATURE

*Megumi Yama*

### Introduction

In the introduction to *Memories, Dreams, Reflections*, Aniela Jaffé (1961/1995: 12) notes that "He [Jung] was well aware that the patient's religious attitude plays a crucial part in the therapy of psychic illness. This observation coincided with his discovery that the psyche spontaneously produces images with a religious content, that it is 'by nature religious.'" I strongly agree with this discovery of Jung's, and I would like to argue that it applies to anyone, regardless of whether they are suffering from a psychic illness or not. Before going any further, I would like to make one thing clear. Although I am interested in religion because of the reason I mentioned above, I am not a scholar of religion but a depth psychologist and psychotherapist with a Jungian theoretical orientation. Having been engaged in clinical work including psychotherapy, supervision and training analysis in Japan for more than 35 years, I have come to realize that the theme of "death" or "soul" always lurks in the background of cases of all kinds, which is connected with something religious; however, by this I do not necessarily mean a given religion or sect.

When the major world religion of Buddhism was introduced to Japan in the sixth century, the indigenous belief was not replaced or regarded as inferior. On the contrary, the primary beliefs of ancient Shintō are still deeply imbued in the Japanese culture and respected by people in everyday life, though largely unconsciously. This fact seems to make the concept of *kami* in Japan ambiguous and unclear. In this paper, I would like to explore Japanese *kami* from the perspective of the idea of holism, exploring the characteristics of *kami* in Shintō in ancient times, referring to the *kami* in the oldest Japanese creation myth.

## *Kami* in Japan

First of all, I would like to show the concept of *kami* in Shintō in Japan especially in ancient times, although I am afraid it may come across as somewhat ambiguous or unclear if we try to understand it by ordinary rational thinking. As soon as I begin to think how I should explain it, I cannot help realizing how challenging it is to articulate something essentially insubstantial (=*kami*) and ambiguous, since the concepts are so fundamentally different from those of monotheistic Judeo-Christian culture. It feels to me to be an important topic because the ambiguous nature of *kami* itself is considered to be not only unique in its religious and cultural meaning but also noteworthy in terms of its deep fixedness in the Japanese psyche. This is the reason why I came to have an interest in the unique concept of *kami* in Japan.

Although the Japanese word *kami* is usually translated into English by terms such as deity, god, or spirit, none of these words precisely captures its full meaning. What makes this concept more ambiguous and chaotic is that due to the syncretization of Japanese religions, the term *kami* is used to refer to both gods and goddesses in Buddhism as well as the innumerable spirits of Shintō. And what is more, the word *kami* is not only used for Japanese *kami* but also to describe religious deities such as Jesus Christ or Yahweh, and all other gods and goddesses in religions and mythologies all over the world. In the long history of syncretization, under the influence of Buddhism, and because of some political and social reasons, many new and different types of *kami* appeared in the Shintō pantheon in addition to ancient Japan's original *kami*.

Satoshi Ito (2012) has elaborately explored the formation process of Shinto from ancient to modern times. According to him, the reasons for the deification of existent people can be roughly classified into two groups. One is to comfort the vengeful spirits of those who were killed because of some political plot or conspiracy. Shrines were founded in fear of their curse—frequent natural disasters, plague, and so on. And the other is to enshrine those who achieved a great deed in order to transmit their achievement to posterity. These shrines were mainly founded in modern times, that is, after 1868.

One of the well-known examples was Sugawara no Michizane (845–903), a bureaucrat and esteemed scholar and poet who was exiled in a plot by a rival member of the Fujiwara clan. In the years after his death, plague, heavy rain and lightning occurred repeatedly, and his chief Fujiwara adversary and the Emperor's son died, while fires caused by lightning and floods destroyed many people. As it was believed they were caused by Michizane's angry spirit, they decided to build a shrine to console his spirit. He was deified as *Tenjin*, which means "heavenly *kami*", a *kami* of learning. Today many Shinto shrines all over Japan are dedicated to him.

The famous examples of the latter reason for deification are Hideyoshi Toyotomi (1537–1598) and Tokugawa Ieyasu (1543–1616), who are both regarded as great unifiers. Hideyoshi was deified with the name of Toyokuni-Daimyōjin, which literally means "Rich Country, Great *Kami*." On the other hand, Ieyasu, the first *shogun* and the founder of the Tokugawa shogunate (1603–1868), was deified with the name Tōshō Daigongen, which literally means the "Light of the East, Great *Gongen*." *Gongen* is believed to be a Buddha who appeared on Earth in the shape of a *kami*.

Since in the case of many *kami* historical, political and psychological factors are entwined in an intricate web, I would like to refer to just the few famous examples above.

Although Shintō is polytheistic as well as animistic, I have been using the word '*kami*' instead of "*kamis*"; this is because we do not usually distinguish between plural and singular in the Japanese language. The *kami* of Shintō are collectively called "*yaoyorozu-no-kami*", which literally means "eight-million-kami" in Japanese and is generally understood to mean an infinite number of omnipresent *kami*. Interestingly, the way in which we should view '*kami*' as a whole and not just as a collection of individual parts may possibly lend itself to an essentially holistic outlook. Even if eight million *kami* were to be collected in one place, it would not make one "*kami*" as a whole (*yaoyorozu-no-kami*: an infinite number of kami).

As Shintō has no founder, no dogma, and no scriptures, it has been debated whether it should actually be considered a religion. Generally, Shintō has been regarded as Japan's indigenous belief-system, which traces its origins back to an ancient animist worship of nature and ancestors. Japanese *kami* in Shintō might be thought to refer to phenomena that inspire a sense of awe and wonder in the beholder. This can be compared to Rudolf Otto's (1917/2010) famous description of the "*Numinous*" as a *mysterium tremendum et fascinans*. It is similar to the view of Norinaga Motoori (1968: 125, 126), the preeminent scholar of Shintō and Japanese classics of the 18th century, who defined *kami* as "a being or a thing which bestows a sense of awe." Increasingly, according to this definition, anything that is animate or inanimate could possibly be a *kami* if only the person observing it does so with a sense of awe. In this sense, I would like to argue that the relationship between the observer and the observed is of utmost importance.

As I mentioned above, the primary beliefs of ancient Shintō are still influencing people in everyday life quietly and largely unconsciously. Since childhood, most Japanese are usually taught to put their palms together and utter the simple 'grace' *itadaki-masu*, which means *I (humbly) receive*, before eating and *gochiso-sama (it was a feast)* when they finish, not to mention being disciplined not to waste even a single grain of rice. They understand on a basic level that they are expressing gratitude for the blessing of food to *kami*; however, which *kami* they are addressing is not at all clear, and few people would even care about it. Many families used to venerate various household *kami,* such as the *kami* of fire, the *kami* of the kitchen and the *kami* of the toilet. These are still known even among the younger generations. There used to be *kami* of mountains, *kami* of rice fields, *kami* of forests, *kami* of wells, and so on, who existed all around us. With the rapid economic development in the 1960s and 1970s, these *kami* seemed to have disappeared from the culture, but I have come to realize that they still reside within people if they go down deep inside of their psyche. The animistic beliefs seem to live on subterraneously, with inanimate items and objects being believed to have souls, as do humans, animals, and plants. The popular Japanese phrase *mottainai* does not necessarily only mean "not wasting" but also conveys the idea that one should respect even small things.

After the introduction of Buddhism in the sixth century, some different types of *kami*, such as the one who was worshiped to allay fears that he might curse someone, developed from within the indigenous beliefs for various political and social reasons, as I mentioned above. This is another reason that the concept of *kami* has become so complicated today. I would like to argue that we might be able to glimpse the ancient layers of the Japanese psyche in the *kami* venerated before the introduction of Buddhism.

Firstly, I would like to explore how Japanese people respond to the topic of "religion" in everyday life. I am pretty sure that most would be embarrassed if they were asked about their religion. At best, most would mumble something hesitantly along the lines of, "Hmm ... I'm an atheist", "... I don't believe in religion" or "Perhaps ... I'm Buddhist."

According to the Japanese National Character Surveys by The Institute of Statistical Mathematics in 2013[1], only 28% of respondents answered "Yes" while 72% answered "No" to the question "Do you believe in religion?" When Japanese hear the word "religion," it is likely that most would have a rather negative image without deep reflection on the topic.

Nevertheless, Japanese people in general often attend Shintō shrines and pray to the *kami* at certain annual events, as well as at important life events, in order to convey gratitude and call for divine protection. However, Japanese usually perform funeral rites according to Buddhist traditions, except in the rather rare cases where the family is Christian. Even so, what may seem strange is that most Japanese would not consciously identify themselves as either Buddhists or Shintōists. Interestingly, this might agree with Hayashi (2010), who investigated the relationship between religiosity and the importance of the "religious mind" in a broader sense in contemporary Japanese societies. She reports: "Although the percent of the people who believe in religion is low in Japan, they tend to value the importance of the religious mind, and the meaning of 'not believing in religion' (in Japan) is different from [its meaning] in Europe" (Hayashi, 2010).

Yamaori (1996/2007, 2, 6), a Japanese scholar of religion, notes as follows:

> Our [Japanese] 'atheism' seems to be just a vague version and apparently different from the convinced atheism such as that which modern western [societies have] produced ... . This is because we seem to have not necessarily performed the "killing of God" as Dostoyevsky or Nietzsche had done ... [After thinking over the matter this way and that, finally Yamaori confesses that] He realized that he himself believes in both *kami*

and Buddha not selectively but almost simultaneously and equally in the depth of the psyche.

Yamaori mentions that the characteristic of the traditional Japanese religious attitude lies not in the "either/or" but the "this and that." Furthermore, he refers to Japanese atheism as "passive atheism", which was delineated from within a mental attitude of "this and that", where the subject is extinguished. According to such a mentality, Japanese seem to have a tendency to accept and contain everything without excluding something for the reason that it does not immediately suit them.

## Characteristics of ancient *kami* in Japan

Now I would like to briefly present some characteristics of ancient *kami*. As I have mentioned, their conceptualization has become ambiguous, complicated and multi-layered over the course of history. In the ancient animistic world, *kami* were not separate from nature, but of nature itself. They were considered to be a manifestation of *musubi* (the interconnecting energy of the universe) and of generativity. *Kami* are considered to reside in mountains, rocks, trees, rivers, waterfalls, and other features of the landscape, as well as in other naturally occurring phenomena, such as wind, lightning, earthquakes, volcanic eruptions, and so on. Also, spirits of human ancestors were regarded as *kami*. In ancient times, when people died, their spirits were believed to ascend to the mountain around the house. These spirits of the dead became *kami*, which could also be called *hotoke* (Buddha) after a certain fixed period, during which memorial services were held regularly. As a result, these spirits successively and gradually lost their individuality and eventually became entirely de-individualized parts of the collective "spirits of ancestors" called "*sorei*" (ancestral spirits), which were also regarded as a collective *kami*. These spirits were invited to the village annually to celebrate events such as New Year's Day with their descendants in the village.

I would like to point out just two important characteristics of the ancient *kami*. The first is the *kami*'s invisibility, the second is their mobility. Under the influence of the arrival of Buddhism, some *kami* were given form as statues or pictures and permanent shrines were erected. Originally, according to Yamaori (1983/2014), invisible *kami* were believed to exist freely in the air, travelling freely from mountain to village, village to river. Yamaori (1983/2014, 30) writes: "Kami have transmigrated to de-individualized *ubusuna-gami*, *kami* of the land of one's birth and the guardian *kami* of the land, by sinking deeply into the internal part of the community." They extinguished their personality through descending into the interior of the land.

However, as the ages passed, certain objects and places began to be designated as the interface of humans and *kami*. There are natural sites that are considered to host unusually sacred spirits and therefore are considered to be places of worship. Such places were called *yorishiro*, where people looked up and worshipped in order to be bestowed with divine power. These venerated objects, together with the surrounding mountains or forests, gradually evolved into permanent shrines, although at first they had been just temporary structures built for a particular purpose. Even today, many shrines feature an original *yorishiro*, usually an enormous tree or a rock, ringed by a sacred rope, called *shimenawa* (Figures 16.1 and 16.2).

I would like to show Ōmiwa Shrine (or Miwa Shrine) in Nara, which is one of the oldest extant Shintō shrines in Japan. It is not exactly known when it was first built, but from the fact that it appears in Japanese myths written in the early 8th century, it is assumed to have been built at least before that. I hope it shows some hints of what the first Shintō shrines were like. The shrine is notable for containing no sacred images or objects, because it is believed that it serves Mount Miwa, the mountain on which it stands (Figure 16.3).

In the earliest shrines the most common *shintai*, literally, body of the *kami* (the *yorishiro* that actually housed the enshrined *kami*), was the nearby mountain

**FIGURE 16.1** Iwashimizu Hachiman Shrine Yawata-city, Kyoto. (By Megumi Yama): *Yorishiro*. This is usually an enormous tree or a rock, ringed by a sacred rope (= *shimenawa*).

**FIGURE 16.2** (By Megumi Yama): The Izumo Daijingu Shrine in Kameoka-city, Kyoto.

**FIGURE 16.3** (By Megumi Yama): Entrance to the Mt. Miwa.

peaks that were the source of stream water, which flowed to the lands where people lived. For the reason I mentioned above, Ōmiwa Shrine has a worship hall (=*haiden*), but no official place for the *kami* to be housed (=*honden*). The very special *Torii*, wooden gate called *Mitsu Torii* (Three Torii), stands behind the inner front of the worship hall; that is between the worship hall and the especially sacred area at Mount Miwa. Although structurally Shintō shrines are usually characterized by the presence of a *honden* (or sanctuary), it is sometimes completely absent, or empty, as in the case of the Ōmiwa Shrine. Instead, *shintai*, which are usually objects such as mirrors, swords, jewels, and so forth, are items to be venerated.

As we have seen, primitive Japanese *kami* hid themselves deep in the mountains where they resided out of view of the people. Through the medium of visual *shintai*, people worship the accumulation of various (*yaoyorozu-no*) *kami* as one entity simply called *kami*. Other polytheistic gods in the world, on the other hand, such as gods in Greek mythology or those in India have unique individualities and characteristic appearances respectively.

## *Kami* in Japanese myth

While no particular scriptures exist in Shintō, the oldest Japanese myth, the *Kojiki* (*Records of Ancient Matters*) written in the year 712, contains a description of the earliest Japanese creation myth. In the very beginning, long before the appearance of the 'First Parents' Izanami and Izanagi, who created the world, many generations of invisible *kami* floated in and out of 'being' one after another. Strictly speaking, they were neither created nor produced but simply 'became' out of nothingness, and one after another they hid themselves. They gradually took the form of *kami*, moving from intangible to tangible, from invisible to visible, from abstract to concrete. Although each embodied a separate *kami*, ultimately, they showed orientation as a whole[2]. The first chapter of the *Kojiki* (Takeda, 1995) begins as follows:

> At the time of the beginning of heaven and earth, there came into existence (成る 'naru' lit. 'became') in Takama-no-hara (the Plain of High Heaven) a *kami* named Ame-no-mi-naka-nushi-no-kami (Master-of-the-Centre-of-Heaven-Kami); next, Takami-musuhi-no-kami (High-Producing-Kami); next, Kami-musuhi-no-kami (Divine-Producing-Kami). These three *kami* all came into existence as single *kami* and their forms were not visible (or they hid their bodies).[3]

These first three *kami* are called "The Three *Kami* of Creation." According to Hayao Kawai (1995: 77–79) they make up the first important triad, which consists of one central deity, Master-of-the-Centre-of-Heaven, who is very important but does essentially nothing, and the other two, who are both 'producing' deities. This part of the myth shows the completion of the foundation for spiritual producing power to work in the Separate Heaven, which also implies that the generation is prepared. Hayao Kawai also points out that Master-of-the-Centre-of-Heaven's name hints at his centrality, though he never appears in the myth narrative again, while the other two play important roles afterwards.

Then where did Master-of-the-Centre-of-Heaven go? I would like to argue that Master-of-the-Centre-of-Heaven hid himself deep in the innermost core of the universe and never appeared again. As a result of what we have seen regarding the ancient *kami* in Shintō, I would like to understand Master-of-the-Centre-of-Heaven as the prototype, as well as the core, of Japan's innumerable *kami*. And even a collection of *yaoyorozuno-kami*, which is eight million *kami*, would never make one Master-of-the-Centre-of-Heaven. As humans, we can never see or have direct contact with this *kami*. All we can do is to have indirect contact through worshiping *shintai* or *yorishiro*.

While several generations of kami 'became' one after another, they gradually took *kami* form. Although each embodies a separate *kami*, ultimately they show orientation as a whole. From within this flow of orientation, the first parents Izanagi and Izanami 'became'. I would like to argue that through this orientation in a connection of seemingly fragmented images an important theme may emerge. Such a concept may finally lead to the Buddhist idea of *jinen*—a state in which everything flows spontaneously, just as it is. Although this idea is based on Buddhism, what we have seen implies that it has something to do with ancient kami in Shintō.

## Conclusion

To conclude, I would like to posit that kami from ancient Shintō beliefs are still living in the unconscious psyche of the Japanese. Ame-no-minaka-nushi, Master-of-the-Centre-of-Heaven, who 'became' as the first kami is hiding him/herself and resides in the centre of universe. He/She is an invisible *kami*, who does 'nothing.' Thus, the Master-of-the-Centre-of-Heaven is not a collection of multiple kami, *yaoyorozu-nokami*. This might imply that the idea of holism is at the core of Shintōism. As we cannot have direct contact with this *kami*, all that we can do is to try to have a relationship with Ame-no-minaka-nushi, as one *kami* as a whole through the channels of multiple kami. To return to a point I made at the start, this relationship depends upon whether or not we have a sense of awe and respect towards *yaoyorozu-no-kami*.

Originally, Japan has been a Great Mother-dominant country. Nowadays the phenomena of *hikikomori* (shut-in) and PDD (Pervasive Developmental Disorders) are widely known topics in Japanese society. "How to establish a subject?" is thought to be an important problem in our field of psychotherapy. The idea I mentioned above may give us a hint with regards to alternative ways of healing. One of these is leaving oneself in the flow of "*jinen*"—doing nothing (though this does not necessarily mean literally "nothing")—and wait attentively for the "time" to come when one receives a sign of connection with *kami* in the sense I mentioned.

## Notes

1 http://www.ism.ac.jp/kokuminsei/table/data/html/ss3/3_1/3_1_all.htm
2 For further detail, please refer to "Ego consciousness in the Japanese psyche: culture, myth and disaster" (Yama, 2013).
3 My translation, which is mainly based on *Kojiki*, translated with an Introduction and Notes by D.L. Phillipi (2002) to which I have made some modifications.

## References

Hayashi, F. (2010). Contemporary Japanese Religious Mind—Based on Survey Data from the Japanese National Character and Other Cross-National Surveys. *Proceedings of the Institute of Statistical Mathematics*, 58, 39–59.
Ito, S. (2012). *Shintō to wa nanika: kami to hotoke no nihonshi. (What is Shintō?: Japanese history of kami and hotoke)*. Chuko Shinsho, Tokyo: Chuokoron-Shinsha.
Jaffé, A. (1961/1995). Introduction. In C. G. Jung, *Memories, Dreams, Reflections*. London: Fontana Press, 12.
Kawai, H. (1995). *Dream, Myth & Fairy Tales in Japan*. Einsiedeln, Switzerland: Daimon.
Motoori, N. (1968). *Kojiki-den*. In *Motoori Norinaga Zenshu dai 9 kan. (Commentary on the Kojiki in the Complete Works of Norinaga Motoori (vol. 9)*. Tokyo: Chikuma-Shobo, 125–126.
Otto, R. (1917/2014). *Das Heilige - Über das Irrationale in der Idee des Göttlichen und sein Verhältnis zum Rationalen*. Verlag C.H. Beck, 4. Auflage.
Philippi, D.L. (Sept, 2002). *Kojiki*. Japan: University of Tokyo Press. 47.
Takeda, Y. (Ed.). (1995). *Kojiki*. Tokyo: Kadokawa-shoten. 21.
The Institute of Statistical Mathematics. (2013). http://www.ism.ac.jp/kokuminsei/table/data/html/ss3/3_1/3_1_all.htm
Yama, M. (2013). Ego Consciousness in the Japanese Psyche: Culture, Myth and Disaster. *Journal of Analytical Psychology*, 58, 52–72.
Yamaori, T. (1983/2014). *Kami to Hotoke: Nihonjin no shukyoukan. (God and Buddha: Japanese view on religion)*. Kodansha gendai bunko. Tokyo: Kodansha. 30.
Yamaori, T. (1996/2007). *Kindai Nihonjin no shuukyou ishiki. (Modern religious Consciousness of Japanese)*. Tokyo. Iwanami gendai bunko. Tokyo: Iwanami-shoten, 2, 6.

# 17

# THE CORE TRUST: THE HOLISTIC APPROACH TO ADDICTION

*Jason Wright*

The CORE Trust was a project working with addicts in Lisson Grove, west London, which developed a structured day program that functioned as a community. CORE stands for: Courage to stop, Order in life, Release from addiction and Entry into new life. I worked there from 1993 to 2006.

There was a range of treatment disciplines that utilised different philosophical constructs. The two principal practices were psychotherapy and acupuncture. These were the main interventions that the founders, Jackie Leven and Carol Woolf, had used to release themselves from addiction and they also formed the central dialogue of the project. During my time at the CORE Trust, we developed a full programme consisting of group therapy three times a day, individual psychotherapy, and complementary therapies. We used the notion of 'community', following the archetypal model that was articulated by James Hillman (1981), to hold together the life of the project. His model focuses upon psyche as soul. It is strongly influenced by the work of Marsilio Ficino (1433–1499), the Florentine, Renaissance Neoplatonist and physician to the Medicis.

CORE originated from within a Jungian and archetypal framework. However, as CORE developed, we incorporated a psychoanalytically developmental approach and focused upon the injuries to self that were evidenced by the client group and their history. Early on, Heinz Kohut's (1971) self-psychology was useful, along with the object relations model, particularly Donald Winnicott's (1960, 1963, 1964, 1968, 1990, 1991) ideas of true and false self and the use of an object. These became powerful tools, enabling critical reflection on how differing components of the CORE community were interacting. Imaginations of projected phase-appropriate self-objects, in the context of an awareness of what part of 'me' was being used, formed a useful practical narrative for structuring interactions between community members and staff. For me, this way of working was framed in a context of dialogue, in the sense that David Bohm (1996, 2003) used the term as a group framework for raising consciousness. This dialogue was set in the communal and archetypal frame. The imaginal thread was a central narrative with its ultimately transpersonal roots. All philosophies in the project were in dialogue as were the community members. The psychoanalytic was one imagination amongst many.

We saw communal use of imagination as the project's most healing function, including how, for instance, we might imagine together a possible future. The sense of belonging created the strongest frame for containment and enabled the client group to change, to find a new life. The means by which this worked was to keep open the question of how the dialogic process unfolded. This notion also held true for the staff team. Each of the volunteers and staff were considered as members of the community and had a responsibility to it. The community was seen as a whole living system, and organism, creative, autopoietic, and emergent as Fritjof Capra (Capra and Luisi, 2014), A.N. Whitehead (1978) or Bohm (1998) might describe it.

The idea of wholeness was based upon the assumption of the individual as whole—mind, body, and spirit—a conception that was fashionable in the mid-1980s when the project began. The founders used talking and complementary therapies to develop the treatment based on their own earlier addiction release, supported by their GP. Following on, we developed a sense of wholeness in a social and environmental context founded in interdisciplinary and communal dialogue—a psycho/spiritual, trans-personal, and participatory model. For my part, this referenced my work with large groups, my experiences in the theatre and notions of participation as described by Peter Brook (1968), which are echoed in the work of Bohm (1996).

This whole was held in mind[1] through Hillman's polytheistic model. C.G. Jung (1875–1961) offered a frame that was able to link both the mystical and the material across a range of philosophic traditions and models broad enough to facilitate dialogue between philosophies in a pluralist context. His notion of the collective unconscious and symbol formation (Samuels, 1986), along with his notion of the transcendent function (Miller 2004), could adequately describe the process of the community particularly when considered in the context of Hillman's (1971, 1975, 1981, 1983, 1989, 1996) archetypal notions of a poetic basis of mind and pathologising, i.e., looking to symptom to find a way forward for the individual or group out of the 'wound' itself. What god, in Hillman's polytheistic terms, is speaking through the wound and how does one engage with this daemon within the symptom?

For people suffering with addiction, who have experienced utter self-betrayal, this is a useful way of imagining, in a collective context, that a new life is possible and to have clues and a practical method for exploring a way forward. From Bohm's (1992, 1996) point of view, dialogue offers the capacity to perceive a new necessity, to pass beyond a fixed, but contingent thought structure to perceive a new reality.

Brook's notion of *The Empty Space* (1968), a description of theatrical space, both sacred and profane, was apposite in imagining a creative environment for healing. I tried to create a space that allowed for a resonance between the therapeutic context and the rehearsal room, opening an absence into which new imaginings of life could become.

In CORE, these Western ideas were held in tension with more Eastern traditions of Buddhist, Taoist, and Yogic thinking, most specifically expressed in the narrative of acupuncture, but also through many of the complementary therapies. To some extent we were forming a syncretic model, searching for a synthesis in an atomised time and in the face of a lethal symptom.

We turned again to more traditional psychodynamic thought influenced by Foulksian (see Foulkes, 1948) group and large group theory, particularly the ideas of Patrick de Maré (de Maré et al, 1991). Group analytic theory is largely psychoanalytically informed and focuses upon the social, positing a social matrix within which the individual is born as a nodal point. De Maré's work is set in this context and focuses on groups over a certain size—sixty plus. His research found that large groups exhibit functions of social rather than family dialogue, which are normally expressed in smaller groups of eight or so. There is a middle group level, 'the median group', of approximately twenty that exhibit functions of both. These were the norm at CORE. De Maré argued that, in large groups, a 'culture' forms much like the psyche in a classical Freudian structure of ego, super ego and id. These he named ideoculture, socioculture and bioculture. He also argued that the group structure was representative of the macro culture, but on a smaller scale. As an overall frame for imagining the processes of CORE it was helpful. However, we augmented this imagination in an archetypal frame, offering a wider range of *dramatis personae* and looking not to heal the individual or group but to heal the *story*, as Hillman (1983) describes. This might be regarded as similar to the Hermetic notion of 'as above, so below,' which added significance to the notion of addressing the narrative that the group acted out as the focus of healing.

I have since developed these approaches with consideration of Bohm's notion of dialogue, Whitehead's notion of process (feeling, consciousness, 'going all the way down', accruing like matter to form more complex components of a system or process) and Capra's exploration of a similar notion through the life sciences—the notion of an autopoietic emergent system, multilayered processes accruing from the subatomic to the social and ecological.

The form of open attention I developed to imagine the process at CORE paid particular attention to Bohm's (1992) ideas of fragmentation and dialogue. Fragmentary thoughts or, feelings, break up what is whole into arbitrary parts as they are a limited and limiting component of experience that can generate 'incoherence' within the whole system by determining what is contingent as necessary. Bohm regards this limiting fragmentation as mediated through 'representation', i.e. an unconscious reconstruction of perceived experience, to give it meaning within a comfortable frame. He deconstructs this in terms of reflex rather than volition, incorporating the body through the endocrine system as well as neurobiology in the context of Pavlovian conditioning.

The notion of trauma work that is currently fashionable in addiction treatment and more widely in psychology could be linked with Bohm's thesis. The processing and recontextualising of traumatic experience at the subcortical level would seem to be at root in the initial stages of addiction treatment but, thereafter, a new imagination of context has to be found. It is my contention that a communal context would be most appropriate for this imagination set within the historical and co-evolving context of the cognitive shift to symbol formation that Yurval Noah Harari (2014) and David Sloan Wilson (2015) refer to as the root of our dominance and diversity as a species on the planet.

Here we might also be reminded of the ideas of Iain McGilchrist (2009) and brain lateralization, or of Brian Lancaster (2004) and his neuro-cognitive deconstruction of the perceptual process to reveal the construction of self as the internally referential process of memory, context and perception. Thought is fragmentary and projective, acting on the perceptual process, but unseen and unknown. Its limiting function is very close to the actions of the left brain as conceived by McGilchrist.

Bohm (1992, 1996, 1998) describes a group process of suspension of thought and proprioception of that thought to become critically aware of the assumptions and antecedents of a representational and fragmenting thought process, a holding in mind and a re-examination of the reflex of thought in the context of the bodily experience, similar to the processes of subcortical healing described in trauma therapies such as eye movement desensitisation and reprocessing (EMDR). He articulates how we negotiate the processes of symbol formation in the group. These symbolic elements will have both personal and cultural roots but are unlikely to be dealt with purely by reason, as thought can be generative of incoherence, particularly when defensive against pain. This is a matter of following the experience of the moment, the thoughts, feelings and associations that arise out of that process in a group context without recourse to dogma or resistance.

In the past, a retreat to dogma often resulted in failures to deal adequately with present experience and hatred, engendering the likelihood of a repetition of previous patterns. Within a sustained community, an attempt could be made to suspend intent toward fragmentation, internal or intrapersonal, that would then allow for the emergence of a new perspective. In other words, an opportunity can be cultivated for representations to be challenged and the creative perception of a new necessity to emerge. From my experience of working within such a frame, I have recognised that the capacity to listen and imagine creatively is far more useful than the capacity to know. Each event is considered from varying points of view and, through dialogue, something develops that points teleologically toward a new individual or communal formation. Here new faith is found. This is set in the context of the whole, specifically of community, but more widely in a spiritual or cosmic whole, as Bohm (1980) suggested of his implicate order.

When the project commenced we were a young, naive staff team full of energy and optimism. Perhaps it was this that provided most of the energy for change. We developed formal and informal structures for dialogue between individuals, groups, philosophies, and practices. These were held in mind in a pluralistic sense as one holds differing theoretical narratives in mind as one practices. Again, this model was informed through large group work. The advantage I found with the development of an archetypal framework was that it was possible to have a fluidity of narrative that could incorporate the transpersonal in a psycho-spiritual context with the transpersonal in a social context; the unconscious in relation to the social unconscious (Hopper, 2001, 2003; Dalal, 2001). Questions of faith were at the core of this work—for the individuals struggling with addiction, the faith to live, and our faith in their capacity to change. This faith was evident in the CORE founders' thinking. Faith was explicit in both the Jungian narratives they built the practice on and the Eastern traditional medicine practices. Analytic models, particularly the socially focused ones, might take a more humanist and empiricist view, but contained faith nonetheless. I would argue that materialist and dualist structures are also acts of faith; rigid faith in the Aristotelian five senses that bracket out other means of knowing and perception, such as intuition or revelation, as William Blake (1757–1827) might describe it.

I have come to understand that addiction presents us with the problem of faith and provides a frame for thinking about the larger faith context in which we find ourselves. In its simplest form, this is the faith that the next moment is possible, not only in the context of limit and what is enough (which was a pressing issue as we grew so rapidly in number) but how, through relatedness, we find the capacity to 'experience something truly satisfying': not just the hit of the latte or the crack pipe, which all too briefly confuses our alienations, but the reciprocal and resonant nature of a shared participatory life, the wholeness in which we may participate. At CORE we worked towards developing a sense of wholeness in context, a wholeness inside reflecting a wholeness outside, akin to Whitehead's finite component, actual event, reflected in an everlasting process. This wholeness we understood to be both material and 'spiritual', or cosmic, as Bohm (1992) puts it.

Western metaphors for spirituality have become subject to materialist humanism, and for that a little threadbare, presenting a crisis of faith. Addiction can be seen as a symptom of this. The Twelve-Step movement says that addiction fills a God-shaped hole. The symptom, addiction, provided just that question of faith; what faith is possible when all is lost including faith in self? How do we regain faith in life when embedded in an atomised and homogenised culture, separated from a traditional sense of wholeness and cohesion? Elsewhere I have argued that addiction—the symptom as we now experience it—is at root a response to capitalism and the fantasy of progress in the West (Wright 2014), a pathology of the enlightenment and the industrial revolution, a cultural symptom of the loss of faith and, in William Blake's terms, the hegemony of reason. It is a response to what Harari (2014) describes as the broken religion of Liberal Humanism.

Looking at it from a practical point of view, it is enough to have faith in the moment lived and that the next moment will happen, until of course it doesn't. Even this faith is difficult, leaving me with the idea that the only thing left to have faith in is faith itself, the ongoing process of becoming. In this critical, postmodern world, all dogma is deconstructed. Without a context to orientate it, critical thinking becomes atomisation. It appears to me that we now need to think of our understanding and experience of context as providing faith. I think Whitehead is helpful with this and points to how, through notions of process, we might rediscover a sense of context in becoming:

> God's immanence in the world in respect of his primordial nature is an urge towards the future based upon appetite in the present. Appetition is at once the conceptual valuation of an immediate physical feeling combined with the urge towards realisation of the data conceptually prehended. For example, 'thirst' is an immediate physical feeling integrated with the conceptual prehension of its quenching.
>
> (Whitehead, 1978, p. 32)

Whitehead challenges us with his use of the word 'God' and all the baggage that it carries, although his is not a God of dogma. It is the notion in this context of appetite for becoming, not a fixed, organising divinity but the universe as it is and an appetite for 'novelty' from that whole system, the possible calling life to into being, a creativity.

Blake, Bohm and Whitehead all focus on an underlying creativity and they emphasise a sense of wholeness. Faith then, in this context, becomes a kind of glue—it glues together meaning and experience, events contextualised in the process. Blake also points in this direction and through his re-working of the *Job* narrative offers insight into re-contextualisation through faith. Blake reworks *Job* to describe the personal and, I would say, the group transition in consciousness. It is a narrative of keeping faith, not literalised faith in dogma, in limited systems of thought, but a more fully experienced participatory faith in the whole, the personal, group and cosmic context within which a new necessity can be perceived.

What most impressed me about CORE was that it fostered goodwill. Much was understood about the hates that were present in the process and how these were to be held and understood as hates present from historical and structural frames. It also helped that the community had a focus around a particular intent, which enabled clarity of purpose, boundary, and practice. One needed to remain attentive, without hubris and with a degree of humility, attentive to the process that one saw unfolding. In this frame we were able to put aside many of our differences and engage in dialogue with each member of the community and their needs.

In my view, the accommodation of this complexity emerged through a certain kind of attention, both internal and external. This was too complex to attend to in any other way than in an intuitive, listening manner. I liken this to Freud's evenly suspended attention where one pays fluid attention to the internal and external process until something arises. One can link this to various meditative practices, both Eastern and Western, and I have framed this in a contemplative context myself.

Bohm uses the idea of proprioception: applying this to a thought and bringing one's attention to the experience of body in the context of that thought. Through this he deconstructs the subject–object fallacy, following each thought back to its antecedents, personal and contextual. Hillman, in the context of soul, would see the frame of our experience being within the world soul, *Anima Mundi*, our pathologies expressions of the daemons or gods, spirits of the world. Both present a resonant connection with an order beyond the personal, yet deeply human. Here I would think of Bohm's notion of participation, our participation in a creative system of which the notion of self is a component contextually negotiated in relationship, forming an aware and resonant whole, which, in the healing community at CORE, we expressed and experienced.

## Note

1 Wholeness is imaginative and occurs through the process of holding in mind to achieve group cohesion. This also refers to Donald Winnicott's notion of 'holding in mind'. It is the group holding in mind both the individual components and the wholeness that forms the coherent and resonant whole.

## References

Brook, P. (1968) *The Empty Space*. London: McGibbons & Kee.
Bohm, D. (1980) *Wholeness and the Implicate Order*. London: Routledge.
Bohm, D. (1992, 2003) *Thought as a System*. London: Routledge.
Bohm, D. (1996, 2003) *On Dialogue*. Ed. L. Nichol. London: Routledge.
Bohm, D. (1998, 2003) *On Creativity*. London: Routledge.
Capra, F., and Luisi, P.L. (2014) *The Systems View of Life*. Cambridge: Cambridge University Press.
Dalal, F. (2001) The Social Unconscious: A Post-Foulkesian Perspective, *Group Analysis* 34:4, 539–555.
de Maré, P., Piper, R., and Thompson, S. (1991) *Koinonia: From Hate, through Dialogue, to Culture in the Large Group*. London: Karnac.
Foulkes, S.H. (1948) *Introduction to Group Analytic Psychotherapy*. London: Karnac.
Harari, Y. N. (2014) *Sapiens: A Brief History of Humankind*. New York: Random House.
Hillman, J. (1971) *Psychology: Monotheistic or Polytheistic?* Dallas, TX: Spring.
Hillman, J. (1975) *Revisioning Psychology*. London & New York: Harper Row.
Hillman, J. (1981) *Archetypal Psychology: A Brief Account*. Dallas, TX: Spring.
Hillman, J. (1983) *Healing Fiction*. New York: Stanton Hill Press.
Hillman, J. (1989) *A Blue Fire*. London: Routledge.
Hillman, J. (1996) *The Soul's Code*. New York: HarperCollins.
Hopper, E. (2001) The Social Unconscious: Theoretical Considerations, *Group Analysis* 34:1, 9–27.
Hopper, E. (2003) *The Social Unconscious: Selected Papers*. London: Jessica Kingsley.

Kohut, H. (1971) *The Analysis of the Self*. New York: International University Press.
Lancaster, B. L. (2004) *Approaches to Consciousness: The Marriage of Science and Mysticism*. New York: Palgrave Macmillan.
McGilchrist, I (2009) *The Master and His Emissary*. London: Yale University Press.
Samuels, A. (1986) *Jung and the Post-Jungians*. Hove and New York: Routledge.
Wilson, D. S. (2015) *Does Altruism Exist?: Culture, Genes, and the Welfare of Others*. Hartford, CT: Yale University Press.
Winnicott, D.W. (ed.), (1960) Ego Distortion True and False Self, in *The Maturational Processes and the Facilitating Environment*. (1990), London: Karnac.
Winnicott, D.W. (ed.), (1963) Dependence in Infant Care, in Child Care and in the Psycho-Analytic Setting, in *The Maturational Process and the Facilitating Environment*. (1990), London: Karnac.
Winnicott, D.W. (1964) The Concept of the False Self, in *Home is Where We Start From: Essays from a Psychoanalyst*. (pp. 65–70) eds. Davis, M., Shepherd, R., Winnicott, C. (1986), Harmondsworth: Penguin.
Winnicott, D.W. (1968) The Use of an Object and Relating through Identifications, in *Psychoanalytic Explorations* eds. Davis, M., Shepherd, R., Winnicott, C. (1989), London: Karnac.
Winnicott, D.W. (1990) *The Maturational Processes and the Facilitating Environment*. London: Karnac.
Winnicott, D.W. (1991) *Playing and Reality*. London: Routledge.
Whitehead, A N. (1978) *Process and Reality*. New York: Free Press.
Wright, J. (2014) *Addiction: Treatment and its Context: Addiction From an Attachment Perspective*. London: Karnac.

# INDEX

Page numbers in **bold** indicate tables. Page numbers in *italics* indicate figures.

*Abraxas/Erikapaios* 63
actants 10–11
active imagination 67
actual level: critical realism 130, 137
acupuncture 180
aetiology of psychosis 56
agential realism 111
Alchemia medica 44
Alchemia transmutatoria 44
alchemy 44, 47
Alexander technique 13
Allen, G.E. 127n21
alterity 141, 142; compatibility of 145
alternative medicine 21
American and British Teilhard Association 23
American society: broader cross-section of 20
analytical psychology 101; as ungrounded science 104–106
ancient *kami*: characteristics of 174–175, *175*, *176*, *177*; *see also kami* in Japan
Anderson, B. 27n11
anima 46–47, 78, 79; integration of perceptions 48
animism: Stahl's 46
*animus* 78, 79
anthology 24
Anthropocene 7, 8, 31; characteristics of 34; defined 34
anti-hylozoism 125

anti-mechanistic theory of organism 8
anti-realism: issues of 114; realism vs. 110–111
anti-realist philosophy 11
*Arcana Coelestia* (Swedenborg) 45
Archer, M. 132
archetype 10, 11, 36, 61, 69, 97, 101–105, 109, 110, 112, 113, 165, 168
*archeus* 47
"A Religion of Evolution" 23
Aristotle 20, 21, 47, 85, 151
Arndt, J. 43, 44
Arnold, G. 43
Ash, M. 3
assemblages 137–138
Atmanspacher, H. 31, 32, 109, 152

Bachelard, G. 92
Badiou, A. 111
Barad, K. 111
Barentsen, G. 10
Bastian, A. 50–51
Batesonian cybernetics 1
Baudrillard, J. 137
Beiser, F. 121
"beloved community" 23
Benedict, R. 20
Benjamin, W. 145
Berengarten, R. 12
Bergson, H. 92

Bertalanffy, L. von 21, 71, 72
Bhaskar, R. 11, 130, 132, 133, 134, 137, 139n1, 139n2, 139n4, 139n5
biocentric attitude 38
biological unity patterns 150
Bishop, P. 126n4, 126n7
Blake, W. 184, 185
Bleuler, E. 55, 56
Bloom, A. 85
'The blue butterfly' 162, 164
*The Blue Butterfly* (Berengarten) 162–163
bodily functions, changes in 46
Boehme, J. 43, 45
Boerhaave, H. 47
Bohm, D. 13, 180, 181, 182, 183, 184, 185, 186
Branka Panić 159–161, 163
Brassens, G. 163
British Council 163
Brooke, R. 77
Brook, P. 181, 182
Bryant, L. 111
Buddhism 170, 171, 173

Cambray, J. 109, 112, 114, 154
Canghuilem, G. 92
Capra, F. 37, 181, 182
Caputo, J. 106
Carson, R. 8, 17–18, 23, 26n5
CAS *see* complex adaptive system (CAS)
child development 83, 85; non-rational nature of 88; on personality 86
Chinese herbalism 13
'Chymie' medical-pharmaceutical 44
civic aim: holistic education 85
civilization 35, 37–38
Civil Rights Act of 1964 22
*'cognitio centralis'* 45
coincidence of opposites *see coincidentia oppositorum*
*coincidentia oppositorum* 55, 61
Cold War animosities 25
Colebrook, C. 125
*Collected Works* (Jung) 67
collective individuation 94
Combes, M. 96
communalism 24
compensation 55
complementarity 55
complementary medicine 21
complex adaptive system (CAS) 153, 154
*complexio oppositorum see* union of opposites
complexity theory 1, 153, 154
conceptual language 146

*coniunctio* 64; double pair of opposites 63; realisation of 63; *Spaltung* to the 58, 59; supreme 63; symbol of 59; 'wholeness' as 60
*coniunctio oppositorum* 9, 55, 58; dialectic of 59
conjunction of opposites *see coniunctio oppositorum*
consciousness 141; heroic ego, overvaluation of 36; human, role of 35; image-thinking 143–144; monotheism of 35; synchronicity 12, 143–144
conscious wish 75
conservative analysis of vertebrate species 34
conversion: in Christianity 49
Corbin, H. 80
CORE Trust 180, 182, 184, 185, 186
'cosmological *coniunctio*' 62, 64
cosmological viewpoints in physics 23
counterculture 20
Craig, E. 77
cranio-sacral therapy 13
critical realism 132, 134, 135–137
critical realist 135, 136; framework 130; ideas of emergence 130; question for 134
Culp, Andrew 78
Cybernetics 21, 33

*Dan mladosti* ('Youth Day') 160
Dannhauer, J.C. 44
*Dark Deleuze* (Culp) 78
de Chardin, T. 8
deep cultural diversity 38
deep ecology 23, 31, 38–39; biocentric 38; and individuation 38, **39**
de Fiori, A. 9
DeLanda, M. 110, 111, 113, 130
Deleuze, G. 7, 10–12, 77, 92, 111, 112, 113, 114, 122–125, 123, 125, 130, 131, 132, 133, 139n3
de Maré, Patrick 182
*Dementia Præcox oder Gruppe der Schizophrenien* (Bleuler) 56
de/re-integration dynamic 9
Derrida, J. 12, 111, 132, 146
developmental holistic activity 77, 78
developmental individuation 10
*Developmental Individuation* 83, 84, 88, 89
*Dial* 22
*Dialectic: The Pulse of Freedom* (Bhaskar) 132
*Dialogues* 20
directed thinking 56

discrimination: gender 19; and poverty 27; racial 19
disenchantment: problem of 3
"disorientation" 68
disparation 93
'divine child' 60
divine immanence 22
'*dream* or *fantasy* thinking' 56
*Dreams of a Spirit-Seer* (Kant) 122
Driesch, H. 3, 127n21
dual-aspect monism 12, *32*, 114, 152
dualism 4
du Prel, C. 141, 143, 144
Durkheim, E. 21
Dusek, V. 3, 4
Dutch Calvinism 43

Earth Day 17
Edinger, E. 83–84, 88
education: personality development 86; purpose of 87; of young 83
*Ego and Archetype* (Edinger) 83–84
ego-Self axis 84, 87, 88, 89, 90
ego-Self relationship 84
Elijah 59
EMDR *see* eye movement desensitisation and reprocessing (EMDR)
emergence 130–131; conceptual understanding of 131–132; holism and 132; holism, teleology and 150–151; ideas of 133
*Emergence and Things in Themselves* (Hornsby) *131*, *134*, *138*
emergent properties 138–139
*Emile: on Education* (Rousseau) 85
empathy 50
empirical level: critical realism 130, 137
empiricism 50
empirics 50
*The Empty Space* (Brook) 182
enantiodromia 37, 55
English Puritanism 43
Enlightenment 50; psychological 23
Eno, B. 134, 139n7
environmentalism 20, 24
epistemic fallacy 130, 136
equality: interracial 23; racial and gender 20
*Eros* 62, 63
Esalen Institute 24
Escamilla, M. 56
'eschatological *coniunctio*' 60, 64
Esfeld, M. 4
ethical holism 10

ethos of containment 25
"eupsychia" 23
European Enlightenment 85
evolutionary theory: Catholicism with 23
experience, personality development 86
*Explanation and Understanding* (von Wright) 151
'external environment' 122
eye movement desensitisation and reprocessing (EMDR) 183

Fach, W. 31
Father of English medicine (Sydenham, T.) 47
Father of General Systems Theory (Bertalanffy, L. von) 21
Father of Protestant Liberalism (Schleiermacher) 50
Fechner, G. 141
Fellows, A. 8
Feyerabend, P.K. 71, 72, 74n6
Ficino, M. 180
*First Outline of a System of the Philosophy of Nature* (Schelling) 102
First World War 57, 59
Flournoy, T. 56
Forbes, S. 85
Fordham, M. 9, 78
fractals dynamics 150
Francke, A.H. 44, 48
Frederick William I 45, 47
Freudian psychoanalysis 69
Freud, S. 56, 57, 68, 72, 75, 78, 84, 107n2, 143, 152, 185–186
Froebel, F. 85, 88
Frosh, S. 95
'fruits of the belief' 49
Fujiwara clan 171
Fukuyama, F. 37
Fuller, M. 22
Fuller, R.B. 8, 18–19, 22–24, 26n7, 26n8, 27n12
Fuller's maps 19

Gaia and psyche 32–38; dynamical correlations between **34**; properties of 33; structural correlations between **36**
Gaia science 23
Gaia theory 8, 31, 33, 39; Cybernetics 33; defined 35
Gaian nervous system 35
Galilean tradition 151
Gebser, J. 87
General System Theory 1, 21, 28n19, 71, 72

generative mechanisms 137
geodesics 18–19
geometric method 50
geoscope 19
German holism: history of 3
German Romanticism 3
Gestalt psychology 20
Geyer-Kordesch, J. 45
Gilbert, J. 22
'God is Love' 42–43
Goethe, J.W. von 109
Goldstein, K. 3
Goss, P. 9
Greek mythology 165
Greek tradition 164
group analytic theory 182
Guattari, F. 77, 92, 123, 130, 131, 132, 133, 139n3

Hamann, J.G. 145
Harari, Y.N. 183, 184
Harman, G. 110, 115n1
Harrington, A. 3
Hartmann, E. von 107n2, 143
Hawking, S. 17, 25, 25n1
Hegelian theory 6
Heidegger, M. 111, 141, 142, 145
Henderson, D. 55
*hermeneutica generalis* 51
hermeneutics 42–45, 50; Francke's 44; pietist 51
Herrnhuter/Moravian churches 43
Hideyoshi Toyotomi 171
hierarchy 5
Hildegard of Bingen 21, 27n15
Hillman, J. 13, 180, 181, 186
Hippocrates 20, 21
historical-critical exegesis 44
Hitler, A. 22
Hoffmann, F. 47
holism: in alternative/complementary medicine 21; in American culture 22, 25; analytical psychology 9–10; in biology 21; communities 23; complex phenomena of life 3; in contemporary life 1; cultural concerns 3; definitions of 2, 4; discourse on 42; emergence 12; ethical 10; in evolution 20; German, history of 3; in Gestalt psychology 20; in Hindu culture 21; history and contexts 7–8; as intellectual and social construct 20; language of 2; Marxist ideology and 3; materialistic 127n21; medical 2; metaphysical perspectives 6; methodological and epistemological principle 5; in natural and social sciences 4; non-materialistic 127n21; philosophy 10–12; in philosophy 20, 21; in post–World War II era 22; practice and arts 12–13; social and political theories 21; teleology and emergence 150–151; and totalitarianism 3; types of 4–6; in Vedanta philosophy 21; Wood's survey of history of 7–8
*Holism and Evolution* (Smuts) 1, 2, 132
holistic: approach 1, 13; health 20; organicism 11; organism 8, 42; reasoning 17; responses to modernity 4; synthesis, Teilhard's 23; system of ideas 72–73; system of methods 72; theology of immanence 21
'holistically informed state' 76
holistic education 9–10, 88; aims of 85; concept of 85–86; Friedrich Froebel on 88; Jean Jacques Rousseau on 86; Johann Heinrich Pestalozzi on 86–88; objective of 84; psychology of 89
*Holistic Thought in Social Science* (Phillips) 4
"Holistic universe" 132
holistic wish: clinical example of 78–79; and human psyche 79–80; principles and theory 76–78; road as holistic migration engine of psyche 80–81
holon 5
holos 20
Holy Spirit 43, 44, 50
Hopcke, R.H. 36
Hornsby, I. 11, *131, 134, 138*
*hotoke* (Buddha) 174
hubris 36, 37; catastrophic 37
human agency 34
human development 36
humankind: method of 71
human nature 87; personality development 86
human organism 73
human psyche 76, 153–154; archetypal movement in 77; contra-sexual influences in 78; holistic wish and 79–80; migratory tendencies in 77, 81; road as holistic migration engine of 80–81; root of holistic wish in 77
Hume, D. 111
Husserl, E. 110
Husserlian phenomenology 144, 147
hylozoism 122, 123

Ieyasu, T. 171–172
*Ignis* (Fire) 63
image-making function: in human psyche 80
image-thinking 141, 142, 145–146; consciousness 143–144; language 144–145; nature 142–143
imagination 48, 51, 68; active 67
*Inans* 63
individuation 8, 9, 34, 77, 132–133; and deep ecology 38, **39**; developmental 10; rethinking 10; sustainable 38–39
individuation process 60, 83, 90, 91; in both Indian and Western cultures 110; Gilbert Simondon on 93–94; philosophical approach to 97; philosophy of 91; rethinking of 96; of *unus mundus* 115
inequities of wealth and power 19
'*infimum malum*': devil as 62
*Instinct and the Unconscious* (Jung) 112
*Interpreting the Universe* (Macmurray) 149, 150
interracial equality 23
intra-psychic activity 79
intuition method 115
irreducible responsibility 8

Jacobi, J. 83, 84, 88
Jaffé, A. 170
Japan: ancient *kami* characteristics in 174–175, *175*, *176*, 177; Buddhism in 170; *kami* in 171–174; *kami* in Japanese myth 177–178
*jinen* 13
Judeo-Christian culture 171
Jung, C.G. 7, 9–10, 11, 12, 31–33, 37–39, 78, 83, 86, 87, 88, 89, 90, 94, 101, 103, 107n2, 107n3, 109, 112, 113, 114, 118, 120, 121, 126n3, 126n12, 130, 132, 133, 141, 149, 152, 153, 154, 167, 168, 170, 181; analytical psychology as ungrounded science 104–106; classic formulation for individuation 77; *Collected Works* 67; epiphany 35; Gilbert Simondon and 97; holistic systems 72–73; microcosm and macrocosm 73; practice of science 68; *Red Book* 55–64, 65n10, 65n19, 65n25, 65n31, 67, 68, 70–71; scientific opinions 69; self-realisation for 34; self-regulation 33; 'therapeutics of presence' 10; 'The Stages of Life' 36; vitalism 11
Jungian conceptual framework 77

Jungian individuation 89
Jungian psychology 36, 39, 91
Jung–Pauli model 11, 110, 115

*kami* 13; in Japan 171–174; in Japanese myth 177–178
Kant, I. 11, 48, 101, 102, 103, 105, 111, 115n1, 118, 122, 123–124, 125, 126n10, 126n12, 126n13, 127n17; biophilosophy and *Critique of Teleological Judgement* 118–122
Kawai, H. 177, 178
Khunrath, H. 44
Klages, L. 141, 144
knowledge 44, 70, 86; acquisition of 87; corrupted order of 86; of God's Grace, 49; of *unus mundus* 115
Koestler, A. 5
*Kojiki* (Takeda) 177
Korzybski, A.H.C. 33
Kraeplin, E. 56

Lancaster, B. 183
Langan, R. 11
language 2, 141; image-thinking 144–145; synchronicity 12, 144–145
Lawrence, C. 2–4
left-leaning 3
Leibbrand, W. 101
Leibniz, G.W. 47, 48, 73, 112–113, 114
Leibniz-Wolffian tradition 50
Leichtman, M. 3
Lenin, V. 3, 21
Leven, J. 180
Levinas, E. 12, 141, 142
Levittown sameness 25
Liberal Humanism 184
*Liber Novus* 57, 68
*Liber Primus* 58–60
*Liber Secundus* 61–62
libido: conception of 57
*Life* magazine 19
living organism: structure of science as 69
long-range deep ecology movement 38
Lovelock, J. 33, 34, 39; Gaia theory 32; speculation 35
Lutheranism 42

McGilchrist, I. 183
Mackey, J. 12
Macmurray, J. 12, 149–150, 151, 152, 153, 154
Màdera, R. 63
*magia naturalis* 44

Maillard, C. 62, 64, 65n30, 65n38
Main, R. 167, 168
Mandelbrot, B.B 36
Marcuse, H. 3
Martin Luther King, Jr. 8, 19, 22
Marxist ideology 3
Maslow, A.H. 8, 19, 20, 23–24, 29n27, 29n31, 89
massacre 160, 165
Master-of-the-Centre-of-Heaven 177, 178
*Mater Coelestis* 62
materialism 134, 143; in physical and chemical sciences 3; social and political consequences of 3
materialistic holism 127n21
material vitalism 123
McMillan, C. 11
mechanism: in physical and chemical sciences 3; social and political consequences of 3
medical-pharmaceutical 'Chymie' 44
Meillasoux, Q. 111
*Memories, Dreams, Reflections* 67, 170
mental disintegration: risk of 78
Merleau-Ponty, M. 92
*metanoia* 31, 39
*Metaphysical Foundations of Natural Science* (Kant) 121–122
metaphysical preoccupations 6
metaphysics 21, 134
metastable equilibrium 93
Methodism 43
military-industrial complexes 19
Miller, B. 8
Miller, F. 56
Miller, S. 30
Milton, J. 164
mind–brain relationship 32
mind-dependent reality 110
mind-matter conundrum 31–33
mirroring 143–144
Mitchell, R. 9–10
*Mitsu Torii* (Three Torii) 177
modernity 4
'modern organicism' 5–6
modern theory of religion 50
monoculture 34
motion: property of 46; regulation of 46
*Motivation and Personality* 24
Motoori, N. 172
Mount Miwa 175, *176*, 177
Muir, J. 22
*mundus imaginalis* 80

Murphy, M. 24
mushroom clouds 19
*Mysterium Coniunctionis* (Jung) 63, 110

'Nada: hope or nothing' 162, 164
Nante, B. 60
Næss, A. 8, 38, 39
natural order 86
Nature 102–103, 106; auto-alterity 103; indeterminacy of 106; productivity 103
nature 141; synchronicity and image-thinking 142–143
*Naturphilosophie* (Schelling) 10, 101, 102, 104; inhibition, actants, derangement 102–103
Nazi Holocaust 165
Nazis 3, 160
neo-materialist philosophy 111
New Age movement 21, 24
New Age religion 23
Nietzsche, F. 92, 101
nonlinear dynamics 150
non-materialistic holism 127n21
"non-sense" 58, 70
Nothingness 62
nuclear fear 25

obligation: darkness of 106
*An Oblique Offering* (Derrida) 132
occupational aim: holistic education 85
Oedipus complex 57
Oetinger, F.C. 45, 50
O Holy Spirit 21
"omega point" 23
Ōmiwa Shrine 175, 177
"One-Ocean World" map 19
'On the Nature of the Psyche' (Jung) 123–124
*On the Psychology of the Unconscious* (Jung) 105
"ontological *coniunctio*" 58, 60, 64
ontological ideas 134
*Operating Manual for Spaceship Earth* 18
organism 42, 119, 121; characteristics of 150; Leibniz's definition 47; vs. mechanism 46–47; self-determined 45; Stahl's definition 45
'organ' of perception 8

pairs of opposites: *Abraxas/Erikapaios* or *Phanès* 63; *Ignis* (Fire) and *Eros/Tree of Life* 62, 63; *Inans/Plenum* 63; *Mater Coelestis/Phallos* 62;

*Nothingness* and *Fullness* 62; serpent/white bird 62, 63; spirituality/sexuality 62; Sun and devil 62; 'terrestrial' and 'celestial' 62
panentheism 6
Panksepp, J. 80
pantheism 6
Paracelsus 44, 47
*Paradise Lost* (Milton) 164
Paul, A. 20, 21
Pauli–Jung conjecture 31, *32*
Pauli, W. 11, 31, 109, 110, 149, 152
Perls, F. 3, 20
personal aim: holistic education 85
personality: child development on 86; development of 83; and sociocultural environment 86
personality development 10, 51
persons: characteristics of 150
Pestalozzi, J.H. 85, 86–88
*Phallos* 62
*Phanès* 63
phenomenological method 50
*The Phenomenology of the Spirit in Fairy Tales* (Jung) 112
Philemon 61–63, 70
Phillips, D. 4–6
philosophical ideas 134
*Philosophy of the Unconscious* (Hartmann) 107n2
'physicotheology' 124
*phyton* 77
Pietism 42–45, 50
pietists 42; application 48–50; devotional literature 43; hymns 43; medicine 45–47; as regenerated congregation 49
Plato 20
Plato's *Phaedrus* 61
*Plenum* 63
*Pleroma* 62, 63
poetry workshops 159, 163
positivism 134; ontological challenge to 137
post-Christian holistic wish 81
post–World War II America 17, 22
pragmatic ontological materialism 134
praxis of Christianity 43
preindividual 94, 96, 97
Preiswerk, H. 56
Price, R. 24
Protevi, J. 140n11
psyche 69, 71, 164–165; chaos of 68; Gaia and 32–38, **34**, **36**; and matter 31; principle of compensation 57; after *Red Book* 57–63; before *Red Book* 55–57; self-regulation 33; Spaltung 56; symbol of psychic function 57; symbol's creation 60; *see also* human psyche
psychic balance 55
psychic equilibrium 60
psychic individuation 93
psychic organism 72
psychic self-regulation 75–76
psychoanalytic movement 68
psychological enlightenment 23
psychological individuality 96, 97
*Psychological Types* (Jung) 63
psychological unity patterns 150
psychology: Gestalt 20; of holistic education 89; Jungian 36, 39; roots of 75; structure of science and 69, 73
*Psychology of the Unconscious* (Jung) 57, 61, 62
psycho-spiritual context 184
psychotherapy 180

quasi-psychological language 103

radical pietist medicine 45–47
rationalistic abstraction 50
realism 11, 114–115, 115–116n2, 134; vs. anti-realism 110–111
real level: critical realism 130, 137
rebirth 42–44
recapitulation theory 88
reciprocal illumination 50
re-conception of nature 12
reconciliation: of opposition 59; of 'thinking' and 'feeling' 59
*Red Book* (Jung) 9, 67; composition period of 55; discourses in 70–71, 73; experience 68, 70–73; practice of science 68; psyche after 57–63; psyche before 55–57; transdisciplinary methodology 68
*The Red Book: Liber Novus* (Jung) 9
reductionism 4, 24
Reformation 42, 44; First 42; Second 42
relational holistic activity 77–78
relations of interiority 113
Renaissance esotericism 3
'Resolution' 59, 60
rethinking individuation 10
revolution in racial relations 22
Rogers, C. 89
Romantic movement 22
Rousseau, J.J. 85, 87; on child's developing personality 86

Saban, M. 10
salvation 21
sanctification 21
Satoshi Ito 171
Schelling, F. 10–11, 101, 102, 106n1; *Naturphilosophie* 102–103, 104
Schelling–Jung intellectual partnership 105
*schizophrenia* 56
Schleiermacher, F. 50
Schonbachler, G. 75, 76, 80
Schopenhauer, A. 101
Scripture 44
*Scrutinies* (*Prügunfen*) 62–63
Second World War 162
*Seelenlehre* (psychology) of Pietism 48
'self' 8, 9, 24, 34, 36, 39, 61, 63, 65n33, 76, 77, 78, 81, 83, 110, 113, 114, 115, 132, 133, 143, 153, 180, 183, 184, 186: comprehensive 38; ego-Self axis 84, 87, 89, 90; ego-Self relationship 84; inspired by Upanishads 38; narrow egoistic 38
self-actualization 24
self-psychology 180
self-realisation 38; primacy of 34
self-regulation 33
self-similarity 36
self-transcendence 143; of consciousness 144
"sense" 58
'*sensus communis*' 45
*Septem Sermones ad Mortuos* 62, 73
Serbia: 'The blue butterfly' 162; massacre in 160; Nazis in 160; poetry workshops in 159, 163; synchronistic experience in 12
Serbian resistance group 160
*Seven Sermons to the Dead* 62–63
sexuality: opposites of 62
Shamdasani, S. 64
*shimenawa* 175, *176*
*shintai* 175–176
Shintō: *kami* in 170, 171, 172, 178; primary beliefs of ancient 172; scriptures exist in 177; shrines in Japan 175, 177; "*yaohorozu-no-kami*" 172
*Silent Spring* (Carson) 17–18
Simondon, G. 10, 91; and Carl Jung 97; individuation 93–94; life of 92–93; preindividual 94; transindividual 94–97
*Sinn see* "sense"
Smuts, J.C. 1–3, 20, 27n13, 132

Sneller, R. 12
socialism 21
social solidarity 24
"*sorei*" (ancestral spirits) 174
'soul,' defined 8
'speech act theory' 143
speed-regulation 35
Spener, P.J. 44
Spinoza, B. 11, 109, 114, 115–116n2; attributes and absolute parity 111–113
"spirits of ancestors" 174
spiritual harmony 24
spirituality: opposites of 62; Western metaphors for 184
spiritual oneness 24
spiritual power 87
spiritual values 20
split personality 56
'The Stages of Life' 36, 37
Stahl, G.E.: animism 46; holistic organism 8, 42, 45, 50; medical and judicial reform 48; pietist application 48–50; and radical pietist medicine 45–47; reception of 47–48; theory of medicine 45, 51; theory of organism 42, 45; theory of phlogiston 45
Stevens, A. 64
Stiegler, B. 92
stratification 130
structure of science and psychology 69, 73
Sugawara no Michizane 171
Šumadija 159
Šumarice 160
'*summum bonum*', Sun as 62
sundry utopian experiments 22
"supreme meaning" 58, 70; 'incarnation' of 58, 60
sustainable individuation 38–39
Swedenborg, E. 45
Sydenham, T. 47
synchronicity 12, 73, 104, 113, 114, 120, 141, 142, 145–146, 159, 165, 167, 168; consciousness 143–144; language 144–145; nature 142–143; in Serbia 12
*Synchronicity: An Acausal Connecting Principle* (Jung) 113, 120
*Systema mundi totius* 63

'technosphere' 35
Teilhard de Chardin, P. 19, 22, 29, 29n26
teleology 33, 153; emergence, holism and 150–151
tension of opposites 55
*Theoria Medica vera* (Stahl) 46, 47

theory: of holistic 45; of medicine 45; of organism 42, 45; of phlogiston 45
Thomasius, C. 48
*A Thousand Plateaus* (Deleuze) 123
"The Three *Kami* of Creation" 177
Tillerson, R. 37
Tillich, P. 85
tipping points 34
Tito, J.B. 160
Toscano, A. 119, 124, 125, 125n1, 126n6
totalitarianism 3, 21
transindividual 94–97
*Tree of Life* 62, 63
Twelve-Step movement 184
Tylor 50

*Über die Psychologie der Dementia Præcox* (Bleuler) 56
*Übersinn see* "supreme meaning"
ultimacy 85, 88, 89; goal of 87
underlabouring 139n4
unhistorical-kerygmatic interpretation 44
union of opposites 55, 60, 61, 63, 64
unity patterns 12, 149–154
universal attitude 71
*unus mundus* 32, 33, 36, 101, 104, 106, 110, 115
Urania 164

van Helmont, J.B. 47
vitalism 118
von Ehrenfels, C., 20
von Franz, M.-L. 33
von Wright, G.H. 12, 149, 151–152, 153
Voting Rights Act of 1965 22

*Wandlungen und Symbole der Libido* (Jung) 56, 57
Weber, M. 3, 4
web of life 17, 18, 22, 23
Weiss, P. 5
Weisz, G. 2–4

'well-regulated freedom' 85
Wertheimer, M. 3, 20
Wesleyan movement 43
Western philosophy: Aristotelian tradition of 146
Western tradition: critique of 141
Whitehead, A.N. 13, 181, 185
whole 17, 18, 141, 146; by Aristotle 21; communal 21; compatibility of 144, 145; experience of 142, 147; by Hippocrates 21; language as a 21; organic 45; organism 21; by Paul 21; by Plato 20; salvation and sanctification 21; Yin and Yang in Chinese 21
wholeness 181, 185, 186n1; *coincidentia oppositorum* 61; of psychic life 55
*Widersinn see* "non-sense"
Wiener, N. 21
Wilson, D.S. 183
Winnicott, D. 13, 186n1
wishing 75–76
Wittgenstein, L. 144
Wolff, C. 48, 49
Wood, L.S. 4, 7
Woolf, C. 180
world-around structures 19

Yama, M. 13
Yamaori, T. 173, 174
Yang 21
*yaoyorozu-no-kami* 172, 177, 178
Yin 21
*yorishiro* 174–175, *175*
Yuasa, Y. 141
Yugoslavia 162–163

Zammito, J. 119, 121, 123, 126n8, 127n17, 127n20
*Zeitgeist* 38
*Zofingia Lectures* (Jung) 11, 118, 120, 122–125, 126n7, 127n21
*Zygon* 23